D1600237

Civil Liberties and Nazis

Civil Liberties and Nazis
The Skokie Free-Speech Controversy

James L. Gibson
University of Houston
and
Richard D. Bingham
University of Wisconsin–Milwaukee

PRAEGER SPECIAL STUDIES • PRAEGER SCIENTIFIC

New York • Philadelphia • Eastbourne, UK
Toronto • Hong Kong • Tokyo • Sydney

Library of Congress Cataloging in Publication Data

Gibson, James L., 1951–
    Civil liberties and Nazis.

    Bibliography: p.
    Includes index.
    1. Freedom of speech—United States.   2. Assembly,
Right of—United States.   3. American Civil Liberties
Union.   4. National Socialist Party of America.
5. Skokie (Ill.)—Demonstration, 1977.   I. Bingham,
Richard D.   II. Title.
JC599.U5G525   1985   323.44'3'0973   84-26320
ISBN 0-03-001634-7

Published in 1985 by Praeger Publishers
CBS Educational and Professional Publishing
A Division of CBS, Inc.
521 Fifth Avenue, New York, New York 10175 U.S.A.

© 1985 by Praeger Publishers

56789   145   987654321

Printed in the United States of America
on acid-free paper

Contents

List of Tables   vii
List of Figures   ix
Preface   xi
Chapter 1: Political Opposition, Tolerance and Democracy   1

   Prerequisites of Democracy   2
   Key Elements of "Democracy"   5
   The Limits of Tolerance in Democratic Societies   9
   The Paradox of American Democracy   12
   The Elitist Theory of Democracy   14
   Limitations of the Elitist Theory of Democracy   16
   The Skokie-Nazi Conflict: An Overview   18
   Chapter by Chapter Overview   18
   Notes   20

Chapter 2: The Context of the Skokie-Nazi Dispute   22

   Skokie   22
   The Nazi Movement in the United States   24
   Skokie's Reaction to Frank Collin   28
   The Reactions of Local Citizens and Leaders   35
   Skokie and Tolerance   41
   Notes   42

Chapter 3: The Nature of the Samples   47

   Research Design   47
   The Elite Nature of the Samples   58
   Notes   69

Chapter 4: The Impact of Skokie on the American
           Civil Liberties Union   71

   The ACLU View of the Response   72
   The Survey View of the Response   74

A Multivariate Analysis of Defection   95
Implications for ACLU   98
Note   104

Chapter 5: Conceptual and Operational Approaches to Political Tolerance   **105**

Measures of Political Tolerance   110
Constraint in Tolerance Belief Systems   129
Discussion   136
Note   139

Chapter 6: The Application of General Tolerance Attitudes: Reactions to the Skokie-Nazi Dispute   **141**

The "Irrationality" of Applied Beliefs   143
Applying Abstract Beliefs to the Skokie Conflict   146
Conclusions   157
Notes   158

Chapter 7: The Behavioral Consequences of Political Tolerance   **160**

Conceptualizing the Attitude-Behavior Relationship   161
Simple Models of the Attitude-Behavior Relationship   164
Conditional Models of the Attitude-Behavior Relationship   171
Conclusions   178
Notes   180

Chapter 8: Conclusions and Implications   **183**

Micro-Level Implications   183
Macro-Level Implications   186

References   **193**
Appendix A: The Skokie Ordinances   **199**
Appendix B: The Questionnaire   **209**
Index   **221**
About the Authors   **227**

List of Tables

Table 1.1 Political Tolerance of the American Public, 1954   13

Table 3.1 Summary of Samples, Response Rates, and Weights   51

Table 3.2 Selected Attributes of ACLU Members and Leaders and Common Cause Members   52

Table 3.3 Differences in Tolerance of ACLU Leaders, ACLU Members, and Common Cause Members   57

Table 3.4 Comparison of ACLU Members and Leaders, Common Cause Members, and the Mass Public on Support for Civil Liberties   62

Table 3.5 Tolerance as Measured by Stouffer Items   66

Table 4.1 Attitudes toward Skokie Ordinances on Nazi Demonstrations   75

Table 4.2 Reasons for Denying Nazis a Permit to Demonstrate in Skokie   78

Table 4.3 Membership Status of Respondents   83

Table 4.4 Major Reasons for Quitting ACLU   84

Table 4.5 Change in ACLU Membership, 1977-1979   84

Table 4.6 Attitudes toward ACLU Defense of Nazi Rights and Defections—ACLU Members   91

Table 4.7 General Libertarianism and Defection Rates—ACLU Members   92

Table 4.8 Ideology and Defection—ACLU Members   93

Table 4.9 Motivation for Joining ACLU and Defections Over Skokie—ACLU Members   94

Table 4.10 Libertarian Predispositions and Defection Behavior—ACLU Members   96

Table 4.11 The Conditional Effect of Religious Affiliation on Defection Rates—ACLU Members   96

Table 4.12 The Conditional Effect of Organizational

	Involvement on Defection Rates—ACLU Members	97
Table 4.13	Issue Consensus	100
Table 4.14	Member Views of ACLU Functions and Priorities	103
Table 5.1	Support for Freedom of Speech	111
Table 5.2	Support for Freedom of Assembly: Heckler's Veto	118
Table 5.3	Support for Freedom of Assembly: Majority Abhorrence	119
Table 5.4	Support for Government Repression	122
Table 5.5	Miscellaneous Civil Liberties	124
Table 5.6	Common Factor Analysis of Miscellaneous Civil Liberties Items	127
Table 5.7	Tolerance as Measured by Stouffer Items	130
Table 5.8	Correlations among Multiple Indicators of Tolerance	134
Table 6.1	Attitudes toward Skokie Ordinances on Nazi Demonstrations	147
Table 6.2	Ordinance Opinion and Willingness to Allow a Nazi Demonstration	149
Table 6.3	Determinants of Willingness to Deny Nazis a Permit to Demonstrate	150
Table 6.4	Determinants of Attitudes toward Skokie Ordinances	151
Table 6.5	Determinants of Attitudes toward Abhorrent Group Demonstrations	153
Table 6.6	Predictability of Opinions on Demonstrations and Communities' Right to Privacy	154
Table 7.1	Intolerant and Tolerant Behaviors	165
Table 7.2	The Direct, Bivariate Relationship of Libertarian Attitudes and Behavior	167
Table 7.3	Explained Variance in the Path Analysis of Tolerance Attitudes and Behavior	168
Table 7.4	The Conditional Impact of Expectations of Violence on the Attitude-Behavior Relationship	173
Table 7.5	The Conditional Impact of Religious Affiliation on the Attitude-Behavior Relationship	175

List of Figures

Figure 1.1   The hypothetical relationship between
             tolerance and democracy   11
Figure 4.1   Change in membership size—Illinois Civil
             Liberties Union   87
Figure 5.1   Relationship of general beliefs to specific
             action   138
Figure 7.1   Path analysis of libertarian attitudes and
             behavior—ACLU members   169
Figure 7.2   The conditional impact of religion on the
             attitude-behavior relationship   177

To Monica
and
Claire

Preface

We are indebted to the National Science Foundation for providing the major financial support for this project (SOC-7825742). The ACLU provided the initial funding for the research and without its cooperation the project could not have been conducted. We are especially grateful to Mr. Jay Miller of the ACLU National Office who encouraged and supported us from the beginning of the project. The University of Wisconsin–Milwaukee provided the support, not insubstantial, that no other agency would. The conclusions and views contained in this book are those of the authors alone and do not necessarily reflect the official positions of NSF, ACLU or UWM. We are indebted to our research assistants—Patricia C. Haeuser and Laura L. Vertz—for their long hours of hard work on the project. Maureen E. Rolfs, Lawrence A. Holt, Carol M. Burzinski, and Gloria J. Palmer also made invaluable contributions. David G. Barnum and George E. Marcus provided us with most helpful comments on portions of this book. The comments of Stephen L. Wasby, as well as his incisive criticism over the entire course of the project, have been particularly helpful. Several of our students have provided most helpful comments on earlier drafts of the book, including Anthony F. Baran, Christopher Emeharole, Fred R. Frey, Michael L. Glover, John W. Gummelt, Scott C. Lummus, Imran Mirza, Timothy K. Newcomb, Leslie Ohr, Lonnie R. Scott, George L. Thompson, Bill A. Whitesides, and especially James P. Wenzel and R. Jeff Zook.

Houston, Texas   J.L.G.
May, 1984   R.D.B.

1   Political Opposition, Tolerance and Democracy

     Politics in the United States is characterized by a curious mixture of tolerance and intolerance. Conflict over the limits of the rights of political minorities has been a recurring element of the 200 years of American political history. While competition for control of power was legitimized fairly early in the development of the American political system (as signaled by the opposition to and repeal of the Alien and Sedition Act of 1798), the system has succumbed to the temptation to limit political competition to those sharing the dominant "consensus" over the direction of public policy with alarming frequency. It seems that the American political system alternately accepts (indeed, even adopts) and represses with equal vigor the views of political nonconformists. This strain between tolerance and intolerance has had an enduring and pervasive influence on the politics of the United States.

     The manner in which this tension is resolved, or even managed, has great consequences for the maintenance of the democratic style of political organization. For when political conflict expands beyond substantive public policy to include conflict over the basic democratic rights of a segment of the citizenry, the ramifications are in no sense minor. The losers in competition over the control of public policy survive to compete again; the continued political existence of the losers in conflict over basic political rights is severely threatened. Without at least some agreement that the basic rights of citizens to political opposition are non-negotiable, normal political conflict evolves into conflict over the very structure of the regime itself. The "zero-sum" quality of such conflict seriously threatens democracies: it is difficult for them to function in the absence of institutionalized guarantees of the rights of access to political power. If we are to understand the factors that contribute to the development and maintenance of democracies, it is quite important to understand the causes and consequences of disputes over democratic rights.

1

Perhaps the single most important determinant of whether political systems are able to resolve and manage conflicts over rights is the level of tolerance in society. Democracies require, more than anything else, that citizens and leaders be willing to tolerate political diversity; without tolerance, majority rule quickly degenerates into majority tyranny. An inquiry into the conditions facilitating democracy must therefore be an inquiry into the beliefs, values, and actions of the members of the polity. This book reports the results of such an inquiry.

The objective of the research reported here is to examine the conditions under which the political majority is willing to extend the rights of democratic citizenship to political minorities. In particular, we focus upon the rights of assembly and speech—rights, we argue, that are essential to effective democracy—within the context of the recent dispute over the efforts of the Village of Skokie (Illinois) to circumscribe the liberty of members of the National Socialist Party of America (Nazis). The Skokie controversy—though in some ways a "limiting case"—dramatizes the conflict of values endemic to democratic societies by raising the question of whether democracies must provide avenues for the expression of "anti-democratic" ideas. How can the political system maintain open political competition while concurrently specifying the breadth of legitimate political debate? Moreover, the Skokie/Nazi dispute highlights the difficulty of the demands democracies make of their citizens; to be tolerant of those expressing abhorrent political views requires that citizens understand and accept the cognitively taxing philosophical underpinnings of democratic thought. Whether, under what conditions, and with what consequences such understanding and acceptance exist among a segment of the politically influential members of American society are the central questions of this research.

PREREQUISITES OF DEMOCRACY

Why do democracies persist? What conditions—social, economic, political, or psychological—give rise to the democratic style of political organization? These are questions that have captured the attention of philosophers for centuries and political scientists for decades. The answers are of extreme importance for mature industrial democracies, as well as for developing nations. Indeed, the very survival of democracy is contigent upon understanding the factors sympathetic to the development of a democratic polity. Only through such an understanding can non-democratic systems be democratized and democratic systems maintained.

While extant understandings of the determinants of democracy are highly varied, at least four major facilitating conditions have been identified. The first line of argument suggests that economic development is a prerequisite to democratization. It has been hypothesized that without high, but not rapid or disjointed, economic development, democracies are unlikely to evolve. Economic development contributes to democracy in several ways. First, advanced economies require certain attributes of the social order, attributes that are also required by democracies. For instance high levels of education and literacy are essential to both developed economic and political systems. Similarly, networks of mass communications are politically and economically advantageous. To the extent that high economic development contributes to the reduction of inequalities in society, democratic development is also facilitated. Economic development seems to contribute to the type of infra-structure that is sympathetic to democracy (Dahl, 1971; Lipset, 1960).

Economic development, or more specifically, economic success, is also useful to democracy because it facilitates the acquisition of more universalistic, less material sets of beliefs among citizens. That is, the satisfaction of economic needs seems to activate, in a Maslovian sense, the desire to satisfy higher order needs such as intellectual and aesthetic needs (Maslow, 1954). While not necessarily sufficient for political activity, efforts to satisfy these higher needs may lead to the levels of political sophistication and involvement that democracies require of their citizens (e.g., Inglehart, 1977, 1980). Thus, economic development may be a powerful stimulant for democratization.

A second hypothesis relates cultural homogeneity to democracy. Societies not rent by serious cleavages in the population (and/or those characterized by cross-cutting cleavages) present fewer obstacles to democratic politics. The central assumption of this hypothesis is that tolerance is essential to democracy and that extreme heterogeneity impedes tolerance. Societies that have been historically characterized by a bedrock of commonality find it easier to engage in the politics of accommodation and compromise. When cleavages reinforce each other, normal political conflict becomes life or death conflict, and normal partisanship may take on tones of zealotry. Homogeneous societies face fewer impediments to democratization.

It has also been hypothesized that certain institutional arrangements and legal structures facilitate the development of democracies. For instance, a long-standing debate exists over the type of party system that most effectively contributes to democratic government. Justifications have been proferred for partyless politics, one-party systems, two-party systems and multi-party systems. The utility of "responsible parties" has also been contested. Similarly, some point to particular legal structures—especially constitutions (e.g., Bagehot, 1966)—as essential to democratic government. Though it is not always clear precisely what structures are considered necessary to democracy, institutional arrangements are thought by some to be quite important.

There is little question that these factors are in some way related to the likelihood of success of democratic regimes. However, structural, historical, institutional, legal, and economic factors—all attributes of *system*—should not be emphasized to the detriment of attributes of the *citizens* of the system. While every type of political regime requires at least some support from its citizens (Easton, 1965), democracies are especially vulnerable to the preferences, whims, and caprices of the members of the polity. "Democratic" institutions rarely function democratically in the absence of a democratic *political culture*. Economic, cultural, and historical factors are important facilitators of democracy mainly insofar as they contribute to democratic beliefs and actions among the citizenry. Without widespread, perhaps even consensual, support for democratic institutions and processes of politics—the democratic "rules of the game"—democracies, more than most other types of regimes, face substantial threats to their existence. As Learned Hand put it:

> I often wonder whether we do not rest our hopes too much upon constitutions, upon laws and upon courts. These are false hopes. Liberty lies in the hearts of men and women; when it dies there, no constitution, no laws, no court can save it; no constitution, no laws, no court can even do much to save it. (Hand, 1959, p. 144)

There is widespread agreement among scholars that the ability of democracies to function effectively is associated with the degree to which citizens subscribe to basic democratic values. But precisely what must citizens believe? That is, what is the content of the political culture on which democracies apparently depend? Unfortunately, there is less widespread agreement on this question. It is therefore necessary to consider in greater detail the nature of the concept "democracy."

KEY ELEMENTS OF "DEMOCRACY"

Philosophers and social scientists have struggled for centuries in their efforts to define the essence of "democracy." Our research effort is not nearly so ambitious and frankly, we would prefer to avoid the task of defining altogether. However, since an implicit definition is assumed throughout anyway, we must make explicit our working approach to the concept. We do this not to foreclose debate on the matter, but rather in an attempt to minimize confusion.

Robert Dahl has put forth a definition of democracy that is useful for our purposes:

> I assume that a key characteristic of a democracy is the continuing responsiveness of the government to the preferences of its citizens, considered as political equals. . . . I assume further that in order for a government to continue over a period of time to be responsive to the preferences of its citizens, considered as political equals, all full citizens must have unimpaired opportunities:
>
> 1. to formulate their preferences
>
> 2. to signify their preferences to their fellow citizens and the government by individual and collective action
>
> 3. to have their preferences weighed equally in the conduct of the government, that is, weighted with no discrimination because of the content or source of the preference. (Dahl, 1971, pp. 1, 2)

Dahl goes on to identify eight institutional guarantees necessary (but not necessarily sufficient) for democracy, including: (1) freedom to form and join organizations; (2) freedom of expression; (3) right to vote; (4) right of political leaders to compete for support; (5) alternative sources of information; (6) eligibility for public office; (7) free and fair elections; and (8) institutions for making government policies that depend on votes and other expressions of preference (Dahl, 1971, p. 3). These can be employed in constructing the two key dimensions of democracy: the inclusiveness of participation and the liberalization of public contestation.

Such an approach to the definition of the concept obviously places great emphasis on political competition; a democracy is a style of government that maximizes the opportunities and avenues of the entire citizenry to compete for control of political power and/or influence over public policy. Crucial to democracy, then, is the ability to compete, to dissent, to challenge the actions of government.

Competition, whether guided by an "invisible hand" or not, is beneficial in two separate ways. First, competition for control of policy is assumed to result in the "best" policy being adopted (in much the same way that the adversary system of justice is assumed to maximize the likelihood of "just" decisions). Only through vigorous debate can the wisdom of particular political choice be carefully evaluated and exposed. Systems that build barriers to political competition have a limited ability for self correction and substantial difficulties with change.

Even if competition does not assist in identifying the correct course of action, it resolves what may be an even more fundamental problem of mass democracies—the problem of legitimacy. All political systems experience difficulties with maintaining the allegiance of citizens whose policy preferences are not satisfied, that is, the losers in the competitive arena. Those who continually lose in politics must be mollified; they must be given some rationale for continued participation in the system. The *processes* of politics provide a solution to this legitimacy problem. If the processes of politics are unbiased—that is, if all preferences are weighed equally in the conduct of the government—then the system is responsive. From responsiveness flows legitimacy. Democracy is an effective remedy for illegitimacy because it allows equal *access*, if not equal *success*, to political power. Failure to control public policy cannot, therefore, be attributed to the fallibility of the system through which policy decisions are made, but rather must be attributed to some other cause (on the effectiveness of the American political system in doing this within the context of widespread unemployment see Schlozman and Verba, 1979). Thus, democracy results in the adoption of the "best" policies, but even if it does not, the openness of the process tends to generate acceptance of the results.

A major problem of democracies (as well as of all systems of organization based on competition: cf. Skolnick, 1967) is to cope with forces tending to circumscribe competition—that is, to institutionalize openness. Toward this end, democratic systems normally attempt to designate access to political power as a "right" of citizenship, and to build legal barriers to infringement of the right. An obvious such example, in the case of the United States, can be found in the Bill of Rights. The Bill of Rights, designed to prohibit general repression of the citizenry by the government, contains several explicit guarantees of access to competition for political power. Perhaps most significant are the guarantees of the rights of political speech and assembly. It is difficult to imagine how competition could be maintained in the absence of free speech and assembly; if the government has the authority to specify the parameters of legitimate debate, and/or to control the process through which ideas are communicated (either to the government or to fellow citizens), then competition succumbs to monopoly. Legitimacy, to say nothing of substantive public policy, suffers under monopolistic control by the government (or any other group in society).

Despite the democrat's fundamental commitment to rights essential to political competition, it cannot be assumed that the rights create social harmony; instead, the result of competition of ideas is more likely cacophony. Indeed, one of the fundamental problems of democracy is to resolve the inherent tension between competition and social discord. There is a strong tendency for the majority to eliminate the discord by stifling the minority. Any system that attempts to maximize opportunities for debate is inevitably faced with the problem of debate that exceeds the boundaries of consensus. Systems that do not allow government to restrain political competition are continually confronted with the possibility that the rights of democratic citizenship will be utilized for anti-democratic purposes. The very openness of the political system presents a podium to those opposed to democracy; freedom for all ideas may include freedom for ideas thoroughly repugnant to the majority and to the principles of democracy.

Are there legitimate limitations to competition among ideas that can be imposed in a democratic polity? This is a question central to the work of almost every political philosopher. Are some ideas so patently false, so dangerous to democracy that government is legitimately impelled to prohibit their dissemination? Must democratic society tolerate all shades of opinion, even opinion that undermines the very foundations of democracy? Any inquiry into the conditions contributing to democracy must confront these difficult questions.

J.S. Mill has provided a rigorous formulation of the problem, and, we argue, an adequate justification for concluding that unrestrained freedom of discussion is essential to democracy. Mill formulates two lines of argument: one to cover the case in which it is conceded that no ideas can be judged, in an absolute sense, to be "wrong," and one to cover the case in which the concession is not granted. Generally, Mill argues:

> . . . the peculiar evil of silencing the expression of an opinion is that it is robbing the human race, posterity as well as the existing

generation—those who dissent from the opinion, still more than those who hold it. If the opinion is right, they are deprived of the opportunity of exchanging error for truth; if wrong, they lose, what is almost as great a benefit, the clearer perception and livelier impression of truth produced by its collision with error. (Mill, 1956, p. 21)

Mill believed that ideas cannot be assumed to be "false," and therefore efforts to stifle the expression of opinion cannot be justified. Moreover, it is not possible to determine which ideas are better without unrestricted debate. Since the truth value of an argument can only be determined through the marketplace of ideas, "truth" cannot be a criterion used to judge whether ideas can be expressed. "There is the greatest difference between presuming an opinion to be true because, with every opportunity for contesting it, it has not been refuted, and assuming its truth for the purpose of not permitting its refutation" (Mill, 1956, p. 24). Truth should not proscribe debate because without debate truth cannot be discerned or even approximated. Indeed, to limit debate is to *weaken* the underpinning, the infrastructure, of the idea:

> The steady habit of correcting and completing his own opinion by collating it with those of others, so far from causing doubt and hesitation in carrying it into practice, is the only stable foundation for a just reliance on it; for, being cognizant of all that can, at least obviously, be said against him, having taken up his position against all gainsayers—knowing that he has sought for objections and difficulties instead of avoiding them, and has shut out no light which can be thrown upon the subject from any quarter—he has a right to think his judgement better than that of any person, or any multitude, who have not gone through a similar process. (Mill, 1956, p. 25)

Further:

> Truth gains more even by the errors of one who, with due study and preparation, thinks for himself than by the true opinions of those who only hold them because they do not suffer themselves to think. Not that it is solely, or chiefly, to form great thinkers that freedom of thinking is required. On the contrary, it is as much and even more indispensible to enable average human beings to attain the mental stature. (Mill, 1956, pp. 41–42)

Political systems that restrain debate out of fear of the persuasiveness of anti-democratic ideas weaken themselves by contributing to citizen commitment to democracy at the level of platitudes, rather than the deeper, more stable commitments that flow from the process of rational thought.

> But when it has come to be an hereditary creed, and to be received passively, not actively—when the mind is no longer compelled, in the same degree as at first, to exercise its vital powers on the questions which its belief presents to it, there is a progressive tendency to forget all of the belief except the formularities, or to give it a dull and torpid assent, as if accepting it on trust dispensed with the necessity of realizing it in consciousness, or testing it by personal experience, until it almost ceases to connect itself at all with the inner life of the human being. Then are seen the cases, so frequent in this age of the world as almost to form the majority, in which the creed remains as it were outside the mind, incrusting and petrifying it against all other influences addressed to the higher parts of our nature; manifesting its power by not suffering any fresh and living conviction to get in, but itself doing nothing for the mind or heart except standing sentinel over them to keep them vacant. (Mill, 1956, pp. 49–50)

The conclusion to be drawn from this conceptualization of democracy is, of course, that tolerance, in the hearts of men and women, as well as in the institutions of government, is essential to effective democratic government. Without tolerance, political competition either cannot exist or is transformed into life or death (zero-sum) battles. Toleration of diverse political ideas, that is, minority political ideas, is essential if democracies are to maintain their openness and responsiveness.

THE LIMITS OF TOLERANCE IN DEMOCRATIC SOCIETIES

But we must return to the question of how much tolerance is necessary. There is frequently confusion in the literature on political tolerance about the nature of the relationship between levels of tolerance and the degree of democratization of the polity. Sullivan, Piereson, and Marcus, for instance, argue that democracies do not require "full and universal" tolerance (Sullivan, Piereson, and Marcus, 1982, p. 5). In particular, they would not wish to see democratic regimes tolerate the "anti-democrat." They assert:

> ...tolerance can be seen as one of *many* important values. And, while the importance of tolerance must be respected, other important values may require accommodations by placing limits on the extent of tolerance to be practiced. Some restraints are thus justified if they are likely to preserve a balance between tolerance and other values. (Sullivan, Piereson, and Marcus, 1982, p. 10)

Thus, perfect tolerance is not necessarily to be equated with perfect democracy.

Our research is *not* guided by any *a priori* assumption about the functional form of the relationship between levels of tolerance in societies and levels of democratization. We do not assume that the two variables are linearly related—that increments in tolerance are associated with like increments in democracy. We believe, with many others, that some sort of relationship exists; some degree of tolerance is essential in order for democracies to function properly. But this relationship my be curvilinear. We are even prepared to consider the Sullivan, Piereson, and Marcus hypothesis that the relationship resembles that depicted in Figure 1.1. That is, beyond some threshold point (to be established empirically, of course), increments in tolerance produce (or are associated with) *decrements* in democracy.

But Sullivan, Piereson, and Marcus write repeatedly of tolerance of "extremist groups" in their discussion of political tolerance in America. They do so mainly as a means of justifying intolerance, for they assert clearly that the "anti-democrat" need not be tolerated in a democratic society. They, with Muller and Seligson (1982), are comforted that intolerance in the United States is directed toward anti-democratic groups, and, of course, that intolerance is not focused upon any single group. Moreover, those who are intolerant assert that their disliked group (that is, their object of intolerance) is undemocratic as a justification for their intolerance. Since a democratic society need not be perfectly tolerant, just as the First Amendment to the U.S. Constitution does not allow all types of speech, the disquieting impact of the findings is mitigated.

However, no evidence is ever presented—by Sullivan, Piereson, and Marcus, nor by Muller and Seligson, nor by any of the subjects they interviewed—that demonstrates that the target groups are in fact extremist. The group most frequently mentioned as the "least-liked group" is "communists." Certainly the Communist Party, U.S.A., is an

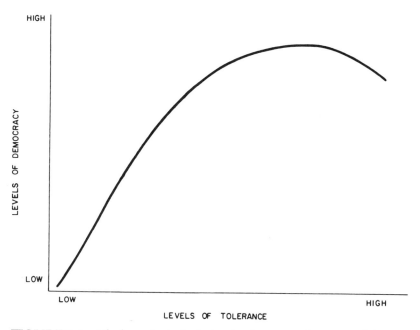

FIGURE 1.1 The hypothetical relationship between tolerance and democracy.

entirely legal entity, one that, for instance, regularly contests presidential elections in the United States. Is the CPUSA an extremist group? More generally, how does the concept "extremist" get operationalized in a scientific fashion? Obviously, these authors find communists to be extremists from the perspective of their own ideological, not scientific, positions. This is probably the single greatest difficulty with their approach to tolerance; to the extent intolerance is permissible under some circumstances, *it is typically the majority that determines the parameters of permissibility.*

Sullivan, Piereson, and Marcus ask respondents to select from a list the group they dislike the most. Various questions concerning intolerance are then asked using the specific "least liked" group as the object or target of intolerance. The second most popular target of intolerance is the Ku Klux Klan, quite possibly an extremist group because of its regular association, at least by the media, with violence. But is this also true of atheists (least-liked by 8 percent), the Black Panthers (6 percent), pro-abortionists (4 percent), anti-abortionists (2 percent), John Birchers (1 percent) and fascists (5 percent)? These groups hardly qualify as extremist.

This also points to the great difficulty of the entire group-based approach to tolerance. Within the context of democratic theory, we postulate that *all groups* ought to be tolerated, but not all *activities*. It is actions, not groups, that are properly prohibited by democratic regimes. If the Ku Klux Klan, or, for that matter, the Republican Party, intends to terrorize citizens with acts of violence, that behavior can legitimately be prohibited and prosecuted. If the Klan intends to engage in legitimate political activity, such as holding demonstrations to protest government policies, then it ought to be allowed to do so. We do not deny that this activity approach to intolerance has some difficulties; however, the advantages over the group-based approach, with its need to determine from the name of the group whether it is extremist or not, should be obvious.[1]

Thus it is our position that one of the most important attributes of a democratic body politic is tolerance: willingness to allow open competition among *all* political ideas. In the absence of tolerance, majority tyranny is an ever-present possibility. The majority cannot be allowed to define some ideas as extremist. Any attempt to understand the conditions favorable to democratic politics must therefore examine the levels of tolerance in society.

THE PARADOX OF AMERICAN DEMOCRACY

But does democracy require that all citizens be tolerant of unpopular political minorities? Perhaps not. Many examinations of tolerance in American society have been conducted, over a number of years, with results that are extremely disquieting. A substantial portion of the American people exhibits an unwillingness to grant the basic rights of democratic citizenship—for example, speech and assembly—to minority political groups. Samuel Stouffer was one of the first to document the low levels of tolerance. In 1954, Stouffer presented several issues of the rights of communists and atheists to a representative sample of the American public. Their responses are shown in Table 1.1. Obviously, the norm of tolerance is now widely held; indeed, a substantial majority of the American people are extremely intolerant! Stouffer's research, conducted at a time of political hysteria, clearly demonstrates the tension between majority rule and democracy.

Nor are these findings solely a function of the peculiar circumstances of post-World War II politics. Findings from research in the late 1950s and early 1960s are consistent with Stouffer's evidence. For instance,

TABLE 1.1. Political Tolerance of the American Public, 1954

	Response	
	No	*Yes*
Should a *socialist*		
be allowed to speak	31%	58%
be allowed to have a book		
in the library	35%	52%
be allowed to teach		
in a university	54%	33%
Should an *atheist*		
be allowed to speak	60%	37%
be allowed to have a book		
in the library	60%	35%
be allowed to teach		
in a university	84%	12%
Should *one who is charged with*		
being a communist but who swears		
that he/she is not		
be allowed to speak	21%	70%
be allowed to have a book		
in the library	22%	69%
be allowed to teach		
in a university	17%	71%
Should *an admitted communist*		
be allowed to speak	68%	27%
be allowed to have a book		
in the library	66%	27%
be allowed to teach		
in a university	89%	6%
have her or his citizenship		
taken away	13%	77%
be put in jail	34%	51%

Source: Adapted from Stouffer, 1955, Ch. 2.

only two-thirds of the residents of Ann Arbor, Michigan (the location of the University of Michigan) would allow an anti-religious speech to take place in their community. A majority would restrict voting rights to tax-payers and would bar a communist from holding or running for office, and a very large majority would allow only the "informed" to vote, and would prohibit a speech by communists (Prothro and Grigg, 1960, p. 285). While the residents of Ann Arbor are somewhat more committed to democratic rights than the residents of Tallahassee, Florida, they fall far short of the ideal democratic citizen.

Survey findings from more recent times are also available. These findings appear to show that levels of tolerance have increased somewhat (Nunn, Crockett, and Williams, 1978; Davis, 1975), but still fall far short of consensus. However, this conclusion must be restricted to tolerance of communists. While the mass public has moderated its views toward communists, other minority political groups—the Ku Klux Klan, the Symbionese Liberation Army, etc.—are tolerated at the level at which communists were tolerated in the early 1950s (Sullivan, Piereson, and Marcus, 1982). Americans demonstrate a strong tendency toward intolerance of political non-conformists, a tendency that seems to be incompatible with the assumptions and demands of democratic theorists.

Such a high level of agreement in research findings is relatively uncommon in social science. The evidence produces a fairly serious paradox—how can relatively democratic institutions and processes coexist with relatively high levels of intolerance in the members of the polity? Obviously, a rethinking of the prerequisites of democracy is necessary. This paradox has led to a fairly substantial restructuring of democratic theory.

THE ELITIST THEORY OF DEMOCRACY

Historically the impetus for the development of democratic styles of political organization stems from abuses of liberty by the leaders of society. Mass political participation was viewed as an antidote to tyranny by the few. However, the problem of democracies in the twentieth century is seen as one of being a tyranny of the many, and the empirical evidence suggests that a majority of citizens in the United States are not favorably predisposed to the protection of minority rights. *The paradox of democracy is that democracy is best maintained by not allowing majority preferences to govern public policy on the rights of political minorities.*

In fact, the American political system is not perfectly responsive to the intolerance of the majority. Many instances can be identified in which public policy is substantially more tolerant of the political activities of political minorities than is public opinion. How is it, for instance, that substantial portions of the faculties of American colleges and universities are atheists, when only 39 percent of the American people would allow an atheist to teach in a college? Indeed, it is possible to argue that politics, under normal circumstances, is controlled by an elite few rather than by the majority. Under some circumstances (e.g., the McCarthy era) the mass public is mobilized in an effort to control public policy; such episodes usually are associated with intolerance. In the absence of mass participation in policy making—the usual state of affairs in American politics— the elite are relatively free to conduct the business of government. Intolerance may exist in the attitudes of the mass public, but only occasionally do these attitudes generate demands on government for intolerant public policy.

The United States is as democratic as it is not because "the people" rule, but precisely because they do not rule. Despite the long-standing presumption that the elite of society are the most probable abusers of democratic rights, it also seems to be the elite who are the "carriers of the democratic creed." For instance, survey research has demonstrated that the elites are far more tolerant than the masses. A 1977 survey reports that 83 percent of a community leader sample can be classified as "more tolerant" whereas only 56 percent of the mass sample is so classified (Nunn, Crockett, and Williams, 1978, p. 149). Those who control and influence public policy in the United States are more protective of the rights of political minorities than the society at large.

These findings, in conjunction with a variety of findings from research on mass voting behavior, have spawned the "elitist theory of democracy." This theory holds that the greater the political involvement of the citizenry, the more likely it is that anti-democratic public policy will be enacted. Democracy in the political system is best maintained by a quiescent mass public; once activated, mass-based politics frequently involves repression of unpopular political minorities. Democratic elitism holds "that political decisions generally adhere to fundamental democratic values and are made according to democratic rules of procedure because political leaders continue to support democratic principles" (Nunn, Crockett, and Williams, 1978, p. 147). Such a position represents a fairly radical reinterpretation of the role of the citizen in a democratic polity.

Elites, then, are said to be the guardians of democracy. Even though political leaders may be drawn from the masses, and are held accountable to the masses, it seems that something about holding a position of leadership in a democratic society is conducive to the development of tolerant beliefs. Some (Key, 1961; Dahl, 1961) have argued that a distinctive elite subculture exists that reinforces the democratic beliefs of leaders and resocializes those holding anti-democratic beliefs.

> This distinctive political stratum is said to arise from and to be perpetuated by the unavoidable exposure of leaders to the nation's democratic heritage and by the necessity of applying those principles in a reasonably coherent and consistent manner. Members of the public, who are less aware of the diverse needs and conflicting interests of the society's heterogeneous population, imagine that they can live their lives without having to concern themselves with decisions which greatly affect the welfare of others. Leaders, whether in public office or in voluntary associations, must make decisions, and they need a set of principles to aid them in the process. Democratic principles, including the rule of democratic restraint, are readily available within America's cultural tradition. (Nunn, Crockett, and Williams, 1978, p. 148)

These norms result in government that is fairly unresponsive to intolerant demands from the citizenry. The paradox of democracy is that democracy is maintained by *not* allowing the will of the majority to determine the allocation of democratic rights in society.

LIMITATIONS OF THE ELITIST THEORY OF DEMOCRACY

The elitist theory of democracy can point to a variety of instances in which a mobilized mass public has demanded repression of political minorities. The most obvious such example is, of course, the McCarthy era. However, many instances of *elite* intolerance can also be identified. The Alien and Sedition Acts of 1798; Lincoln's suppression of due process rights; the post–World War I "red scare"; the incarceration of Japanese-Americans during World War II; the host of repressive acts by the national government during the 1940s and 1950s (e.g., Caute, 1978); and Watergate are all incompatible with the theory of elite commitment to democratic rights. Nor is repression limited to national political leaders—local community leaders, of which 83 percent are "more tolerant," have a long record of efforts to stifle dissent by political minorities. Certainly Mayors Daley and Rizzo must be considered as members of an elite. Local school boards are continually embroiled in issues involving freedom of information. The extensive history of civil liberties litigation, as well as civil rights litigation, in the United States almost always involves efforts by local and state elites to repress minorities. Repression may be initiated by mass activism, but, at a minimum, elite complicity has been widespread.

Indeed, even some of the strongest evidence supporting the elitist theory of democracy must be given careful scrutiny. For instance, the "red menace" of the late 1940s and early 1950s was *not* salient to the masses. Stouffer reports that 30 percent of a mass sample in 1954 could not identify a single correct name—not even Senator McCarthy's name—when asked to identify "any of the Senators or Congressmen who have been taking a leading part in [the congressional committees investigating Communism]" (Stouffer, 1955, p. 85). He also reports that local elites were strongly supportive of extending political rights to Communists. Most likely, then, it was the national elite, *acting without stimulation from a mobilized mass public*, who were responsible for the repression. Indeed, recent analyses of the era document the widespread agreement on the part of liberal and conservative leaders on the desirability of oppressing leftists (e.g., Navasky, 1980, and especially Caute, 1978). While it may be generally true that the national elite is more supportive than the local elite of the rights of political minorities, there are frequent and well-documented instances of substantial portions of the national elite failing to support democratic norms. Elite self-interest generates general support for minority rights, but minorities that challenge elite hegemony rarely are the beneficiaries of elite support.[2]

It is clear that, though elites may be more favorably predisposed toward protecting the political rights of minorities, there are conditions under which elite-directed repression occurs. The conditions occur regularly and, because elites have superior resources, motivations, and access to political power, the consequences for the maintenance of democracy are great. Understanding the attitudes and actions of the "politically relevant" stratum of society is critical to understanding the conditions under which democracy flourishes.

Thus, it is doubtful that unanimous support among the ordinary citizens of democracies for democratic norms is necessary. Instead, it may only be necessary that a significant portion of the citizens be receptive to democratic appeals from the leaders of society. Even a democratic elite may occasionally succumb to the temptation to oppress unpopular political minorities, however. Thus, the important research question concerns the conditions under which elite intolerance materializes and prevails over public policy.

THE SKOKIE-NAZI CONFLICT: AN OVERVIEW

The purpose of our research is to develop a theory of the conditions under which elites are mobilized in support of, or in opposition to, efforts of political minorities to exercise rights of democratic citizenship. Because it is normally thought that democracy can only be protected by a vigilant elite, our inquiry focuses upon a particular dispute—that over the efforts of the Village of Skokie, Illinois, to prohibit a demonstration by members of the National Socialist Party of America (Nazis)—in which repression seems to have been supported, if not initiated, by members of the elite. The Skokie-Nazi conflict presents a challenge to the elitist theory of democracy, a challenge that must be understood if the theory is to be used to account for the levels of democracy in American society.

The particular controversy in Skokie is itself important as an example of the recurrent rights conflict in local politics. However, the dispute extended well beyond the borders of Skokie, raising serious issues of constitutional law and having a major impact on the oldest and largest libertarian interest group in the United States. For many members of this group—the American Civil Liberties Union (ACLU)—Skokie presented a context in which they were unable to support the rights of an unpopular minority political group. Further, opposition to minority rights extended beyond attitudes; a substantial number of members of ACLU took action to support the limitation of the rights of the Nazis. The consequences of the members of such a group opposing minority rights are substantial; if the members of ACLU, presumably one of the most democratic segments of the elite, are unwilling to support minority political rights, then it is quite unlikely that the remainder of society—elite and mass—will rally to the support of democratic rights. Issues that generate so much dissension among the elite can contribute greatly to the development of democratic theory.

CHAPTER BY CHAPTER OVERVIEW

In the next chapter we examine the specific context of the civil liberties dispute in Skokie. The chapter is essentially an overview of the entire controversy. We first look at Skokie itself to see why a Nazi demonstration there would be any different from one held in any other city. We also briefly examine the Nazi movement in the United States so that we can place the Nazi "threat" in perspective. The events themselves are documented and a brief synopsis of the legal decisions generated by the dispute is presented. And, finally, we look at Skokie's politics in an attempt to determine why the Village's political citizens and elites reacted the way they did to this tiny band of extreme rightists.

Chapter 3 is partially technical in nature. Since the book is based on an analysis of an extensive survey of ACLU and Common Cause members, it is necessary to report the sampling procedures, the weighting of the responses, and other such procedures. And, since the book is about elite tolerance, it is also important to establish that the members of ACLU and Common Cause are, in fact, elites. This we do by comparing the social characteristics of the respondents with the social characteristics of elites as defined in other major studies. Finally, we compare the attitudes of our respondents with a recent survey of the mass public to see if they are, in fact, more tolerant of potential activities of unpopular political groups.

The Skokie-Nazi dispute was reported to have had a nearly devastating impact on the ACLU. In Chapter 4, we examine the consequences of the controversy for the organization. We first consider ACLU's estimate that it lost about 15 percent of its membership over its decision to defend the Nazis. We examine the knowledge the members had of the issue, their attitudes toward ACLU's position, and the reasons why they held these attitudes. We then assess the overall impact Skokie had on the organization *in relation to other controversial civil liberties issues.* Finally, we turn our attention to those who actually quit over Skokie. We examine their personal characteristics, libertarian attitudes, and their attitudes toward the ACLU in order to account for why they quit or did not quit the organization.

In Chapter 5 we are concerned with the more general concept of political tolerance. Initially, we take issue with the ways other researchers have measured political tolerance. Tolerance has rarely been conceptualized as a system of beliefs. It has typically been assumed that tolerance is a single dimension. We show that this approach is far too simplistic; tolerance is a syndrome of beliefs. Free speech, for example, does not have the same meaning as freedom of assembly. Our analysis suggests that it is useful to distinguish between two types of civil liberties: rights of political opposition, and rights related to freedom from intervention in certain aspects of the private lives of citizens.

It is commonly observed that general attitudes are not well translated into opinions within specific situations. In Chapter 6 we assess the extent and causes of inconsistency in the opinions and beliefs of the elites and assess the degree of congruence between abstract civil liberties attitudes and specific reactions to the Skokie dispute. We find that, among elites, abstract commitment to democratic norms played a very significant role in structuring responses to the conflict. Furthermore, to the extent that slippage occurs, it is in the failure of those with intolerant attitudes to adopt intolerant positions in specific situations.

Chapter 7 holds a unique position in research on political tolerance in that we examine the relationship between tolerance attitudes and *actual behavior*. We were fairly successful in accounting for the process of mobilizing attitudes into behavior and found that contextual stimuli make it easier for some to act, while making it more difficult for others. By combining general attitudes, specific opinions, and perceptions of the context of the dispute, intolerant political behavior is reasonably well predicted.

In the final chapter we consider the implications of the model, holding that contextual stimuli raise and lower hurdles or impediments to political behavior. Based on the findings of the project, we suggest modifications to the elitist theory of democracy. We conclude with some comments on the roles of interest groups in protecting liberty in democratic societies.

NOTES

1. There are other difficulties with the Sullivan, Piereson, and Marcus approach, especially insofar as the relationship between tolerance and democracy is concerned. In allowing the subjects to select their own least-liked group, Sullivan, Piereson, and Marcus are tapping the extreme limits of intolerance. But their approach almost predetermines a finding of "pluralistic intolerance." They discover that there is some considerable diversity in the groups picked as least-liked, but they do not know the nature of the relationship between "liking" and intolerance. At what point along the "liking" scale do people become intolerant? *Sullivan, Piereson, and Marcus are able to demonstrate that at the end of the "liking" continuum, people are intolerant, but they cannot ascertain how much "dislike" is necessary in order for an intolerant response to be given.* Thus, although everyone may pick a different group as most disliked, this does not mean that a group that is relatively disliked will nonetheless be the object of intolerance. Sullivan, Piereson, and Marcus present data that are a little curious on this point. In the 1976 Twin Cities survey, the subjects were queried about six activities. Table 2 (Sullivan, Piereson, and Marcus, 1979) reported the

percentage tolerant for the least-liked and second least-liked groups. For three of the activities, the least-liked group was tolerated less than the second least-liked group, which is to be expected. But on one activity, they were tolerated at equal levels, and on two activities the second least-liked group was tolerated *less* than the least-liked group. None of the differences is great, but, at the very least, these data hint of a curious relationship between liking and tolerance. Of course, they can provide some evidence on this point with the Stouffer items included in their survey for comparison purposes. But even this is flawed to some degree because they do not know how disliked the Stouffer groups are. If they did, it would be an important question to determine the empirical relationship between "like-dislike" and tolerance. These considerations make their findings of "pluralistic intolerance" suspect.

2. Elites generally tend to be *more* supportive of the civil liberties of political minorities than are the masses. However, this statement must not be taken, as it so often is, to mean that a pro-democratic elite consensus invariably exists. Systematic data on this point are a bit sketchy, to be sure, but a tentative conclusion can be drawn from McClosky and Brill's recent survey of a variety of elite groups. This survey reveals not only tremendous differences among various segments of the elite, but also a wide variety of issues on which a democratic consensus fails to materialize. For instance, the percentages scoring as "most tolerant" on the civil liberties scale are 33.5 percent for a mass public sample, 35.7 percent for a sample of police officials, 62.8 percent for a sample of community elites, and 85.9 percent for a sample of legal elites (McClosky and Chong, 1980, Table 3). Our own data, to be considered fully in later chapters, reinforce the view that elite consensus is far from automatic. It is quite easy within the context of the great differences between elites and masses to underemphasize the fact that elites are frequently less than democratic.

2   The Context of the Skokie-Nazi Dispute

The burden of our arguments concerning the conceptualization and operationalization of political tolerance to be presented below is that tolerance results from the application of conflicting values to particular circumstances. Moreover, the relationship between tolerant attitudes and tolerant behavior is surely one of contingent consistency: attitudes are only conditionally related to behavior. The relationship is contingent upon a variety of contextual factors, factors that emanate from the specific civil liberties conflict. Thus, analyses of tolerance that rely on contrived, and relatively abstract questionnaire items cannot provide a complete understanding of tolerance attitudes and behaviors. As Zellman argues: "The hypothetical concrete situations that elicit civil liberties attitudes lack the actor specificity, articulated context, and threat salience that is present in real-life situations involving dissent" (Zellman, 1975, pp. 34–35). The Skokie-Nazi dispute provides just such a real-life situation.

Because the specific context of civil liberties disputes is so important to understanding the dynamics of political tolerance, we provide in this chapter a description of the major events in the Skokie controversy. Substantial detail is given to the three ordinances adopted by Skokie. The constitutional and legal issues involved in the various litigation between the Nazis and Skokie are also reviewed, and careful attention is given to the role of the ACLU in the matter. Finally, so as to complete the review of the major actors in the dispute, we examine the role of the Skokie leaders and citizens in the dispute.

SKOKIE

Skokie is a middle-class suburb of Chicago, located a few miles north of the City and just west of Lake Michigan. Although technically a village, Skokie hardly portrays that image, housing some 70,000–80,000 people. It is a part of Chicago's inner ring of suburbs and, like so much of the North Shore, is hardly distinguishable from its neighbors.

To the casual observer, Skokie is a hodgepodge of small apartments, commercial strips, and single-family homes. In anticipation of forecast growth, the Village was divided into 25-and 35-foot lots in the 1930s and 1940s (League of Women Voters, 1959), a fact accounting for much of the Village's unplanned and crowded appearance.[1] Although Skokie's present population is well short of the 200,000 anticipated in the early 1940s, it is hardly a typical bedroom suburb. Excluding Chicago, Skokie is second in the state in industrial production, third in industrial sales, fourth in retail sales (Skokie Chamber of Commerce, 1977), and now has virtually no undeveloped land.

Skokie has also experienced major cultural change, becoming an important center of Jewish culture in the Chicago area. In the years before World War II, the residents of Skokie were almost entirely non-Jewish. In fact, most of its early settlers were German, and it is thus not surprising that many residents supported Nazi Germany and that membership in the German-American Bund was not inconsequential. The migration to the suburbs after the War brought a large number of Jews to Skokie, many of whom were moving from Chicago's inner-city neighborhoods in response to the immigration of blacks from the South. Houses in Skokie were reasonably priced and downtown Chicago was readily accessible from the Village.

Today, over one-half of the population of Skokie is Jewish. Ten synagogues are supported (Chicagoland's Community Guide, 1970), and the Village is the home of the Hebrew Theological College, a divinity school for the study of religion and the Hebrew language. The Village is also the home of the Brisk Rabbinical Academy, another institution ordaining rabbis. More importantly, Skokie remembers Nazi Germany. It has the highest number of Holocaust survivors of any city in the nation outside New York City. It is the home of hundreds of survivors of the Holocaust and of thousands of families with relatives who died in the Nazi concentration camps. Thus, Skokie was ideal for a controversy with Frank Collin and the Nazis.

As vulnerable as Skokie appears to be to the Nazis, it is still somewhat surprising that they were as successful as they were at creating a major, well-publicized controversy. After all, Collin's National Socialist Party of America, the Nazi group involved in the dispute, cannot count more than 20 or 30 members. Do the Nazis really pose a socio-political threat that merits such great concern? Of course, this question cannot be easily answered, but, so as to put the Nazis in some perspective, a brief review of Nazism in the United States is in order.

THE NAZI MOVEMENT IN THE UNITED STATES[2]

The Nazi movement in the United States began after World War I with the rise of the German-American Bund. It reached its zenith of power and influence in 1937 and 1938. At that time, it had approximately 8500 members and 5000 to 6000 anonymous sympathizers. The Bund formed the basis of Hitler's support in the United States and espoused Hitler's nationalism, doctrine of Aryan superiority, and, of course, his virulent anti-Jewish doctrine. A division of the Bund, the Ordnungs-dienst, or OD, was a paramilitary unit patterned after Hitler's SS. The OD were fully-uniformed elites—outfitted with the typical Sam Brown belts and the swastika arm bands associated with Nazi Germany. The movement, however, died very shortly after Pearl Harbor and the United States declaration of war on the Axis powers. The Treasury Department seized Bund records and arrested many Bund leaders, a number of whom were convicted for engaging in subversive activities, or for violating the 1940 Selective Service Act. Deportations were also not uncommon.

Nazism in the United States remained dormant for many years, for fairly obvious reasons, until it was revived in the 1950s by George Lincoln Rockwell. Rockwell, a former Lieutenant Commander in the U.S. Navy, worked with a variety of right-wing causes during the 1950s, and, with the assistance of Harold N. Arrowsmith, Jr., a wealthy businessman, created the National Committee to Free America from Jewish Domination. Arrowsmith provided a house in Arlington, Virginia, as a headquarters for the organization, and purchased printing equipment to publish material purporting to show Jewish intrigues and complicity in historical events. Arrowsmith eventually withdrew his support and Rockwell then renamed the organization the American Nazi Party.

The Party was organized along paramilitary lines, with the national commander (Rockwell) acting as Führer. In addition to the Commander, the organization had majors, captains, lieutenants and storm troopers (the lowest echelon). The storm troopers wore khaki shirts and trousers, paratrooper boots, fatigue caps, and swastika arm bands. All party members were required to take the following oath:

In the presence of the Great Spirit of the Universe and my loyal Party comrades, I hereby irrevocably pledge: To Adolf Hitler, the philosophical leader of the White Man's fight for an idealistic and scientific world order against the atheistical and materialistic forces of Marxism and racial suicide, I pledge my reverence and respect. To the Commander of Adolf Hitler's National Socialist Movement, I pledge my faith, my courage, and my obedience. To my Party Comrades, throughout the world, I pledge my absolute loyalty, even unto death. To myself, as a leader of the White Man's fight, I pledge a clean and manly life of honor. To the United States of America, I pledge my loyalty and my careful compliance with its Constitution and laws until those which are unjust can be legally changed by winning the hearts of the people. To my ignorant fellow white men, who will hate and persecute me because they have been so cruelly brainwashed, I pledge my patience and my love. To the traitors of my race and nation, I pledge swift and ruthless justice. (Bell, 1973, p. 113)

From his headquarters in Arlington, Rockwell controlled an organization of a few hundred members with units in Boston, Chicago, Dallas, Los Angeles, and Oakland.

Rockwell and his followers used shock tactics to capture mass-media exposure, and thus to give the impression that the organization was larger and stronger than it actually was. As the Party's notoriety increased, Rockwell began a series of nationwide lectures at colleges and universities and increased the production of books, articles, and other printed material. The basic theme emerging from the party literature was a combination of anti-black and anti-Jewish sentiment. Writings dealing with the supremacy of the Aryan race were few, however. Instead, the emphasis was on White supremacy in an attempt to broaden the Party's appeal.

Rockwell was killed by a former party member in 1967, shortly after renaming the Party the National Socialist White People's Party (NSWPP). He was then replaced by Matt Koehl, the commander of the Party's Chicago unit. Koehl changed the direction of the Party, moving away from dramatic, publicity-focused events, to concerns with defining doctrine and organizing converts.

Like many extremist organizations, the NSWPP spawned several splinter groups. Most such groups are lead by individuals who have been purged from the Party. John Patler, Rockwell's murderer, formed the American National Party after having been expelled from the

NSWPP. James Madole, another Nazi, led the National Renaissance Party in New York. Koehl, before beginning an association with Madole, and later Rockwell, founded and led the National States Rights Party, a small, but affluent, splinter group in Reedy, West Virginia, and a homosexual Nazi organization, the National Socialist League, in Los Angeles.

The most relevant of these splinter groups is, of course, Frank Collin's National Socialist Party of America. Collin has a few followers in Missouri, Texas, and California, but the major part of the organization is composed of the 20 or 30 members in the Marquette Park area of Chicago. Collin was apparently forced out of the NSWPP in 1967 when the *New York Times* reported that his father, Max Collin, was a Jew.

Of the current Nazi leaders, Collin comes closest in style to George Lincoln Rockwell. Though he hardly commands the physical presence of Rockwell, he has Rockwell's flair for using the media. Collins' organization is small and is without major resources, but has commanded a great deal of attention. Hamlin points out that:

> The absence of large numbers of followers and big money hasn't diminished Collin's activity over the years.... It is that activity and the disproportionate press coverage it receives which took Collin down the road to Skokie, creating one of the most heated free speech controversies of the decade, bringing Frank Collin press clippings and news footage beyond his wildest dreams, and catapulting him from local notoriety in Chicago to national news. (Hamlin, 1978, p. 10)

Publicity notwithstanding, the Nazi movement in the United States since World War II has been small. During the ten or eleven years that the movement was headed by Rockwell, there were never more than 400–500 contributors. Collins splinter organization in Chicago is tiny even by these standards. Why then, it might be asked, is there such a great amount of concern over such an insignificant number of Nazis?

There are a number of reasons for the concern, not the least of which is the abhorrent Nazi political philosophy. Rockwell publicly espoused the use of gas chambers for Jews. His biography is replete with such statements. He explicitly admitted that he was "an exponent of gas chambers for Jewish (and all other) Communist traitors" (Rockwell, 1963, p. 10), and estimated that "about eighty percent of adult Jews will be found guilty of treason and have to be gassed..."(Rockwell, 1963, p. 17).

Although there are no more than 1000 to 1200 Nazis throughout the country, their media exposure provides them a visibility far disproportionate to their numbers. Running for local public office (Nazis have been on the ballots in Baltimore, Chicago, Milwaukee, St. Louis, and San Francisco) has been a particularly effective publicity stratagem. Hamlin notes the success Frank Collin has had in exploiting the Chicago media.

> Collin is all but made for television. Just as a bad auto accident makes for good news footage—scenes which are both fascinating and repulsive—so Frank Collin makes for a good item on the evening news. His symbols make him instantly recognizable. He is visual, noisy, interesting, emotional and there is always some sort of action near him. He is all that a news director could ask for, and the results are not surprising. Frank Collin is more easily recognized by most Chicago-area residents than any of the last five Republican candidates for the office of mayor of Chicago. And Collin has gotten a whole lot more press than all five of them combined. (Hamlin, 1978, p. 9)

Thus, to many, the Nazis do not seem to be the insignificant political movement suggested by their number.

Finally, there is a concern over the effects of Nazism on zealots and the emotionally unstable. Many of those associated with Nazism are capable of cruel and violent actions against individuals. During 1977 alone, a number of unrelated events took place that illustrate this brutality. Consider the following: a Chicago Nazi murdered a Jew by forcing him to inhale hydrogen cyanide. Several months earlier a Nazi follower in New York killed five people. Later that year, several of Collin's followers were indicted for attempted murder following a confrontation with members of the Jewish Defense League. A Nazi in North Carolina fired several shots into a crowd of blacks attending a Labor Day picnic (Neier, 1979, pp. 21–22). And, of course, in that same state the Nazis and communists have clashed violently. Similar events occur several times every year throughout the country. These sporadic instances of violence have a greatly disproportionate psychological impact.

Thus, to many Frank Collin's small group represented a very real threat, especially in Skokie. Nazis espouse a philosophy of discrimination and death. They stir memories of one of the great horrors of mankind. Their successful use of the media gives them the appearance of a political group more substantial than their true number. And overt acts of violence are prevalent enough to fuel the fears and insecurities of Jews and others. Thus it is not too difficult to understand how Frank Collin was able to have such an impact on the leaders and residents of Skokie.

SKOKIE'S REACTION TO FRANK COLLIN

The Skokie-Nazi dispute actually began in Chicago. The headquarters of Collin's Nazis is located in a small building in an area close to Marquette Park on Chicago's south side. The area around Marquette Park has been the site of a number of racial confrontations in recent years. Racial tensions run high, focusing on the issue of residential integration. Blacks moving away from the center of Chicago have attempted, without palpable success, to move into the area. Black marches in Marquette Park have generated adverse reactions from the white community, including counter-demonstrations and violence. Confrontations of this type are, of course, made-to-order for the Nazis, and Collin and his group have demonstrated and marched in the area on numerous occasions.

In 1976, however, the parameters of the dispute started to change. In an attempt to quiet the area around Marquette Park, the Chicago Park District began to enforce an old, largely dormant ordinance. The law required that an insurance bond of $250,000 be posted before the Park District would issue a permit to demonstrate. Collin, effectively rendered impotent by the Park District's action, turned to the American Civil Liberties Union for legal assistance and it responded. In May 1976, the ACLU filed suit in the U.S. District Court on Collin's behalf challenging the Park District's restriction on the freedom of assembly and speech.

The lifeblood of Collin and his movement is publicity, for he has little to offer other than the visibility associated with media exposure. While awaiting trial in federal court, Collin was effectively denied access to the media. He had no cause of any great interest. In an effort to regenerate media attention, he wrote in early 1977 to a number of Chicago suburbs, including Skokie, requesting permission to hold a suburban demonstration protesting the Chicago policy. Most of the communities ignored Collin's request; one did not.

The Skokie Park District responded to Collin's inquiry by informing him that his organization would be required to post a $350,000 insurance bond in order to hold a rally. Collin again called on ACLU, and another lawsuit was filed on his behalf. Collin also sent another missive to Skokie, announcing his intention to demonstrate in front of the Skokie Village Hall on May 1, 1977, for about half an hour in protest of the Skokie Park District insurance requirement. He advised the Village that the Nazis would carry signs with slogans such as "White Free Speech," "Free Speech for White Americans," and "Free Speech for the White Man," but would make no derogatory remarks either orally or in writing directed at any ethnic or religious group. Collin also advised the Village that his group would be in Nazi uniform and that the uniforms included a swastika emblem on the arm band.

When news of this reached the residents of Skokie, many became upset. Local organizations adopted two resolutions: one to deny the Nazis the right to march, and another calling for a counter-demonstration on May 1st a few blocks from the Village Hall. Twelve to fifteen thousand people were expected to participate in the counter-demonstration. Village officials were fearful of violence, and four days before the scheduled march filed a petition asking the Circuit Court of Cook County (a state court) to enjoin the Nazis from parading in uniform. The complaint alleged that the public display of the swastika constituted a symbolic assault against a large number of Skokie residents.

> The threatened march of the defendants [the Nazis] has aroused the passions of thousands of individuals of Jewish faith or ancestry within the Village and more particularly has aroused the passions of the survivors of the Nazi concentration camps who are taking measures unknown to the plaintiffs [the Village of Skokie] to thwart the threatened march. The march of the defendants on May 1, 1977, is a deliberate and willful attempt to exacerbate the sensitivities of the Jewish population in Skokie and to incite racial and religious hatred. Said march, if not restrained by Order of this Court, constitutes a grave and serious threat to the peace of the citizens of the Village of Skokie. By reason of the ethnic and religious composition of the Village of Skokie and the circumstances alleged above, the public display of the swastika in connection with the proposed activities of the defendant, National Socialist Party of America, constitutes a symbolic assault against large numbers of the residents of the Plaintiff village and an incitation to violence and retaliation. (From Skokie's complaint asking for the issuance of an emergency injunction, quoted in Neier, 1979, pp. 44–45.)

The Circuit Court convened on April 28th, with Circuit Court Judge Joseph Wosik presiding. Testimony for Skokie that a counter-demonstration against the Nazis might become uncontrollable included statements by one concentration camp survivor that he did not know if he could refrain from attacking Collin when he saw the swastika. Judge Wosik issued an injunction barring the Nazis from engaging in any of the following actions on May 1, 1977, within the Village of Skokie: "Marching, walking or parading or otherwise displaying the swastika on or off their persons; distributing pamphlets or displaying any materials which incite or promote hatred against persons of Jewish faith or ancestry or hatred against persons of any faith or ancestry, race or religion" (quoted in Neier, 1979, pp. 45–48). The ACLU, representing Collin, appealed the order, but, on the following afternoon, the Illinois Appellate Court denied its motion for a stay of the injunction against the march.

Collin was not deterred, however. After hearing of the Appellate Court's decision, Collin announced that the Nazis would march the very next day, Saturday, April 30th. The court order had specified only that no march should take place on May 1st. On the morning of the 30th, the attorney for the Village of Skokie was successful at convincing Circuit Court Judge Harold Sullivan to modify Judge Wosik's injunction so as to ban the march without limitation as to date or time, pending further order of the court. Since Collin's motorcade was already underway, the police intercepted Collin at the Skokie exit of the expressway and informed him of the new court order. Collin turned back.

On May 2nd, Skokie adopted three new ordinances intended to control demonstrations within the Village. The three ordinances, 994, 995, and 996 are reproduced in Appendix A. Ordinance 994 required demonstrators on the Village streets to secure a permit at least 30 days in advance and to post liability insurance of $300,000 and property damage insurance of $50,000. The ordinance also provided that permits would be issued only if the Village manager found "the conduct of the parade, public assembly, or similar activity will not portray criminality, depravity, or lack of virtue in, or incite violence, hatred, abuse or hostility toward a person or group of persons by reason of reference to religious, racial, ethnic, national or regional affiliation." Furthermore, the ordinance allowed the Village trustees the discretion to waive any of its provisions. Ordinance 995 made it a crime to disseminate any material "which promotes and incites hatred against persons by reason of their race, national origin, or religion...." Markings and clothing of symbolic significance were also prohibited. Ordinance 996 prohibited persons from engaging "in any march, walk or public demonstration as a member or on behalf of any political party while wearing a military-style uniform." All three ordinances were adopted unanimously.

Collin applied on June 22, 1977, for a permit under Ordinance 994 to hold a march on July 4th in front of the Village Hall. Since he could not secure the $350,000 insurance, he requested that the Village waive the requirement, or that it help him find an insurer. Skokie declined both requests, and consequently the ACLU filed suit in federal court to invalidate the three ordinances.

Collin's announced intention to demonstrate again provoked the community, and, although the Nazis did not appear on July 4th, the Jewish Defense League did. Thirty-one JDL members with black helmets marched in military formation in a parking lot at the Jewish Community Center. About 2,000 people were on hand as observers. News and photographs of the event were published widely.

In mid-July, the Illinois Appellate Court modified the injunction against the Nazi march. The Nazis would be allowed to demonstrate. Skokie had contended, relying on *Brandenburg v. Ohio*, that display of the Nazi uniform was the symbolic equivalent of a public call to kill all Jews, and consequently that it constituted a "direct incitation to immediate mass murder." It also contended, relying primarily on *Chaplinsky v. New Hampshire*, that Nazi uniforms are the equivalent of fighting words, and hence were not protected by the First Amendment. The Court was not persuaded. Although the Court's opinion asserted that there was a virtual certainty that thousands of irate Jewish citizens would physically attack the Nazis, it held that the mere presence of hostile spectators could not justify the restraint of First Amendment activity. However, the Nazis would not be allowed to display the swastika. The Court's logic was:

The swastika is a symbol [that] is inherently likely to provoke violent reaction among those of the Jewish persuasion or ancestry when intentionally brought in close proximity to their homes and places of worship. The swastika is a personal affront to every member of the Jewish faith, in remembering the nearly consummated genocide of their people, committed within memory, by those who used the swastika as their symbol. This is especially true for the thousands of Skokie residents who personally survived the holocaust of the Third Reich. They remember all too well the brutal destruction of their families and communities by those wearing the swastika. So, too, the tens of thousands of Skokie's Jewish residents must feel gross revulsion for the swastika and would immediately respond to .

the personally abusive epithets slung their way in the form of the defendant's chosen symbol, the swastika. (*Village of Skokie v. National Socialist Part of America*, 366 N.E. 2d 347, Illinois Appellate Court, 1977, quoted in Neier, 1979, pp. 51–52.)

Thus, the Appellate Court held that the display of the swastika was inherently likely to evoke violent reactions and that "the Village of Skokie [had] met its heavy burden of justifying the prior restraint imposed upon the defendants' planned wearing and display of the swastika."

Once more, ACLU appealed, this time to the Illinois Supreme Court, arguing its case in September of 1977. This appeal was somewhat more successful: on January 27, 1978, the Court ruled in a 7–1 vote that neither the march nor the swastika emblem could be prohibited. Quoting at length from *Cohen v. California*,[3] the Court explained that, as offensive as the display of the swastika may be, it is symbolic political speech intended to convey the beliefs of those who display it. The display cannot be precluded because it may

provoke a violent reaction by those who view it. Particularly this is true where, as here, there has been advance notice by the demonstrators of their plans so that they have become... "common knowledge" and those to whom sight of the swastika banner or uniforms would be offensive are forewarned and need not view them. A speaker who gives prior notice of his message has not compelled a confrontation with those who voluntarily listen.

Thus, the injunction was vacated. Only the problem of the ordinances remained.

Here too, however, the ACLU litigation was beginning to produce results. Federal Judge Bernard M. Decker of the Federal Court for the Northern District of Illinois declared all three of the ordinances unconstitutional (see *Collin v. Smith*, 447 f. Supp. 676, N.D. Ill., 1978). The insurance requirement was unconstitutional because it posed an impossible obstacle to the free exercise of First Amendment rights in Skokie. He noted that there was uncontradicted testimony that the NSPA could not obtain the requisite insurance "because insurance companies are simply not interested in writing the kind of policy required due to the unknown risks involved" (477 F. Supp. at 684), and, even if the insurance were available, its premium could be as much as $1000 for each event. Thus, the requirement was a "drastic restriction on the right of freedom of speech and assembly [which] is an abridgement 'in the guise of regulation'" (447 F. Supp. at 685), and imposed a "virtually insuperable obstacle to the free exercise of First Amendment rights in the Village of Skokie, which obstacle has not been proved to be justified by the legitimate needs of the Village and which may be disposed of at the uncontrolled and standardless discretion of the Village government" (447 F. Supp. at 686).

The racial slur provisions of ordinances 994 and 995 were held to be vague and overbroad and to impose an unconstitutional prior restraint on speech. Judge Decker argued that the issue was not "whether there are some ideas that are completely unacceptable in a civilized society," but rather whether "the danger that allowing the government to punish 'unacceptable' ideas will lead to suppression of ideas that are merely uncomfortable to those in power" is greater than "the danger that permitting free debate on such unacceptable ideas will encourage their acceptance rather than discouraging them by revealing their pernicious quality." He noted that the United States Supreme Court has adopted the position that the expression of a particular idea may not be suppressed unless it is both intended to and likely to incite imminent unlawful conduct (see *Brandenburg v. Ohio*[4]). Such was obviously not true of the proposed Nazi demonstration. Moreover, the prohibition was unconstitutionally vague because it made it unreasonably difficult to distinguish speech intentionally inciting hatred, which Skokie claimed was prohibitable, from speech instigating social unrest, which is clearly protectable. Finally, the group libel ordinance denying a permit for a public assembly because the participants are expected to incite hatred or hostility toward a race or religion or portray criminality was deemed to be an unconstitutional prior restraint on free speech.

Judge Decker also struck down the ban on demonstrations in military-style uniforms, declaring that the banning of the display of symbols, repugnant or not, is unconstitutional. He was not persuaded by Skokie's contention that military-style uniforms offended both the notion of civilian control of government and the moral standards of the Village residents, instead asserting that:

The First Amendment embraces the freedom to advocate even that government ought to be violently overthrown, let alone that it ought not be controlled by civilians. Thus, the banning of a symbol which is repugnant to a 'tradition' which all Americans are free to reject and openly criticize is clearly unconstitutional. The reference to Skokie's standards of decency and morality is apparently an attempt to invoke the 'community standards' test applied in obscenity cases.... However, to be obscene, speech must in some way be erotically stimulating.... Plaintiffs' wearing of uniforms is political speech, which, as the Court has often emphasized, 'need not meet standards of acceptability'.... The court finds Ordinance #996 to be patently and flagrantly unconstitutional on its face. (447 F. Supp. at 700)

The efforts of Skokie officials to prohibit a demonstration by the Nazis were resoundingly rebuffed in the district court opinion.

Skokie's counsel appealed Judge Decker's decision to the Seventh Circuit Court of Appeals, relying heavily on *Beauharnais v. Illinois.*[5] On May 22, 1978, the Court strongly affirmed Judge Decker's decision (*Collin v. Smith,,* 578 F. 2d 1197, 7th Cir., 1978). Although not precluding the possibility of punishing or preventing nonpersonal insults, the Court relied on the fact that Skokie had taken the position that neither the Nazis nor their audience would create violence, and therefore held that the fighting words doctrine of *Chaplinsky v. New Hampshire*[6] did not support the application of Ordinance #995 to the proposed demonstration (578 F. 2d at 1203). Skokie's claim that mental anguish, or "menticide," would be inflicted upon the community by the Nazis was similarly rejected because of the great difficulty of distinguishing speech that might inflict psychic trauma from speech that merely induces conditions of unrest, creates dissatisfaction with present conditions, or even stirs people to anger. Moreover, whatever protections from offensive speech as might apply were not relevant because the potential audience was far from captive. After the decision of the Circuit Court of Appeals little of substance was left of the Skokie ordinances. The final knell was heard when Skokie unsuccessfully appealed to the United States Supreme Court, which denied certiorari. Thus, the Skokie ordinances were nullified.

Frank Collin and his Nazis never actually marched in Skokie, however, because the obstacles were also removed from their attempt to demonstrate in Chicago. In June 1978, a U.S. District Court judge ordered the Chicago Park District to issue Collin a permit to demonstrate in Marquette Park. After negotiations, Collin restricted his demonstration to the Federal Building Plaza in Chicago and to Marquette Park. Thus, the Skokie dispute ended.

THE REACTIONS OF LOCAL CITIZENS AND LEADERS

The possibility that the Nazis would march on the thoroughfares of Skokie generated no small amount of consternation within the Village. And the reactions of local citizens—masses and elites—are important within the broader context of the elitist theory of democracy. We therefore believe it is important to devote some attention to the local politics of the dispute. Because David Barnum has written such a thorough account of the dispute, it is useful simply to reproduce his report of the major elements of the Skokie reaction to the Nazis.

∫ ∫ ∫

PUBLIC OPINION AND ELITE BEHAVIOR IN THE SKOKIE CONTROVERSY

The policy-making process in the Skokie free speech controversy was characterized by an initial phase—governed by an original consensus among public officials and community leaders in Skokie that the Nazis should be allowed to march—and a subsequent phase—governed by a new consensus among public officials and community leaders, formulated in response to public pressures, that every available legal means should be adopted to try to prevent the Nazis from marching. Moreover, the Skokie free speech controversy as a whole generated a distinctive set of interactions involving, on the one hand, public officials, community leaders, and the general public, and, on the other hand, public officials and the courts.

The Original Consensus

The original consensus among public officials in the Skokie controversy consisted of two parts. When Village officials first learned, in March of 1977, that Frank Collin intended to come to Skokie, some of the officials—including the Village Counsel and one or two members of the Board of Trustees—indicated that in their opinion the Nazis probably had a right to march in Skokie. Their opinions were based less on a

---

Source: David G. Barnum, "Decision Making in a Constitutional Democracy: Policy Formation in the Skokie Free Speech Controversy." *Journal of Politics* 44 (May 1982). Footnotes omitted.

strong personal or professional commitment to freedom of speech than on a rough familiarity with constitutional decisions of the U.S. Supreme Court and other courts. They felt that the courts in the past had taken the position that demonstrators had a right to march, despite community hostility, and would so rule in the Skokie case if called upon to do so. The second and more widely shared view among public officials—which was related to the first—was that the best strategy for handling the situation would be to allow the Nazis to come to Skokie but ignore them. The consensus was that opposition to the march would be counter-productive, because the Village would eventually lose in court, but even if a court fight to prevent the Nazis from coming to Skokie were a success, or at least succeeded in postponing the day on which the Nazis came, the intervening publicity would represent a greater prize to Frank Collin than would coming to Skokie itself.

The New Consensus

The original consensus among public officials in the Skokie controversy collapsed almost immediately—within three or four weeks of its inception—and was replaced by the unanimous view among the public officials that every possible avenue of opposition to the proposed Nazi march should be explored. The exploration soon focused on two strategies, however, both of which involved transferring ultimate responsibility for resolution of the issue to the courts. On April 28, 1977, the Village sought and obtained in state court an injunction against the proposed May first Nazi march. Then, on May 2, 1977, at its regular weekly meeting, the Board of Trustees voted unanimously, and without any discussion at the meeting itself, to pass three ordinances designed to prevent the Nazis from marching. The ordinances, however, were immediately challenged in federal court on grounds of unconstitutionality.

The reasons for the new "antidemocratic" consensus among public officials in the Skokie controversy were mixed. On the one hand, many of the officials—including some who were Jewish but had not previously had extensive contact with survivors of the Nazi Holocaust—became aware for the first time of the depth of both fear and hostility on the Nazi issue among survivors and others in the community. This realization led in some cases to a genuine sympathy for the feelings of the survivors and to a belief that those feelings should take precedence over the alleged First Amendment rights of the Nazis. It led in other cases to a realization that enormous violence was unavoidable should the Nazis come to Skokie and therefore to a conclusion that the free speech issues in the Skokie case were, at best, academic. In either case, however, it produced support for efforts to prevent the Nazis from marching. Among elected officials, of course, there was an additional reason for supporting the new consensus, namely, that continued support for the position that the Nazis should be allowed to come and go without publicity would be tantamount to committing political suicide. Irrespective of the precise distribution of public opinion in the Skokie controversy, dedicated opponents of the Nazi march could easily organize a campaign to produce the electoral defeat, or perhaps even the recall, of a dissenting public official—or such, at least, was the subjective perception of the officials themselves.

Public officials justified their opposition to a Nazi march in a variety of ways. One common argument was that the primary responsibility of a public official in a situation such as that which Skokie faced was to prevent violence and property damage from occurring in the community, even if the source of these dangers was some of the citizens of Skokie or other opponents of the Nazis. Another widely held belief was that responsibility for the probable violence could be imputed to the Nazis themselves, because they were coming to Skokie with the intention of provoking violence or because a demonstration by Nazis in Skokie, regardless of its purpose, would constitute "fighting words" in a constitutional sense. Finally, public officials subscribed to two arguments—one emphasizing the exceptionally brutal character of the Nazi regime in Europe and a second emphasizing the fact that the Nazis, if they came to power, would destroy the very freedom of speech for which they themselves were asking—which were designed to differentiate the Nazis from all other groups and to portray them as uniquely undeserving of First Amendment protection.

It thus appears that the motivations of those who joined the new consensus and the reasons they gave for joining it were varied. However, the consensus itself was essentially unanimous among public officials and community leaders in Skokie. It endorsed the propriety of committing all of the available resources of the Village of Skokie to the battle to prevent the Nazis from marching in the community. In this sense, it was an antidemocratic consensus of unambiguous scope and content. At the same time, however, the consensus did not endorse the use of all possible *means* to prevent the Nazis from marching in Skokie. In fact, it endorsed only the use of legal means. Moreover, those who were in

charge of publicly announcing and explaining the legal steps which were
being taken were always careful to emphasize that the decisions of the
courts, whatever they were, would be obeyed. Therefore, the consensus,
while it was unapologetically "antidemocratic" on the free speech
issues involved, was scrupulously "democratic" on the remaining constitutional and political issues in the case.

Public Officials, Community Leaders, and the General Public

Relations among public officials, community leaders, and the general
public in the Skokie controversy conform to much of what we know
about the nature of decision-making in a complex democracy. The first
people to learn that Frank Collin intended to hold a demonstration in
Skokie were the Village officials. Upon discovering, with some chagrin,
that the Village had no ordinances which could serve to regulate, let
alone to prevent, such a demonstration, Village officials got in touch
with various community leaders, in particular leaders of the Jewish
community and various Jewish organizations, and together they pro-
pounded the strategy of letting the Nazis come to Skokie but ignoring
them when they did. The strategy broke down, however, as soon as the
public was informed of the proposed visit by the Nazis to Skokie, at
which point the Village hastily prepared to go to court to seek an
injunction against the march and hastily enacted three ordinances,
which, although they were certain to be tested in court, were aimed, in
the meantime, at preventing the Nazis from marching.

Once this strategy was adopted, it became important to enlist the
support of the community, including those who would not be satisfied
with the use of merely legal means to prevent the Nazis from marching,
but it also became important for Village officials to preserve for themselves a somewhat free hand in the implementation of the strategy and
to avoid undue publicity about the daily developments and decisions in
the case. An exchange which occurred at the regular public meeting of
the Board of Trustees on April 25, 1977, just three days before the
Village entered state court to seek an injunction against the Nazi march,
is indicative of the dilemma of Village officials and their response to it:

Village Counsel: The Village is planning for every contingency
and is pursuing the possibility of legal action to
prevent the Nazis from marching. However, it
has been the policy of the Village and it will
continue to be our policy throughout that it is
not, we think, in the overall public interest to

discuss the specific details and plans of every-
thing the Village intends to do out in public.
We prefer not to do that. You must rest assured
and have confidence and trust in the statement
I have made.

Citizen: You can't tell us any specific actions you plan
to take?

Village Counsel: I cannot.

Citizen: So it's left up to the citizens of the community?

Village Counsel: No, it is left, first, up to the duly elected
government of this community. And this
government will act in accordance with the
best interests of the citizens of this community,
taking into consideration all that is being said
here tonight. Rest assured on that.

The responsibility for planning and implementing the strategy to
prevent the Nazis from marching, and, after various court decisions
went against the Village, the responsibility for planning the massive but
peaceful counter-demonstration, were kept within a relatively small
circle of public officials and community leaders in Skokie and the
Chicago metropolitan area. It is entirely possible that because of the
extensive network of Jewish organizations in the Skokie community,
"grassroots participation" by citizens in the effort to prevent the Nazis
from marching was in fact more widespread than it would have been—in
Skokie or anywhere else—in connection with any other, more "typical,"
urban issue. At the same time, the need to foster and implement a
compromise solution to the threat of a Nazi march—one which respected
the wishes of a majority of the community and in particular the wishes
of the survivors but also abjured any resort to violence—meant that all
the key decisions in the controversy had to be reached among individuals
who shared a willingness to transform the issue into one which was
capable of legal resolution and willingness to accept the decisions,
whatever they might be, of the courts.

Public Officials and the Courts

The consensus among public officials in the Skokie controversy
included agreement on the necessity of referring the issue of the Nazi
march to the courts and the necessity of abiding by whatever decision
was reached by the courts. None of the public officials believed that a
decision of the courts that the Nazis had a right to march would

represent a definitive statement of the truth in any metaphysical sense. The prevailing view among public officials in the Skokie case was that courts are human institutions, which often make incorrect decisions, but that such decisions, eventually, will be corrected. Most of the public officials concluded that the reason the courts decided against the Village—three out of five courts which rendered decisions in the Skokie litigation decided against the Village—was that the prevailing interpretation of the First Amendment at this juncture of American constitutional history is abnormally rigid or absolutist in content and that Skokie was simply ahead of its time in trying to acquaint judges with certain particularly subtle arguments relating to the proper meaning of the First Amendment in a civilized society.

Be that as it may, there was, on the part of the public officials, no reluctance, nor even any regret, about submitting the issue to the courts. Such an alternative offers public officials—in Skokie or elsewhere—several advantages. First, it means that they can rely on strictly legal means to further their opposition to a public demonstration by an unpopular group. Second, it means that they can enjoy all the political advantages of publicly opposing a demonstration by an unpopular group while simultaneously divesting themselves of the ultimate responsibility for deciding the issue. Third, it means that the stigma of a decision in favor of the right of an unpopular group to hold a public demonstration will fall upon the courts rather than upon themselves. Most of the public officials in the Skokie controversy argued, at least in retrospect, that the courts were the proper forum in which to decide an issue such as that with which their community was faced. Such deference to the courts, however, can have a number of wellsprings, especially among legislators. It can represent genuine enthusiasm for a constitutional arrangement which places ultimate decision-making responsibility for certain issues in the hands of the most politically insulated institutions in the society. Thus, it can represent a belief that courts are indeed necessary, on occasion, to save the society, and even its elected officials, from themselves. It can also represent, however, a permanent preference for letting someone else make the hard and unpopular decisions in the constitutional democracy. Thus, it can represent a convenient and corrupting method of escape from responsibility for public officials who are unwilling to accept their share of the burden of preserving the fundamental procedural norms of the democracy. It is difficult to know, in any given controversy, what motive or motives are actuating a particular legislator or group of legislators.

What is clear is that the structural characteristics of the American democracy permit elected officials and other public officials to withhold consensual support for a democratic norm such as the right of unpopular groups to hold peaceful demonstrations—indeed to join in a popular challenge to such a norm—without necessarily jeopardizing the prospect that the norm itself will be duly applied to a specific situation. The Skokie case should also caution us, however, that this conclusion may be valid only on the condition that public officials do not also withold consensual support for the democratic norm of reliance on the courts for the resolution of civil liberties issues and obedience to the decisions of the courts, whatever those decisions might be, in such cases.

ʃ ʃ ʃ

SKOKIE AND TOLERANCE

Thus, Barnum is willing to assert, perhaps grudgingly, that the Skokie ordinances were anti-democratic. We are willing to assert directly and with little qualification that support for the Skokie ordinances is an intolerant and anti-democratic position. Note that we are required to take no position on the matter of the Nazis themselves, in part because it is an unanswered empirical question as to whether the Nazis are anti-democratic. We do not defend Nazi ideology; if members of the Nazi Party, or of the Jewish Defense League, engage in criminal acts then all democratic theories would support their prosecution. But the issue for democratic theory is not the Nazis; rather the issue is the ordinances and whether *speech* of the type prohibited in the ordinances can be properly proscribed by democratic regimes. To reiterate, Skokie required $300,000 of public liability insurance and $50,000 of property damage insurance. Repression in the guise of regulation, has a long history in American law. Demonstrations creating "an imminent danger of a substantial breach of the peace, riot, or similar disorder" were prohibited, as were demonstrations portraying "criminality, depravity or lack of virtue in," or inciting "violence, hatred, abuse or hostility toward a person or group of persons by reason of reference to religious, racial, ethnic, national or regional affiliation." The dissemination of material "which promotes and incites hatred against persons by reason of their race, national origin, or religion" was also proscribed. Demonstrations while wearing "military-style" uniforms were made illegal. And there were serious procedural defects in the ordinances as well. It is our position that these prohibitions are of a breadth and importance sufficient to constitute a non-trivial encroachment on the rights of political opposition.

Within our understanding of the free speech/assembly continuum, the Skokie ordinances do not enhance these important rights. Support for freedom of speech/assembly is a propensity to extend guarantees of the right to speak and to assemble to more ideas, under more circumstances. It is unnecessary to claim that opposition to the Skokie ordinances is the "right" position. Instead, commitment to civil liberties is a continuum ranging from a position allowing no speeches/assemblies under any circumstances to one allowing all speeches/assemblies under all circumstances. Clearly, the Skokie ordinances tend toward the restrictive end of this scale.

Thus, the Skokie-Nazi conflict provides an interesting opportunity to study elite and mass support for the civil liberties of an unpopular political minority within a fully-specified, and *real* context. As a case-study test of the elitist theory of democracy, Skokie is ideal.

NOTES

1. In 1940 the Village, then known as Niles Center, had a population of only 7,172. In that year the Village changed its name to Skokie in recognition of its location at the gateway to the Skokie Valley.

2. This section draws heavily on an excellent history of American Nazism by Leland V. Bell (1973).

3. *Cohen* exemplifies the Supreme Court's current approach to the issue of "fighting words." Paul Cohen was convicted under a California statute that banned "maliciously and willfully disturb[ing] the peace or quiet of any neighborhood or person by offensive conduct." The California Court of Appeals construed "offensive conduct" as that behavior tending to provoke others to violent acts or to disturb the peace.

Cohen was arrested for wearing a jacket bearing the slogan "Fuck the Draft" in a Los Angeles courthouse corridor. The jacket was a means of expressing Cohen's strong negative feelings about the Selective Service and the war in Viet Nam. While Cohen's message caused no disturbance, the California Court of Appeals felt it reasonable to assume that it might have done so and affirmed the conviction.

The United States Supreme Court overturned the conviction. The Court felt that the doctrine of "fighting words" was inappropriate to Cohen's case for, although his language might often be used in a personally inciting manner, it had here not been directed at a particular person. The Court was less concerned with the particular words or message uttered than with the context in which they were communicated.

Cohen raised a second issue germane to the Skokie case, that of captive audiences. Counsel for California had argued that Cohen's message had been forced upon unwilling viewers and that the state had therefore appropriately restricted the communication of that message in the courthouse. It could be similarly argued that a Nazi demonstration in residential Skokie inflicted the anti-Jewish expression on those who lived in the area. Yet the Court in *Cohen* was unwilling to condone suppressing a speaker in order to protect the feelings of the audience, noting that viewers could "avoid further bombardment of their sensibilities simply by averting their eyes" (403 U.S. at 21).

On the matter of symbolic speech, in *Tinker v. Des Moines Independent School District*, 39 U.S. 503 (1969), students in both junior and senior high schools were suspended for wearing black armbands to protest the Vietnam War. Lower federal courts upheld the school board's action on the grounds that it was a reasonable measure to prevent a disturbance within the school. The Supreme Court reversed the decision below, however, viewing the action of the school system as a direct threat to First Amendment rights. There was no evidence, according to the Court, that the armbands provoked violence or interfered with the school's work. The Court held that anticipation of a disturbance is not enough to overcome the right to freedom of expression.

> Any departure from absolute regimentation may cause trouble. Any variation from the majority's opinion may inspire fear. Any words spoken, in class, in the lunchroom or on the campus, that deviate from the views of another person, may start an argument or cause a disturbance. But our Constitution says we must take this risk.
>
> If a regulation were adopted by school officials forbidding discussion of the Vietnam conflict, or the expression by any student of opposition to it anywhere on school property except as part of a prescribed classroom exercise, it would be obvious that the regulation would violate the constitutional rights of students, at least if it could not be justified by showing that the students' activities would materially and substantially disrupt the work and discipline of the school. [Here,] the prohibition of the silent, passive witness of the armbands, as one of the children called it, is no less offensive to the constitution's guarantees.

Thus expression, even if not strictly spoken speech, can be protected by the First Amendment.

4. Brandenburg, a leader of the Ku Klux Klan, was convicted under an Ohio Criminal Syndicalism statute of "advocat[ing] the duty, necessity or propriety of crime, sabotage, violence, or unlawful methods of terrorism as a

means of accomplishing industrial or political reform" and "of voluntarily assembl[ing] within any society, group or assemblage of persons formed to teach or advocate the doctrines of criminal syndicalism." In a filmed speech Brandenburg stated: "We are not a revengent organization, but if our President, our Congress, our Supreme Court, continues to suppress the white caucasian race, it's possible that there might have to be some revengence taken."

The Supreme Court reversed the conviction, distinguishing between advocating violence as a means of accomplishing political reform and inciting imminent lawless action. The Court held that the mere advocacy of violence as a means of accomplishing reform is constitutionally protected, although, of course, the state can prohibit specific violent actions in pursuit of revolution.

5. Beauharnais was convicted under a state statute prohibiting the manufacture, publication or exhibition in a public place of any publication portraying "depravity, criminality, unchastity, or lack of virtue of a class of citizens, of any race, color, creed or religion [which exposes such citizens] to contempt, derision or obloquy or which is productive of breach of the peace or riots." Beauharnais organized the distribution of an anti-integration leaflet that was derisive of blacks. The United States Supreme Court affirmed his conviction, holding that defamation of groups may be unprotected by the First Amendment in the same way as is the libel of individuals.

The Court affirmed the notion, expressed in *Chaplinsky* (see note 6), that a state can constitutionally prohibit obscenity, libel, or fighting words. And "...if an utterance directed at an individual may be the object of criminal sanctions, we cannot deny to a state power to punish the same utterance directed at a defined group, unless we can say that this is a willful and purposeless restriction unrelated to the peace and well-being of the state" (343 US at 258). Because Illinois had endured a great deal of racial tension and violence, much of which was provoked by racial slurs, the Court found it a reasonable exercise of the police power of the state to attempt to curb such defamation.

Counsel for Beauharnais argued that the "rational basis" test used by the Court was inappropriate and that in order to convict the jury must have found that the leaflet was likely to produce a clear and present danger of serious harm. The Court disagreed with this position, however, on the grounds that libelous utterances were not constitutionally protected and that it was therefore unnecessary to employ the "clear and present danger" of violence test.

The vitality of *Beauharnais* as a precedent was questioned by the United States District Court in *Collin v. Smith*. The Court first offered two rationales in support of the *Beauharnais* approach to group libel: that defamation might be viewed as damaging the reputations of the individuals belonging to the group and that such libel has such a tendency to produce violence that a further showing of personally provocative use is unnecessary. The Court found the first theory untenable because of the evolution of the laws of libel and defamation since *Beauharnais* had been decided (particularly, *New York Times v. Sullivan*). Moreover, the District Court held that the line of precedent concerning "fighting words" did not support a position that speech could be restricted for no further reason than an inherent tendency to lead to violence.

6. In 1942, in *Chaplinsky*, the Supreme Court held that certain types of speech could be restrained as "no essential part of any exposition of ideas and... of such slight social value as a step to truth that any benefits that may be derived from them is clearly outweighed by the social interests in order and morality" (315 U.S. at 572). One such category of speech includes insulting or "fighting" words. A unanimous Court affirmed a conviction under a statute construed by the state court to bar "words likely to cause an average addressee to fight." Chaplinsky, a Jehovah's Witness, denounced organized religion while proselytizing on the streets of Rochester, New Hampshire. Despite a city marshall's warning to "go slow" because his listeners were irate at the attacks on other faiths, Chaplinsky continued his activities. When a disturbance occurred, he was arrested. As he was being led to the police station, Chaplinsky called the city marshall a "god damned racketeer" and a "damned fascist."

The Court found that "fighting words" lacked sufficient value to society to justify tolerating the harm inflicted by them. Speech such as Chaplinsky's was not significant for its content. It was not part of any exchange of ideas; it served only to revile. Moreover, such speech was in itself hurtful, by its "very utterance inflict[ing] injury or tend[ing] to incite an immediate breach of the peace." Thus, quite in keeping with earlier announcements of constitutional policy on free speech, a balancing test was applied.

The Skokie case is factually distinguishable from *Chaplinsky*. In the latter, it was the language that was offensive and insulting, not the ideas being communicated. In contrast, the Skokie demonstrations were feared because of the anticipated impact of the views conveyed. Additionally, while Chaplinsky spoke directly to an individual, the city marshall, a Nazi march in Skokie might be considered to lack the same personally insulting quality. But regardless of the differences between the situations, *Chaplinsky* does serve as an example of certain speech being determined constitutionally suppressible in order to preserve social order.

Later the Supreme Court had decided an issue perhaps more directly relevant to the Skokie case. In *Terminiello v. Chicago*, 337 U.S. 1 (1949) the Supreme Court, in a 5-4 decision, overturned a breach of peace conviction. While speaking in a meeting hall, Terminiello, a suspended Catholic priest, viciously criticized certain racial and political groups. He referred to Communists and Jews as "slimy scum," "snakes," and "bedbugs." Violence ensued.

At trial, the ordinance was construed to ban conduct that "stirs the public to anger, invites dispute, brings about a condition of unrest, or creates a disturbance, or if it molests the inhabitants in the enjoyment of peace and quiet by arousing alarm." The lower court focused on the effect of the defendant's speech and found that, under the circumstances, he had indeed disturbed the peace. The conviction was affirmed by both the Illinois Appellate and Supreme courts.

The United States Supreme Court avoided any inquiry into the nature of Terminiello's speech, for it found the ordinance as construed to be overbroad and hence unconstitutional on its face. In support of this decision, the majority explained that "a function of free speech under our system of government is to invite dispute. It may indeed best serve its high purpose when it induces a condition of unrest, creates dissatisfaction with conditions as they are, or even stirs people to anger.... That is why freedom of speech, though not absolute, is nevertheless protected against censorship or punishment, unless shown likely to produce a clear and present danger of a serious substantive evil that rises far above public inconvenience, annoyance, or unrest" (337 U.S. at 4).

3   The Nature of the Samples

In this chapter we provide some detail about the subjects upon whom this research is based. After a brief description of the survey methodology, we examine the attributes of the members and leaders of ACLU and Common Cause with an eye toward understanding whether they should be treated as elites or masses. We also provide some data on the relative tolerance of these subjects as compared to members of the general public.

RESEARCH DESIGN

This research is based on data from a survey of the membership and leadership of the American Civil Liberties Union and of Common Cause. Questionnaires were distributed to a sample of approximately 15,000 members of ACLU; the entire membership of the boards of directors of the state affiliates of the Union; and a sample of 3,000 of the ordinary members of Common Cause. The sampling and mailings varied greatly in complexity and, because of certain complications, some detail must be provided on the process.

The ACLU Membership Survey

Two completely independent samples were drawn from the ACLU membership. The first sample consisted of approximately 10,000 subjects; the second consisted of 5,000 subjects. The first sample represented four different strata of approximately 2,000 subjects each:

    1. ACLU members who failed to renew their memberships (renewal dates between June 30 and November 30, 1977).

    2. Members who responded to a special contribution appeal structured around the Skokie crisis.

    3. Members who did not respond to the special appeal.

4. Individuals who joined ACLU for the first time in the period from June 1977 through June 1978.

In addition, the *universe* of individuals resigning or having their memberships terminated in 1977 for any reason was selected. This stratification in the sampling process was designed to insure that there would be a number of individuals engaging in intolerant (e.g., quitting) and tolerant (e.g., making a special contribution) behavior adequate to sustain statistical analysis. These subjects were mailed questionnaires in July 1978.

The company that maintained ACLU's membership list at the time selected the sample. Rather than using a truly random procedure, they selected the first N names satisfying the stratum criterion. Inasmuch as the list of members had vestiges of alphabetical order, and because new members were at the time being added to the end of the membership file, the samples selected were skewed toward members with last names beginning with the early letters of the alphabet and, for the new member stratum, those who had joined at a particular time. Moreover, for reasons that are still not clear to us, the self-reported membership status of the subjects only roughly corresponds to the membership status defining the stratum. For example, only 41 percent of the subjects coded on the list as having quit ACLU reported on the questionnarie that they had in fact quit (and only one-half of these quit over the Skokie issue). Fully 75 percent of the non-renewers reported that they were active members of the organization. Approximately one-half of the "new" members reported being a member of the organization for more than one year. And although most of those thought to have contributed to ACLU's special Skokie appeal did report making extra financial contributions to the Union, only 58 percent claimed (at a different point in the questionnaire) to have made donations to organizations in support of the efforts of the Nazis to demonstrate. Of course, there are a variety of explanations for these discrepancies, including: (1) possible miscategorization of the membership list; (2) faulty memories on the part of the respondents; (3) ambiguity in some of the categories (e.g., non-renewers may consider themselves members even though they had not yet renewed and consequently had been dropped from the active member rolls of the organization); and (4) processing errors on our part. In any event, the stratum defining variables are sufficiently suspect that we have not relied upon them for any purpose.

Since we could not estimate the amount of bias associated with the erroneous sampling process, a second, truly random sample was selected and another survey was initiated. This sample represents people who were active members in June 1977, or who joined ACLU during the period between June 1977 and June 1978, a total of approximately 5000 people. Questionnaires were mailed in September 1978. A second copy of the questionnaires was sent in April 1979 to nonrespondents in this second sample, new members from the first sample, and the universe of those writing letters of resignation.

The ACLU Leadership Survey

An effort was also made to survey all members of the boards of directors of the state affiliates. In addition to the Washington, D.C. affiliate, 44 states had a functioning state board in early 1978. Delaware, Idaho, North Dakota, Wyoming and West Virginia had no boards. Five states (California, Missouri, Ohio, Pennsylvania, and Texas) are divided geographically into two affiliates, both of which were surveyed. In most states the questionnaires were not mailed directly to the board members. Instead, they were distributed to the members by the affiliates' executive directors at their board meetings. Given previous controversies within the ACLU over making lists of names and addresses of the members of the boards available (e.g., to the Federal Bureau of Investigations), we felt that this was the least obtrusive method of contacting the directors. Three state affiliates—Alaska, Arkansas and Louisiana—never responded to the intial letter requesting assistance (a letter that, it should be noted, had the endorsement of the National Office). An additional two states—New Jersey and Michigan— agreed initially to participate, but no questionnaires were ever returned to us. This survey method means, of course, that we cannot be certain that all directors received the questionnaires (for example, some directors do not attend all of the board meetings; there are vacancies on the boards; etc.).

The Common Cause Membership Survey

The sample of Common Cause members is much more easily defined. A strictly random sample of approximately 3,000 members of the organization was selected, and questionnaires were mailed in September 1978. Nonrespondents received a follow-up mailing in April 1979.

Response Rates

Calculations of response rates are usually somewhat arbitrary and always result in approximations rather than in precise figures. In this research, many of the common problems attending these calculations are exacerbated. For instance, the ACLU and Common Cause membership lists contain institutional members as well as individual members. Moreover, the ACLU has experienced considerable difficulty in maintaining its mailing list, resulting in an unknown but no doubt substantial number of incorrect addresses, deceased members, etc. in the membership files. Since the questionnaires were mailed at the third class, nonprofit rate, the Post Office made no attempt to forward the mail. The sample address lists were cleaned as much as possible, and response rates have been calculated on the basis of adjusted denominators. Nevertheless, these figures must still be considered as only conservative estimates of the true rate.

There are other factors that undermine the reliability of the calculated response rates. For instance, many people hold joint memberships in ACLU, and in some of these instances two members received only a single questionnaire. As with all surveys of this type, we are uncertain whether the individuals completing the questionnaire are the same individuals to whom the questionnaire was addressed. Typical logistical problems in mailing, exacerbated by the use of identification numbers on the questionnaires, affected this project. Consequently, these calculations are subject to a substantial number of caveats.

The response rates for the general membership samples of ACLU and Common Cause are 43 and 47 percent, respectively. The higher rate for the Common Cause survey was unexpected and undoubtedly reflects the difference in the quality and accuracy of the two mailing lists. Further, the ACLU rate is depressed by the oversampling of new members, only 37 percent of whom responded, and of members who had failed to renew their memberships in the organization (rate = 31 percent). Table 3.1 shows the response rates for each of the strata.

Approximately 1,600 questionnaires were sent to the state affiliates for distribution to their directors: 584 of these were returned, for a response rate of 37 percent. The rate varies substantially by state, but the mean across the states is 39 percent. (This figure includes states that initially agreed to participate even though they did not return questionnaires, but it excludes affiliates refusing from the beginning to participate.) In view of the constraints under which the survey was conducted, this is a quite conservative estimate of the true rate.

Because very little is known about the characteristics of ACLU and Common Cause members, it is not possible to assess the representativeness of the sample respondents. However, the sample data reveal

TABLE 3.1. Summary of Samples, Response Rates, and Weights

	Total	Adjusted	Returned	Response rate %	Probability of selection	Final weight	Weighted (N)
ACLU							
Non-renewers	1902	1855	568	30.6	1	3	1704
Contributors	1893	1890	1101	58.3	1	2	2202
Non-contributors	1911	1904	909	47.7	1	2	1818
New members*	1914	1904	680	35.7	1	3	2040
Resigners*	2132	2107	866	41.1	1	2	1732
Active members—							
June, 1977*	3999	3680	1646	44.7	.0350	64	105,344
New members*	1000	837	328	39.2	.0465	55	18,040
Common Cause							
Members*	3059	3057	1427	46.6	.0153	140	199,780

*Received two mailings.

Source: James L. Gibson and Richard D. Bingham, "On the Conceptualization and Measurement of Political Tolerance," American Political Science Review, Vol. 76, No. 3, September 1982, p. 619.

TABLE 3.2. Selected Attributes of ACLU Members and Leaders and Common Cause Members

Attribute	ACLU Members	ACLU Leaders	Common Cause Members	
			ACLU Members	Not ACLU Members
% living in a single state	18.7	14.1	19.0	19.2
% living in a single country	73.8	70.8	71.6	75.2
% Republican	4.0	2.1	4.8	15.5
% Democrat	60.9	77.5	62.9	47.6
% members of Common Cause	47.7	36.1	100.0	100.0
% members of NAACP	18.3	27.4	40.1	4.6
% involved in many organizational activities	22.7	95.8	19.3	20.6
% joining over Watergate	6.3	4.9	14.7	15.9
% rating some social issue as more important than civil liberties	26.8	14.8	28.0	50.2
% saying some source of information other than ACLU is more important than ACLU information	20.1	8.9	15.3	70.8
% with college degree	71.0	76.7	69.3	67.1

% non-Jewish	78.6	72.7	75.5	85.0
% nominal member of the organization	25.4	0.0	24.1	25.3
% quitting over Skokie	5.9	0.3	—	—
% member of the organization for greater than 10 years	47.5	23.9	65.1	72.6
% with no World War II experience with the Nazis	65.2	57.8	61.1	70.7
% under 40 years old	43.7	44.2	17.9	19.8
% over 60 years old	18.8	13.4	39.5	40.3
Religious Affiliation				
% none	35.6	38.8	25.7	18.4
% Catholic	7.7	5.6	4.4	11.8
% Jewish	17.9	20.0	21.6	13.2
% Conservative Protestant	11.2	7.5	18.9	25.2
% Liberal Protestant	15.9	20.2	18.4	15.1
% other Protestant	8.3	5.3	8.3	13.2
% other	3.5	2.6	2.7	3.1
% black	1.4	2.0	1.7	1.5
% "liberal" (self identification)	46.1	40.9	53.8	35.1

few surprises about the demographic attributes of the respondents (see Table 3.2). The most striking attribute of the respondents is their demographic homogeneity. Only tiny proportions of them are from an ethnic minority. Relatively few are very young or very old—a large majority are between 30 and 59 years old. Approximately two-thirds are male. A majority of respondents hold professional jobs, and include substantial numbers of academics and lawyers. While ACLU members and leaders generally differ little with regard to their occupations, leaders are much more likely than members to be attorneys. These subjects also have unusually high levels of education. In terms of religious affiliation, Catholics are under-represented with respect to national figures; Jews and Unitarians/Universalists are over-represented; but a plurality have no religious affiliation. Indeed, data on the frequency of attendance at religious services suggest that religious affiliation is for many a nominal label: only 14 percent attend religious services weekly, while over 50 percent attend less than annually or never. Most do not consider themselves members of a particular ethnic group. Generally, these data reveal that ACLU and Common Cause members are almost uniformly middle class: the typical member is middle-aged, middle class, and white. In most respects the ACLU leadership mirrors the characteristics of the membership. Though not typical of the total United States population, these subjects are probably fairly representative of the membership of center-left interest groups.[1]

Weighting

Table 3.1 also demonstrates that the probabilities of selection for the various subsamples were greatly dissimilar. Because the sampling process that selected the first four samples was defective, these subjects must be considered to have had a probability of selection of one. That is, because they are not randomly selected samples, they must be treated as if they were populations. Similarly, the population of resigners was selected so that each of them had a probability of selection of 1. However, only 3,680 of the approximately 105,000 active members (i.e., omitting those in the process of joining or resigning) in June 1977, were selected, resulting in a probability of selection for each subject of .0350. With such disparate probabilities, it is essential that the responses be weighted. Accepted practice (cf. Kish, 1965) is to weight by the inverse of the probability of selection.

It is difficult at both the conceptual and methodological levels to specify the size of the ACLU membership. The conceptual problems revolve around the definition of "member." Failure to pay one's dues does not necessarily result in being dropped from the organization's rolls, especially in the short run. This is owing in part to the fact that members are not prompt in renewing memberships, but also in part to the fact that ACLU has experienced considerable difficulty in maintaining accurate records of its membership. Consequently, in weighting, it was necessary to rely on an estimate of the total number of members in each category. The following assumptions were made. First, the total active membership at any given time is approximately 105,000 (omitting those in the process of joining or resigning). Second, in the period from June 1977 through June 1978 it was assumed that approximately 30,000 new members were added to the rolls. Finally, the total membership of Common Cause was estimated at approximately 200,000.

Because the response rates of the strata differ, it is essential to apply an additional corrective weight. This weight is the inverse of the probability of responding, that is the response rate. Such a procedure makes the assumption that the non-responders are not dissimilar to responders. Nevertheless, weighting within the subsamples is the most reasonable of the alternatives. The final weights applied to the cases are simply the product of the inverses of the probabilities of selection and the probabilities of responding. The last column of Table 3.1 shows the weighted N that is used throughout the analysis.[2]

We have carefully considered whether the inclusion of the defective samples in this analysis affects any of our substantive results. Conceptually, the defective samples can be taken to represent the universe of individuals fulfilling the de facto stratum definitions, and universes can always be used to supplement samples so long as the weighting scheme is appropriate. Empirically, there are only miniscule differences between the propositions from the univariate frequencies of the strictly random samples and the univariate frequencies from all samples, reflecting of course the very small weights attached to respondents from the defective samples. The only alternative to the strategy we have adopted is to omit the defective samples, but since this would be of no substantive consequence we have included them, properly weighted, in the analysis.

Joint Membership in ACLU and Common Cause

In much of our analysis we have segregated the Common Cause respondents according to whether they are also members of ACLU. Over 33 percent of the Common Cause respondents claim membership in ACLU (compared to 48 percent of the ACLU members claiming membership in Common Cause), a figure no doubt higher—because of the salience of the Skokie issue to ACLU members—than the true figure for all Common Cause members. This segregation allows us to create a much more refined picture of the attitudes and behaviors of that segment of the elite that is not composed of libertarian activists.

There are fairly substantial differences in the attitudes of the members of the four groups. On each of the attitude and opinion variables used in this analysis the leaders of ACLU are markedly more likely to adopt a tolerant position. The leadership mean is approximately one-half standard deviation (i.e., the standard deviation of the universe) higher (more tolerant) than the mean for the ordinary ACLU members. Also in every instance the ACLU membership sample scores as slightly more tolerant than the portion of the membership of Common Cause that is also a member of ACLU. These differences are slight, only rarely exceeding a quarter of a standard deviation between the respective groups means, but because they are consistent across the five attitude and three opinion variables we suspect that the differences are meaningful. Finally, the Common Cause members who are *not* members of ACLU are in every instance the least tolerant of the four groups. The distance between the means of this group and the ACLU leadership means typically exceeds a full standard deviation. Table 3.3 summarizes these data.

These differences most likely reflect selection effects. Although we have no way of discounting the possibility that the ACLU leaders are "resocialized" to more tolerant values, the lack of contact among the regular members of ACLU and Common Cause makes this resocialization hypothesis unlikely. That is, without some exposure to the presumably more tolerant segments of ACLU, the ordinary member is hardly likely to experience attitude change. It is possible that exposure to ACLU literature has some effect in this direction, but it seems more plausible that these people are joining the organizations that reflect their values prior to joining. Common Cause members are less likely to adopt the quite tolerant positions of the typical ACLU member and therefore they feel less predisposed to join the Union.

Measurement Error

The most serious problems facing those who study public opinion are all related to measurement error. In this research, there is little reason to believe that measurement error is less than is common in questionnaire-based opinion research. For instance, the social desirability

TABLE 3.3. Differences in Tolerance of ACLU Leaders, ACLU Members, and Common Cause Members

Mean Score	ACLU Members	ACLU Leaders	Common Cause Members		Overall Mean	Overall Std. Dev.
			ACLU Members	Not ACLU Members		
Favor ACLU's position on Skokie	.68	1.17	.66	.11	.44	.88
Skokie Ordinance Opinion	.83	1.27	.67	.25	.56	.71
Allow Nazi Demonstration	.30	.46	.26	.06	.19	.44
Free Assembly-Abhorrent Groups	3.58	5.13	3.17	1.33	2.58	3.32
Free Assembly-Heckler's Veto	.76	1.61	.45	-.08	.35	1.52
Freedom of Speech	.32	.68	.13	.00	.15	.73
Stouffer Tolerance	.98	1.30	.81	.32	.68	.94
Political Oppression	.31	.56	.07	-.33	.00	.95

57

of tolerance no doubt influenced some of the subjects to give answers to our questions that were more tolerant than their true beliefs. In designing the questionnaire items we were conscious of this problem and have made every attempt to legitimize the more intolerant responses. Nonetheless, we are certain that our efforts are less than perfectly successful.

We also suspect that a certain amount of "instrument reactivity" was present. That is, the subjects learned something about civil liberties as they worked their way through the questionnaire and the learning affected their responses to later questions. We would not be at all surprised to learn, for instance, that reactions to the Skokie affair, especially for those who had little prior exposure to or interest in the issue, were affected by the earlier more general questions concerning civil liberties.

And of course there is a second sort of social desirability affecting the responses. As educated, middle class people, the subjects no doubt value consistency and consequently may have conformed their later responses to the more specific items to their responses to the more abstract questions. For instance, a certain amount of dissonance would be created for one who answered earlier questions favoring freedom of speech for all types of speech but then gave an anti-free speech response in the case of the Nazis. We know from some reports from our subjects this happened. We have, however, no way of estimating the magnitude of the problem.

Most of the measures we employed in this research were multiple item scales, a strategy that minimizes measurement error. We have also been quite concerned about the validity and reliability of our scales (see Chapter 5). In the final analysis, however, we are simply unable to assess the degree to which measurement error affects our substantive conclusions.

THE ELITE NATURE OF THE SAMPLES

We posit in this research that ACLU and Common Cause members and leaders can be thought of as "elites." This position reflects the following considerations: (1) elites have been defined in extant literature as those possessing resources that are convertible into political influence, and ACLU and Common Cause members possess such resources; (2) elites have been defined as political activists, and ACLU and Common Cause members are considerably more politically active than typical members of the mass public; (3) elites have been defined as those holding positions of power within political organizations and institutions, and ACLU leaders clearly fall within that category; and (4) in terms of political tolerance, ACLU and Common Cause members hold attitudes much more characteristic of elites than of members of the mass public. We will in this section consider each of these claims further.

Extant Conceptualizations of Political Elites

As McClosky and Brill (1983, pp. 236-243) observe, there is much confusion over the definition of the term "elite." Part of the confusion is associated with the fact that different researchers have been forced by the difficulty of data collection to operationalize "elite" in different ways. For instance, Stouffer (1955) and Nunn, Crockett, and Williams (1978) identified elites as the leaders of local political, social, and economic organizations, ranging from the chairpersons of the county political party organizations to the regents of the Daughters of the American Revolution. McClosky (1964) focused on delegates to the 1956 Democratic and Republican national conventions. More recently, McClosky and Brill (1983) report the most exhaustive operational definition of elite produced to date: they include legal elites (e.g., criminal attorneys, judges), other community or opinion leaders (e.g., mayor or city council members, religious leaders, influential college professors, newspaper editors or publishers, etc.), members of various national organizations (e.g., the American Civil Liberties Union), and those listed in *Who's Who* and *Black Who's Who*. Thus, in existing research there has been fairly heavy emphasis on positions that provide individuals with resources that are potentially convertible into political influence.

A less defensible approach to identifying elites is one that simply segregates mass samples into those who have resources and those who do not. Typically, the segregating variable is the level of education (e.g., Prothro and Grigg, 1960). Presumably, it is thought that those with relatively high levels of education have access to the resources necessary for political influence.

Perhaps McClosky's understanding of the concept "elite" is closest to the manner in which we employ the term. For McClosky, elite refers to

> those people who occupy themselves with public affairs to an unusual degree, such as government officials, elected office holders, active party members, publicists, officers of voluntary associations, and opinion leaders. The [concept does] not apply to any definable

> social class in the usual sense, nor to a particular status group or profession. Although the people [the concept designates] can be distinguished from other citizens by their activity and concerns, they are in no sense a community, they do not act as a body, and they do not necessarily possess identical or even harmonious interests. (McClosky, 1964, p. 363)

Thus, "elite" is an analytical concept.

> It represents...a classification imposed by political observers and research investigators to enable them to select those individuals or groups in society who have to some appropriate degree marked themselves off from other men and women by their greater involvement and participation in public affairs, their higher levels of political interest and knowledge, and the greater saliency with which they invest public issues. (McClosky and Brill, 1983, p. 237)

Thus, at the conceptual level it is obvious that the leaders and members of ACLU and Common Cause satisfy at least some definitions of the concept "elite."

The Resources of ACLU and Common Cause Members

Some indication of how the members and leaders of ACLU and Common Cause compare to the population as a whole can be attained through a comparison with the subjects responding to the 1977 General Social Survey. Only a few attributes can be compared, but even within the limitations of the data, it is possible to see clearly that these subjects are appropriately treated as elites.

Table 3.2 reports that over two-thirds of the members and leaders of these organizations have college degrees. A college education is typically taken as evidence of elite status. In the General Social Survey over 14 percent of the respondents report having a college degree. This is our clearest evidence of the elite status of these subjects.[3]

The Activism of ACLU and Common Cause Members

By virtue of their political activism, these subjects may also be considered elites. In terms of political activities, simply being a member of a political organization or club may well qualify one as an activist. Only 4.8 percent of the GSS sample claimed membership in an organization such as ACLU or Common Cause. And most members of both organizations participate in organizational affairs beyond mere dues paying.

With regard to political activity, 66 percent of the ACLU members, 40 percent of the Common Cause members, and 85 percent of the ACLU leaders have participated in a demonstration. In comparison, the 1973 General Social Survey reports that 9.5 percent of the mass public have picketed for a labor strike; 4.3 percent have participated in a civil-rights demonstration; 4.9 percent in an antiwar demonstration; 0.4 percent in a prowar demonstration; and 5.3 percent in a school-related demonstration.

Thus, in terms of the resources and motivations necessary for political influence, these subjects are much more similar to elites than to masses.

ACLU Leaders

Even if the argument that ACLU and Common Cause members are elites is not entirely satisfactory, there can be little doubt that ACLU leaders possess the qualities of the traditional definition of elites. Stouffer, for instance, was interested in local elites, whom he defined as those holding institutional positions of potential political influence. Thus, he included in his operational definition of local elites the following: mayors, presidents of Chambers of Commerce, chairmen of Community Chests, presidents of large labor-union locals, chairmen of Republican and Democratic county central committees, commanders of American Legion posts, regents of Daughters of the American Revolution, presidents of local women's clubs, chairmen of school boards and library boards, presidents of local councils of the Parent-Teachers' Association, presidents of bar associations, and publishers of locally-owned newspapers (Stouffer, 1955, p. 17). Obviously, members of boards of directors of the ACLU state affiliates are as elite as Stouffer's regents of the Daughters of the American Revolution! Thus, by virtue of their leadership positions alone, these people are elites in the classical sense.

The Political Tolerance of ACLU and Common Cause Members

The new measures of political tolerance that we introduce below have been put neither to a sample of the mass public nor to another elite sample so it is not possible to assess the degree to which the tolerance of ACLU and Common Cause members is similar to other elites or masses. We are able, however, to compare the responses of the ACLU/

TABLE 3.4. Comparison of ACLU Members and Leaders, Common Cause Members, and the Mass Public on Support for Civil Liberties

Percent Supporting the Right	ACLU Leaders	ACLU Members	Common Cause Members		Mass Public[a]
			ACLU Members	Not ACLU Members	
Group: Communists					
Speech	99.9	98.8	98.1	94.8	55.5
Teach	75.0	87.2	75.1	66.3	42.9
Publish	96.9	97.2	97.4	93.7	57.8
Demonstrate	98.2	90.5	85.8	70.2	—[b]
Group: Atheists					
Speech	99.6	98.6	97.2	94.8	62.3
Teach	98.9	94.8	89.9	79.9	38.8
Publish	99.1	97.3	97.9	95.0	60.4
Demonstrate	97.9	89.8	85.9	71.8	—
Group: Militarists					
Speech	99.1	93.8	91.6	85.3	50.5
Teach	93.8	83.2	74.8	61.9	34.0
Publish	97.1	95.3	93.3	90.3	57.3
Demonstrate	95.7	81.2	74.9	59.6	

Group					
Group: Ku Klux Klan					
Speech	98.7	91.5	89.9	81.4	—
Teach	92.6	81.3	75.6	63.3	—
Publish	96.2	93.6	93.3	88.8	—
Demonstrate	95.7	81.2	69.4	52.0	—
Group: Racists					
Speech	—	—	—	—	58.6
Teach	—	—	—	—	40.8
Publish	—	—	—	—	63.7
Demonstrate	—	—	—	—	—
Group: Nazis					
Speech	99.4	93.8	94.0	87.4	—
Teach	92.6	79.9	71.3	59.5	—
Publish	97.3	93.7	91.3	88.8	—
Demonstrate	96.4	80.2	76.4	58.6	—
Group: Homosexuals					
Speech	—	—	—	—	61.8
Teach	—	—	—	—	49.3
Publish	—	—	—	—	58.7
Demonstrate	—	—	—	—	—

[a]The mass public results are taken from the 1977 General Social Survey.
[b]Dashes indicate that the item was not asked.

63

Common Cause survey with the responses of a mass sample to the traditional Stouffer measures of tolerance.[4] Table 3.4 reports the data of interest for the comparison.

It is obvious that, to the extent that these items are valid measures of support for civil liberties, the responses of ACLU and Common Cause members are much more similar to the typical results of elite surveys than they are to the typical results of mass surveys. The leaders of ACLU are nearly unanimous in their responses to each of the scenarios: only a tiny few would deny communists, atheists, militarists, Klansmen, or Nazis the right to speak, teach, publish, or demonstrate.[5] There is a libertarian consensus among the members of ACLU: in every instance posed, three-fourths of the members give a tolerant response. Nearly all of the members of ACLU would allow representatives of each of these groups to speak and to publish, although not insignificant minorities would prohibit militarists, Klansmen, and Nazis from teaching and demonstrating. Generally, Klansmen and Nazis are the most disfavored groups: about one-third of the ACLU members would deny Klansmen and Nazis the right to engage in at least one of the four activities, whereas the figure denying some activity to atheists—the most favored group—is 15 percent. Similarly, teaching and demonstrating are less favored activities than speaking and publishing.

The responses of members of Common Cause exhibit more variation. First, it should be noted that there are substantial differences in the responses to the more conflictual scenarios of Common Cause members who are also members of ACLU than of those who are not. This is especially apparent on the items referring to demonstrations. For instance, only 59 percent of those who are members of Common Cause but not of ACLU would allow a demonstration by Nazis, whereas 76 percent of those who are members of both organizations give tolerant responses. We cannot be certain whether this reflects selective recruitment—only the more libertarian individuals are motivated to join ACLU—or whether there is some socialization toward more libertarian values after joining the organization, or both, but as the items pose a greater degree of conflict between values, "pure" Common Cause members are less likely to be willing to support the exercise of the liberty.

Although there is never an instance in which pure Common Cause members are as supportive of political repression as the mass public, this group is far from being consensually united on these issues. Most Common Cause members would allow speeches by members of these five political minority groups, and having a book advocating the philosophy of the group in a public library seems to present little threat. However, holding public demonstrations is a quite different matter. While an extraordinary majority would allow a Klansman to make a speech, only a bare majority would allow the speech if it were in the context of a public demonstration. Over 84 percent of the ACLU-Common Cause members would deny none of these five groups the right to speak; for pure Common Cause members the figure is 72 percent. However, the comparable figures for demonstrations are 64 and 45 percent, respectively (with an even more substantial decline for teaching in a college or university). Thus, the proportion of respondents who would allow members of all five groups to engage in all four activities is not large.

These items can be compared to the Sullivan, Piereson, and Marcus approach to tolerance. Let us *assume* that Sullivan, Piereson, and Marcus are correct in asserting that the variation in willingness to repress political groups is a function of variation in the degree of dislike (or threat) of the group. Thus, on the question of free speech, these subjects have been queried concerning five groups, presumably varying in acceptability to the respondent. For those tolerant of all five groups no general conclusion about tolerance can be drawn because there might still be other political minorities that are more disliked than any of the five listed groups and these groups might stimulate an intolerant response. Indeed, it may even be incorrect to assume that those giving a tolerant response to all five groups are any more tolerant at all than those giving an intolerant response to one or more groups. Within the context of a *post facto* attempt to create a measure of political tolerance comparable to the Sullivan, Piereson, and Marcus measure, those with perfect tolerance scores must be considered as including tolerant individuals *and* individuals who have not been given a proper opportunity to demonstrate their intolerance. Thus, the percentage of respondents giving at least one intolerant response can be taken as a minimal estimate of the level of intolerance within the group. These data are shown in Table 3.5.

Several conclusions can be drawn from Table 3.5. First, the upper portion of the table indicates the percentages of respondents who are perfectly tolerant (at least in terms of the four activities) of the five groups. These figures represent the maximum possible estimate of the percentage that is actually perfectly tolerant. That is, these figures may be taken as estimates of the percentage of respondents who do not

TABLE 3.5. Tolerance as Measured by Stouffer Items

Percentage "Perfectly" Tolerant	ACLU Members	ACLU Leaders	Common Cause Members		Mass Public[a]
			ACLU Members	Not ACLU Members	
Group-based tolerance					
Atheists	85.3	95.4	79.1	60.6	32.9
Communists	79.6	72.4	65.1	46.4	32.8
Militarists	71.6	87.1	61.2	44.0	28.4
Nazis	68.2	87.5	58.2	41.1	—[b]
Klansmen	63.5	83.3	55.8	37.9	—
Homosexuals	—	—	—	—	40.2
Racists	—	—	—	—	31.2
Activity-based tolerance[c]					
Speaking	88.6	97.8	84.8	72.8	33.0
Publishing	88.4	92.9	85.3	77.6	38.7
Demonstrating	70.1	91.2	64.6	45.8	—
Teaching	65.1	65.4	49.9	36.9	33.0

[a]The mass public results are taken from the 1977 General Social Survey. Great care in comparing the group-based tolerance results of the mass public survey to the ACLU and Common Cause survey must be exercised inasmuch as the mass public sample was not asked about whether members of the group should be allowed to hold a demonstration. This is of special consequence because demonstrating is not a well-tolerated activity.

[b]Dashes indicate that the item was not asked.

[c]For each of the groups, up to four activities were considered:

1. "If such a person wanted to make a speech in your community against/in favor of _____, should he/she be allowed to speak?"
2. "Should such a person be allowed to organize a march against/in favor of _____ in your community?"
3. "Should such a person be allowed to teach in a college or university?"
4. "If some people in your community suggested that a book he/she wrote against/in favor of _____ should be taken out of your public library, would you favor removing the book?"

consider the group to be among their least-liked, *plus* those who are actually perfectly tolerant. Thus, the 85.3 percent of ACLU members who are perfectly tolerant of atheists includes those who are intolerant of others but not atheists and those who are tolerant of all groups. But because the percentage tolerant of all groups is a constant, the ranking of groups on observed percentage that is perfectly tolerant amounts to a ranking of groups in terms of the percentage counting the group among the least-liked. Thus, atheists are least least-liked by ACLU and Common Cause members and leaders, whereas Klansmen are most least-liked by ACLU and Common Cause members. The communist aberration for ACLU leaders is no doubt a function of measurement error (see note 5 to Chapter 3). Thus, we see an important divergence for the Sullivan, Piereson, and Marcus finding on the opinions of members of the mass public. Their subjects were more likely to select left-wing targets of intolerance than right-wing targets (Sullivan, Piereson, and Marcus, 1982, p. 86), whereas ACLU and Common Cause members are more likely to select right-wing than left-wing groups. This should not be surprising when the relative distribution of liberal-conservative self identifications is taken into consideration (see note 3 to Chapter 3).

It is also interesting to note that tolerance is far from perfect, even among ACLU members. Over one-third of the members would support some sort of repression of Klansmen, despite the fact that on any given activity less than one-fifth would not allow Klansmen to engage in one of the activities. Among Common Cause members, the figures are even more strongly in favor of political repression: less than 40 percent of the pure Common Cause members support the right of Klansmen to speak, publish, demonstrate, and teach. Only ACLU leaders are generally tolerant of each of the five groups.

Nonetheless, Common Cause and ACLU members are substantially more tolerant than the mass public in general. The differences between the mass public figures and the figures for the leaders of ACLU are enormous. Only in a few instances of comparison to the pure members of Common Cause does the mass public not distinguish itself by its intolerance.

The insensitivity to the specific group under consideration can also be seen in these results. Militarists are tolerated slightly less, homosexuals somewhat more, but generally there is little difference in intolerance that is associated with the nature of the target group. Perhaps for most, atheists, communists, militarists, homosexuals, and racists all fall within the "very disliked" range of the scale.

There is substantial variability in attitudes toward the different activities. Speaking and publishing are fairly well supported by all, but demonstrating and teaching in colleges and universities are apparently much more difficult to support.

If, as argued above, it is possible to assume that these figures represent *minimal* levels of intolerance, then these data are not very supportive of the presumption that elites are consensually and strongly supportive of the rights of political opposition. However, careful scrutiny of extant research on the tolerance of political elites suggests that the empirical basis of the elitist theory of democracy is not overwhelming. It is true that Stouffer observed fairly substantial differences between local elites and the mass public, but it has been suggested recently that the gap is closing (Nunn, Crockett, and Williams, 1978). Careful examination of more recent data reveals a number of instances in which elites are not consensually supportive of civil liberties (for example, McClosky and Brill, 1983). And, of course, Jackman (1972) argued about a decade ago that even Stouffer's findings on elite-mass differences may have reflected demographic differences in the elite and mass samples, and a special form of measurement error in which the social desirability of tolerance played a key role in elite responses. As we have argued in Chapter 1, there is ample historical evidence that elites have not always, if even usually, supported the rights of unpopular minorities. *Thus it may well be that the general elite consensus on democratic values is illusory; only to the degree that elites can reason out a fairly simple and socially appropriate response to highly simplified and purified questionnaire items are they necessarily more tolerant than members of the mass public. Some elites are tolerant—and that tolerance may be critically important to the maintenance of democratic public policy—but elite consensus on democratic values may neither exist nor matter.* These issues are considered more fully in Chapter 8. For the moment, however, there can be little doubt that, on these measures of political tolerance, these subjects are considerably more tolerant than the mass public.

Summary

Thus, from a variety of perspectives, these subjects are not representative of the typical mass public. On the other hand, we do not claim that they are representative of the elite; instead, we only claim that they have attributes that qualify them as elites.

NOTES

1.   In 1970, ACLU conducted a survey in order to construct a profile of its membership. Comparison of our data with the 1970 survey reveals remarkable similarity in most of the characteristics we have considered (education, religion, and gender). Our data indicate a slight decline in the percentage of members who are educators and a slight decline in attorneys. There is perhaps more significance in the data on member ages. In the eight years separating the two surveys the average age increased by six years. The percentage of members under 30 has declined by nearly 15 percentage points. Whether this is an artifact of the response rates or whether it reflects the fact that ACLU is most successful at appealing to a particular and probably atypical cohort (see Jennings and Niemi, 1981) cannot be known from these data.

2.   We are indebted to Mr. Charles Palit of the University of Wisconsin for assistance in resolving some of the difficult sampling and weighting issues.

3.   Other differences not directly related to elite status are apparent. For instance, while only 2.3 percent of the GSS respondents reported being Jewish, between 12 and 22 percent of the ACLU/Common Cause respondents are Jewish. Catholics are substantially underrepresented in these two organizations (24.8 percent of the GSS respondents claim to be Catholics). Similarly, blacks are greatly underrepresented: 11.6 percent of the GSS respondents were black, whereas virtually none of the members of ACLU and Common Cause is black.

Politically, Democrats are overrepresented in the ACLU samples, with only 44.6 percent of the GSS respondents claiming Democratic affiliation. On this measure, the members of Common Cause are much more similar to the members of the mass public.

Of the GSS sample, 44.1 percent are under 40 years of age, a figure similar to ACLU members and leaders. Common Cause members, however, tend to be considerably older than the mass public in general.

Finally, and not surprisingly, both ACLU and Common Cause members are substantially more liberal in their self-identifications than is the mass public. Only 11.6 percent of the GSS subjects accept the "liberal" label, whereas from one-third to one-half of the ACLU/Common Cause subjects accept the label.

4.   It should be noted prior to considering these data that, when supplemented with an item on demonstrations, the Stouffer items performed reasonably well in comparison with the more rigorous measures of political tolerance introduced below.

5.   It may appear that the responses to the question of whether a communist should be allowed to teach constitute a possible exception to this conclusion. We believe not; instead, the responses to this item are heavily

influenced by measurement error. In personal interviews, this item is typically reflected in an attempt to assess the degree of acquiescence bias ("yea-saying") and our questionnaire adopted this strategy. This was a mistake. Before considering communists as the object of intolerance, the subjects were presented with the standard series of four items referring to "somebody who is against all churches and religion" and to "an admitted member of the Ku Klux Klan." The teaching item read: "should such a person be allowed to teach in a college or university?" For the communists, the item read: "suppose he/she is teaching in a college. Should he/she be fired?" The teaching item for "an admitted member of a para-military organization" and "a member of the Nazi Party" reverted to the "allowed to teach" form. The frequencies convince us that many of the ACLU leaders assumed that the items concerning communists were parallel in form to the set of items to which they had just responded, and that they meant to give a tolerant response to the communist teaching item. After answering the first two sets of questions, they no doubt concluded that they would deny communists *none* of the activities and they therefore simply copied the response pattern from the prior questions. The effect on the ACLU and Common Cause members is similar, although probably not as great, owing to generally lower levels of tolerance.

4   The Impact of Skokie on the American Civil Liberties Union

It is widely assumed that the Skokie-Nazi dispute had a debilitating, if not devastating, impact on the ACLU. Press accounts at the time of the incident (e.g., Mann, 1978) made it appear that the ACLU was on the verge of collapse as an organization. Great numbers of members supposedly opposed the decision to allocate organizational resources to defend the rights of hated Nazis, and no small proportion of these were reported to have quit the organization in disgust. Frank Collin and his Nazis not only generated a great deal of *angst* in Skokie, but in the ACLU as well.

If in fact ACLU lost a number of its members as a result of its decision to defend the Nazis, then the incident might be taken as evidence in opposition to the elitist theory of democracy. After all, that theory asserts that it is the elite who stand as guardians of the rights of unpopular minorities. If ACLU members and leaders—no doubt among the most libertarian of elites—were unwilling to support the organization in its efforts in what, after all, has been characterized as "an easy case in law" (Lucas, 1978, p. 10), then some modification of the theory of elite beneficence is in order.

It should not be presumed, however, that popular accounts of the impact of the dispute on the organization are necessarily accurate, and, indeed, there are a variety of reasons to suspect that they are not. The sole source of information about the magnitude of the response to its position is the ACLU itself. The Union could easily have miscalculated the magnitude of negative reaction for several reasons: (1) their records on their membership were, at this particular time, in abysmal condition, making it difficult to know with any certainty the number of people falling into any particular membership category; (2) the psychological impact of the letters the ACLU received was disproportionate to their number both because of the emotional intensity of many of the letters, and because of the ease with which a stack of mail, even, say 1000 letters, can be thought to be an enormous quantity despite the fact that it represents a tiny proportion of the membership; (3) it was in the self-interest of the organization to appear to be under seige; and (4) second doubts various leaders were having about the wisdom of the decision made them receptive to perceiving a groundswell of opposition. Thus, it will be fruitful to attempt to derive some independent estimate of the impact of the dispute on the organization, and that is the purpose of this chapter. We shall begin with a review of official ACLU accounts concerning member response to the Skokie-Nazi affair and then proceed to a fairly detailed examination of the reactions—behavioral and attitudinal—of members to the dispute as revealed through our survey.

THE ACLU VIEW OF THE RESPONSE

That there was any significant response by the ACLU members to the organization's decision to defend Frank Collin was a complete shock to ACLU officials. From the first days of the controversy, when ACLU attorney Goldberger announced the Union's intention to appeal the restraining order issued by Judge Wosik, the Chicago ACLU office received hundreds of angry phone calls denouncing its position. David Hamlin, the executive director of the Illinois Civil Liberties Union at the time, provides the following account of public reaction immediately after it became known that the ACLU was representing Frank Collin:

> The office was alive with tension. The calls of protest were coming into our telephone system so rapidly that the system could not carry all of the calls. . . . The calls quickly fell into a pattern. Nobody called to express their support of ACLU's position; the only calls which did not protest our work were those from reporters. Virtually all of the callers identified themselves as Jewish, and a substantial majority of all the calls went beyond the issues of the controversy itself into territory that was at once surprising and shocking. . . . The anger which ran through most of the calls was more than sufficient to create an air of siege in the office, but the anger was not the most common element in the calls. . . . While hundreds of people called ACLU to protest our actions in the case, not one of them knew the basic facts in the case. . . . The barrage of calls had left us in a corner, so we argued our position from an increasingly hard-line posture, a posture which would do nothing to further anyone's understanding

of the issues....Shellshocked...I went home for the weekend. (Hamlin, 1980, pp. 64–70)

After a short period of time, the phone calls turned to letters, "angry letters, disappointed letters, hateful letters, and lots and lots of letters of resignation" (Hamlin, 1978, p. 27). While the ACLU might have expected such negative reactions from the general public, Union officials were astounded by the response of its members to the Skokie case.

The National Office of the ACLU felt similarly besieged. Aryeh Neier, National's executive director, provided this grim assessment of the impact of the controversy:

> More than 4,000 ACLU members responded to the publicity about the Skokie case by sending in angry letters of resignation. Some returned their membership cards, probably not noticing the First Amendment is printed on it. Others sent in postcards, oblivious to the fact that the stamps said, "The Right of the People Peaceably to Assemble."
>
> Several times the number who wrote letters of resignation silently allowed their memberships to lapse. All told, the case probably cost the ACLU about 30,000 members—15 percent of its membership—and about $500,000 a year. (Neier, 1979, p. 79)

But ACLU had suffered membership defections in the past. For example, it lost a significant number of members in 1960 when it defended another Nazi, George Lincoln Rockwell. The difference in the leaders' perceptions of the impact on the organization, however, may be traced to general membership trends. While ACLU may have lost the same percentage of members in 1960 over the Rockwell defense, the *impact* on the organization was perceived to be substantially different. In the early 1960s, ACLU was experiencing a great upsurge in membership as the country's fears of joining an organization that defends the rights of communists (indeed, an organization falsely labeled by Senator McCarthy from Wisconsin as a communist-front organization) abated somewhat. Thus, the Rockwell resignations were lost in a sea of new members. Such was not the case in 1977, however (though we challenge this perception below). In the context of a general decline in membership, the Skokie dispute was perceived to be the "straw that broke the camel's back."

Thus, the leaders of the ACLU have fairly definite views about the magnitude of member defections from the organization. We can now assess the degree to which those views are consonant with the results of the survey.

THE SURVEY VIEW OF THE RESPONSE

Before considering the results of the survey of the ACLU membership and leadership a critical caveat must be reiterated. Our ability to generalize all of the survey results is considerably undermined by the response rate to the mail questionnaire (see Chapter 3 for details on the survey and response rate). This is of course a common limitation of all mail surveys. Unless one is willing to assume that those who responded to the questionnaire constitute a random sample of all those receiving a questionnaire, and hence that respondents and non-respondents differ little, the enormously useful assumptions of sampling and probability theories are inaccessible. We doubt that respondents perfectly mirror the universe—at the very least, they probably tend to be those to whom the issue is more salient. But, on the other hand, there is likely less bias in the sample results than in generalizations made from ordinary, unstructured observations of reality. Thus, while we concede that sampling error is far from negligible, we strongly suspect that the sample projections are at least more accurate than the more subjective estimates of ACLU officials.

What were the opinions of ACLU members on the issues in the dispute? At the center of the conflict over the right of the Nazis to hold public demonstrations are the Skokie ordinances (see Appendix A). The ACLU members and leaders were questioned on their reactions to the insurance bond and "group libel" provisions of the Skokie ordinances, with the results shown in Table 4.1. Though it is inaccurate to characterize the opponents of the ACLU position on Skokie as representing a "massive" segment of the organization, they do comprise a substantial minority. Within ACLU, 21 percent of the members and 5 percent of the leaders failed to oppose both ordinances. There is similar variation in the responses to whether a permit to demonstrate should be issued to the Nazis. One-fifth of the ACLU members would deny a permit but the leaders are virtually unanimous in their view that the demonstration should be allowed. Thus, ACLU members consensually

TABLE 4.1. Attitudes toward Skokie Ordinances on Nazi
Demonstrations

	ACLU Members	ACLU Leaders
Ordinance to deny demonstration permits if "group libel" would occur		
Strongly favor	2.6	0.7
Favor	8.7	1.3
No opinion	2.7	0.7
Oppose	36.9	15.3
Strongly oppose	49.1	82.1
	100.0	100.0
	(129,258)	(1,272)
Ordinance requiring insurance bond		
Strongly favor	1.7	0.3
Favor	8.0	1.4
No opinion	5.8	1.7
Oppose	37.9	18.2
Strongly oppose	46.6	78.3
	100.0	100.0
	(129,292)	(1,270)
Should the permit be granted?		
Yes, grant	78.7	95.4
No opinion	2.8	0.9
No, deny	18.5	3.8
	100.0	100.0
	(129,129)	(1,275)

NOTE: Ns have been weighted to reflect probabilities of selection and response rates. Details on the weighting may be found in Chapter 3.

Source: James L. Gibson and Richard D. Bingham, "Skokie, Nazis, and the Elitist Theory of Democracy," *Western Political Quarterly*, Vol. 37, No. 1, March 1984, p. 39. Reprinted by Permission of the University of Utah, Copyright Holder.

opposed the repressive Skokie legislation, and ACLU leaders were nearly unanimous in their opposition.

It is likely that many members were unaware of the specific provisions of the Skokie ordinances. This suspicion was confirmed: only 44 percent of the members knew of the group libel ordinance and only 39 percent knew of the insurance requirement. Comparable figures for the leaders are 72 and 78 percent, for the two ordinances, respectively. Statistical analysis reveals, however, no relationship between awareness of the ordinances and substantive opinions of the ordinances.

Rationales for Opposing the Nazi Right to Demonstrate

As reported in Table 4.2, there is considerable variation in the rationales put forth for denying a march permit to the Nazis. The most popular reason for the denial stems from the belief that the maintenance of public order is more important than (and, implicitly, incompatible with) the proposed Nazi demonstration. Over 60 percent of ACLU members opposing the demonstration cite the threat of violence as an explanation of their position. One attorney asserted:

> I believe in the right to free speech, in the right to assemble, etc., of *any* person or group, unless there is a clear indication that the purpose is to incite violence. I believe that the Skokie situation was as clear an example of a group's desire to incite violence and worse, as you can have. This was clear from the beginning, and was finally proven when after winning the legal action, the Nazis called off the Skokie march.

And:

> The words "peaceably to assemble" from the First Amendment are too often forgotten. In my opinion the Nazis stated purpose of marching in Skokie was far from having one thing to do with the keeping of the peace. Nor would any move by the Klan to demonstrate in full regalia in a Black community in either the South, or the North. Nor for that matter was the Jewish Defense League intending anything peaceful when they planned to confront the Nazis in Skokie or when they attempted to do so in Chicago.

The few ACLU leaders opposing the Nazi demonstration unanimously cite potential violence as a rationale.

The "fire in a crowd theater" argument was also well-represented. For example,

> I think the biggest mistake made is that it has been characterized as a "First Amendment controversy." It is not. The Nazis are not operating within the First Amendment. Yelling "Fire!" in a crowded theater is not "protected speech"; specifically threatening to kill an

individual or a group of individuals, who are identified, and urging their killing, is not "protected speech"; a symbol such as the swastika, which specifically represents that theory and approach and belief and credo is not "protected symbolic speech."

A not insignificant number of subjects in each category cited a "right" of local communities to control the content of demonstrations within their boundaries. Most do this within the context of a potential for "psychological harm" to be done to members of the community (analogous to the B'nai Brith allegation). For example, one subject defended her position with the following comments:

> People like the Nazis, who are a form of fascism, should be allowed to publish materials and make speeches, but they shouldn't be allowed to march in Jewish neighborhoods or agitate hatred and violence. This is not a civil right. "Civil" means a respect for life, or having a sense of justice; it also means being a humanitarian. You have to be if you have respect for life or have a sense of justice. To allow a Nazi group to taunt or harass a Jewish group would be the same thing as allowing the police or FBI or CIA to use torture.

Others asserted a community right to privacy. For example:

> There is a difference... between holding a march in Marquette Park and holding such a march in downtown Chicago and in holding such a march in Skokie. Each presents a different situation. There is something particularly heinous and despicable about subjecting people who are survivors of the Holocaust to seeing again the same symbols as caused them so much pain and suffering. It may not be a "right" recognized yet in the law, but there should be a right of "mental privacy" which would protect someone in such a situation. Therefore, I think that the Nazis being allowed to march in Marquette Park is objectionable, and I believe that it can be prohibited under the First Amendment, but I can understand and accept their marching where there are, in fact a number of people sympathetic to their ideas and concept.

Similarly:

> Nazis are an abomination and deserve no defense. The right to assemble peaceably to obtain a redress of grievances is really the only Constitutional guarantee toward groups. Nazis have no legitimate

TABLE 4.2. **Reasons for Denying Nazis a Permit to Demonstrate in Skokie**

Reason	ACLU Members	ACLU Leaders
Maintenance of public order is more important		
Prohibit the march to prevent violence	23.5%	47.1%
Nazis intend to incite the crowd	38.8	58.8
Like fire in a crowded theater	3.3	—
Fighting words	0.5	5.9
Community has the right to prohibit marches within its boundaries		
They can march but not in Skokie	6.6	5.9
Community standards prohibit march	1.7	—
Psychological harm to residents	15.2	17.6
Skokie passed a law	0.0	—
Nazis aren't residents of Skokie	0.4	—
Content of Nazi speech/ideology justifies prohibition		
No "redeeming social value"	8.0	—
Nazis would destroy the First Amendment	4.6	—
Nazis advocate genocide	11.2	5.9
Nazis destroy American way of life	0.4	—
Racists shouldn't be allowed to demonstrate	6.5	5.9
Nazis have no rights	4.2	5.9
Nazis are the enemy—World War II	5.9	—
Don't encourage the growth of the Nazi Movement		
Gives them media exposure	0.5	5.9
Don't encourage growth	1.1	—
Other	0.0	—
	132.7%[a]	158.8%
	(18,988)	(34)

[a]Columns total to more than 100% owing to the multiple responses. Those who would grant the permit have been omitted from this table.

NOTE: Ns have been weighted to reflect probabilities of selection and response rates. Details on the weighting may be found in Chapter 3.

Source: James L. Gibson and Richard D. Bingham, "Skokie, Nazis, and the Elitist Theory of Democracy," *Western Political Quarterly*, Vol. 37, No. 1, March 1984, p. 40. Reprinted by Permission of the University of Utah, Copyright Holder.

grievances here. They are allowed to live and work unmolested here for the most part. If a community wishes to refuse them the right to demonstrate in support of their beliefs, no right of theirs is being violated.

Some see privacy in a more restrictive physical sense:

When you have a demonstration that denies me free use of my property or business or denies me access to any public services, then you interfere with my rights to disagree and continue to live a normal life. Where two equal rights collide, neither can bury the other but both must give a little to allow both to function to the fullest.

And:

Freedom of speech should not give a person the *right* to *make others listen.* Marching on the public streets comes close to forcing others to listen, because the "speech" takes over public areas where others may prefer not to be subjected to the marchers' expression of free speech. Freedom of speech does not give a guy the right to invade my privacy. And I am entitled to some of that privacy in public places too. The right to parade on public streets involves more than freedom to speak. It involves the question whether the marchers have the right to inflict their freedom of speech on others who don't want to listen.

Another major strain in the responses concerns the specific content of the Nazi ideology and the (presumed) content of the speech. Some likened Nazi ideas to obscenity, declaring that Nazi speeches have no "redeeming social value." For instance:

Many people in that community [Skokie] claimed the Nazi march represented an "obscene" event surely as much as the open sale of pornographic material. If the courts are going to leave the latter up to community standards, why not the former? I find the distinction made by the courts here very difficult to comprehend. Perhaps other aspects of the case (i.e., the very high bond, etc.) colored the case so unfortunately as to preclude a clearer interpretation of obscenity.

Others asserted that because the Nazis advocate the destruction of the First Amendment, they surrender their rights of free speech:

On the basis of their policies as well as history, Nazis obviously had intent to deprive Jews of their civil rights, possibly lives. Their intent was to threaten, not persuade the population. A loaded gun pointed at people is not sanctioned by the First Amendment. We do not have to grant civil rights to a group which, as a matter of policy, will use these to threaten other people's lives and civil rights.

Some would deny the Nazis civil liberties because they believe the Nazi advocacy of genocide is unprotected by the United States Constitution. A small number referred to Nazi atrocities in World War II in support of their position. We even encountered the argument that the Nazis have no rights because the U.S. is still technically at war with Nazi Germany.

> This country never signed a peace treaty with the "Grossdeutsche Reich," Hitler's bygone, but legally-established empire internationally recognized in its time. Consequently, the American Nazi party uses enemy symbols, and offers assistance and comfort to this country's enemy. The U.S. criminal code, if applied, would take care of such deeds.

> The last "führer" of the "Grossdeutsche Reich" is still alive, but never was invited to negotiate and sign a peace treaty with the United States. Former Admiral Doenitz, convicted at Nuremberg and eventually imprisoned at Spandau, presently quite often is invited as a lecturer at gatherings of Nazi veterans in Western Germany.

> Actually—legally—Germany as such was "pacified" by the four powers, i.e., the United States, Great Britain, France, and the U.S.S.R. Many documents speak of a forthcoming peace treaty, but none ever was concluded.

Finally, a small group would deny the permit as a means of denying the Nazis valuable publicity.

Thus, most members of the ACLU justified their position of intolerance of the Nazis in terms of potential harm—physical or mental—to the residents of Skokie. This harm was weighted more heavily than the freedom of the despicable political minority. And most members tried to provide constitutional legitimacy to their opinions. Apparently in an effort to reduce cognitive dissonance, most of those supporting the Skokie position searched, sometimes quite creatively, for a constitutional theory compatible with their preferred outcome. Most individuals can identify, or suggest, a rational-legal basis for their intolerant positions.

Rationales for Supporting the Nazi Right to Demonstrate

A much less variable set of responses was given by those who would allow the demonstration. Over 90 percent of each of the two groups gave a First Amendment rationale for their position. Many relied on the "marketplace of ideas" sentiment:

> The democratic system is based on the idea that people have the ability to decide for themselves about various things concerning their government . . . and that people will decide what's best and right in the majority of cases whether they're fed lies or not. But to make intelligent choices we need a free exchange of ideas. This is why at all costs we must defend the First Amendment.

Some referred to basic "human rights," while others supported the right of the Nazis for fear of a "domino" effect. Many of the legal/constitutional responses were accompanied by vigorous statements of negative opinion toward the Nazi ideology itself. Generally, those supporting the rights of the Nazis to demonstrate relied on conventional and well-known arguments in doing so.

Behavioral Responses to the Issue

Opinions on civil liberties issues may be misleading if behavior only infrequently flows from attitudes, and it is behavior that is of interest to us and to the ACLU. It is conceivable that a significant minority of the members of the ACLU took action against the organization, action that was intended to cripple its ability to aid in the defense of the rights of the Nazis. If all of the 17 percent of the membership and 5 percent of the leadership who opposed the organization's position took action against it, then the organizational consequences could be devastating. Certainly this is what the national leaders of ACLU perceived to be the case. Reliable estimates of the magnitude of the defections are therefore essential.

Table 4.3 shows the reports as given by the members themselves of their current and intended membership status. Most ACLU members had not recently changed their membership status. Only 4.3 percent of the members reported that they had recently joined the organization. Over one-half of these, representing nearly 3,000 new members, asserted that the Skokie issue motivated them to join.

At the time of the survey, 10 percent of the respondents had recently resigned, failed to renew their memberships, or intended not to renew. This group is about evenly divided between those upset over Skokie and those upset over other issues, but we estimate that over 5,600 members quit primarily because of the ACLU defense of Nazi rights. For another 1,400 the Skokie dispute was a contributing factor. A tiny percentage of the leadership resigned and the overwhelming majority of these leaders quit over issues unrelated to Skokie. Thus, while there can be little doubt that the volume of mail, as well as its emotional intensity, was perceived by ACLU and others to be alarmingly large, our research does not come close to uncovering the 30,000 "lost" members claimed by ACLU National.

Our subjects reported that they resigned from the ACLU because of a variety of issues not directly related to the Skokie (see Table 4.4). Foremost among these is financial, with many of the defectors claiming to be unable to afford the membership fee. Beyond this, almost 18 percent of the defectors referred to "personal" or general reasons. This is a heterogenous group, including members who felt that the ACLU should have taken their own individual cases.

None of the other categories of reasons was mentioned by more than 10 percent of the defectors. However, some of the responses are susceptible to additional categorization. For instance, the responses "ACLU isn't responding to pressing issues," "ACLU has moved beyond the first amendment," "ACLU defense of KKK," and "ACLU defense of Nazis" are all related to the organization's activity in defense of the rights of extreme rightists. Capital punishment is also a controversial issue. In general, though, it is true that no single issue comes close to generating the defections that were associated with Skokie. Indeed, the aggregate effect of all other issues is no greater than the effect of Skokie.

Official ACLU membership figures can be used to consider further the magnitude of the reaction. Since ACLU became actively involved in the Nazi-Skokie conflict in May 1977, the most appropriate comparison of the size of the membership would be from pre-1977 to the present. Unfortunately, reliable data are not available prior to calendar 1977, so all comparisons must be based on that year. Because the impact of the incident was felt continuously from mid-1977 through the end of 1978,

TABLE 4.3. Membership Status of Respondents

Membership Status	ACLU Members		ACLU Leaders	
Neither Recently Joined Nor Resigned	85.8%		96.1%	
Recently Joined	4.3		1.8	
Over Nazi Issue		53.6%		0.0%
Over Other Issues		36.8		100.0
Over Both Issues		9.5		0.0
		100.0%		100.0%
		(5546)		(23)
Recently Quit, Will Quit	10.0%		2.1%	
Over Other Issues		45.7%		84.6%
Over Nazi Issue		43.6		0
Over Both Issues		10.8		15.4
		100.0%		100.0%
		(12,939)		(26)
	100.0%		100.0%	
	(129,794)		(1254)	

Source: James L. Gibson and Richard D. Bingham, "Skokie, Nazis, and the Elitist Theory of Democracy," Western Political Quarterly, Vol. 37, No. 1, March 1984, p. 42. Reprinted by Permission of the University of Utah, Copyright Holder.

the use of 1977 as a base comparison year tends to underestimate the effect. No preferable alternative is available, however.

The Union did experience some change in the size of its membership in this period (see Table 4.5). At the end of 1977, it had 122,736 active members. The number declines to 117,008 in 1978, but then rebounds to 129,237 by the end of 1979. The average (of the state affiliates) percentage change in total active members from 1977 to 1978 was –9.7 percent. The comparable figure for 1978 to 1979 is +12.5 percent, and +1.6 percent for the two-year 1977 to 1979 period. Interestingly, the figures for new members demonstrate a contrary trend. In 1978 there were over 10,000 more new members than in 1977, but in 1979 there were approximately 2,000 fewer new members than in 1978. These figures are reflected in the growth rates for the affiliates—the average percentage increase in new members from 1977 to 1978 was 38.6 percent, whereas the figure for 1978 to 1979 was 0.7 percent. Trends in membership renewals are quite different—a decline in renewals occurred in 1977 to 1978, followed by a nearly identical increase in 1978 to 1979.

TABLE 4.4. Major Reasons for Quitting ACLU

Reason for Quitting	ACLU Members	ACLU Leaders
ACLU is too expensive	26.4%[a]	—
General or personal	17.9	13.3
Abortion	8.1	13.3
Capital punishment	7.1	—
ACLU has moved beyond the First Amendment	6.8	—
ACLU isn't responding to pressing issues	5.8	33.3
Reverse discrimination	5.3	—
ACLU interference in Gary Gilmore case	5.2	—
ACLU office discourtesies	3.8	40.0
ACLU defense of Nazis	3.8	—
ACLU gave names to FBI	2.7	—
ACLU defense of KKK	2.6	—
Corporal punishment in schools	2.5	—
Women's rights	1.3	13.3
Other	15.6	
	114.9	113.2
	(5199)	(15)

[a]Percent of those quitting ACLU for reasons other than Skokie giving this response. Columns total to more than 100 percent owing to multiple responses.

TABLE 4.5. Change in ACLU Membership, 1977–1979

	Percentage Change		
	1977–1978	1978–1979	1977–1979
52 State Affiliates			
Total Active Members	− 9.7	12.5	1.6
New Members	38.6	0.7	42.8
Renewals	−11.0	12.0	0.0
25 Large Affiliates			
Total Active Members	− 7.4	10.7	2.6
New Members	42.0	− 5.2	33.0
Renewals	−10.1	10.8	− 0.4

These membership figures suggest several conclusions. First, the Skokie controversy had some negative impact on the membership. Renewals declined substantially, but this decline was counterpoised to some degree by an *increase* in new members. Second, the ACLU rebounded in 1979, primarily by cutting the non-renewal rate. If all of the change in membership were attributable to Skokie (and it obviously cannot be), then the net effect of the issue approaches zero.

It should be noted that there are some differences in the conclusions supported by the survey data and those supported by the aggregate membership data. The survey implies a net loss in members that can be attributed to Skokie, whereas the aggregate figures imply an overall (i.e., not Skokie-specific) net gain (although direct comparison must be limited because the survey has a rather imprecise time frame). The survey appears to have missed the surge of new members that was occurring simultaneously with the selection of the samples. It is also unclear that the new member samples provided to us by ACLU actually were drawn from the new member population. For instance, of the first "new member sample" only 19 percent reported that they had recently joined the organization. For the second new member sample, the figure is also approximately 20 percent. In terms of defectors, it must also be noted that it is not easy to quit ACLU. The survey indicates that somewhat less than 20,000 members were in the process of quitting in late 1978 and early 1979. At the end of 1978, ACLU reports 29,000 members as "suspended." Part of this difference is attributable to the exclusion in the survey of institutional members and members who quit for non-programmatic reasons (e.g., death). Thus, while precise numbers may be quite difficult to reconcile, for a variety of reasons, it does seem likely that about one-half of those quitting in this period did so over Skokie.

A further indication of the limited magnitude of the defections can be seen by examining the membership figures of the Illinois affiliate of the ACLU. Given the salience of the issue for the Illinois affiliate and its members, it might be expected that impact of the dispute would be easily discernible. Figure 4.1 reports data on the size of the affiliate for the period from 1966 to 1980. The parabolic line represents the predicted scores from a quadratic regression of the membership figures on time. It is important to note that the regression is based only on the data for the period 1966 to 1976. The data reveal that there was a significant surge in the membership in the Nixon-Watergate-Vietnam era. It also appears, however, that most of these members had been lost *prior* to the Skokie controversy. In 1968, the Illinois affiliate had 8,560 members; in 1976, the figure was 8,465. And while the membership declined in 1977 by 1,969 members, the prediction based upon the 1966-1976 trend (i.e., based on the regression) was that the membership would decline by 1,263 as compared to the predicted membership in 1977, and 1,464 as compared to the actual membership in 1977. *Thus, given the assumptions of the analysis, the maximum possible loss attributable to the Skokie dispute is on the order of 500 members.* It seems likely that defections attributable to this secular trend were erroneously attributed to the Skokie dispute by the leaders of the ACLU. Indeed, the Skokie controversy seems responsible for *reversing* the pattern of declining membership. Based on the 1976 projections and assuming that the 1966-1976 trend remained in effect, the Illinois affiliate should have had only 1,541 members in 1981! Instead, it had 8,277 members. In Illinois at least, the effect of the Skokie dispute was a net gain in the sense that, while the membership did not increase from 1976 to 1980, it did not decline nearly as much as expected. Frank Collin may have been a blessing in disguise for the Illinois affiliate.

Our research cannot, and was not designed to, assess whether the financial impact of the Skokie-Nazi conflict on ACLU was minor or extraordinary. When an organization has been through a period of financial stagnation and the concomitant budget cuts, it may find the impact of even marginal additional cut-backs devastating. Hamlin reports, for instance, losing five of the thirteen employees in the Illinois office because of Skokie (Hamlin, 1980, p. 132). Our estimates of the size of the membership defection do little more than set the parameters for the severity of the impact on the organization. Nonetheless, it is likely that the leaders of the ACLU overestimated the negative member reaction, and failed to anticipate the substantial positive member counter-reaction.

Attributes of Defectors

The ACLU leadership, especially Neier, had some pretty definite views about the type of members who defected. First, it was believed that the organization had the virtually unanimous support of both its national and state leadership. Second, Neier suggested that members who termed themselves "progressive" or "radical" might have been more inclined to leave the organization. These members found it difficult to justify the allocation of scarce organizational resources to the defense of one of the gravest of enemies of civilized society. This position is

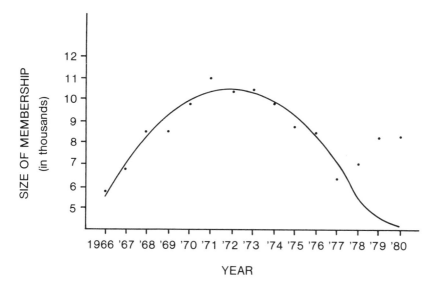

$$\hat{y}= -711167.9+(20055.72 * YEAR) - (139.3357 * YEAR^2)$$
$$R^2= .948$$

FIGURE 4.1. Change in membership size—Illinois Civil Liberties Union.

most clearly represented by the National Lawyers Guild in its accusation of the ACLU as engaging in "poisonous evenhandedness:"

> To say that progressive people such as anti-war activists, communists, anarchists, and anti-imperialists, are to be treated in the same way and accorded the same defense by the ACLU as is accorded to Nazis, Fascists (such as the Reverend Moon) and to the Klan will ultimately weaken support for civil liberties amongst progressive and militant people in struggles in this country. Support for one side, the progressive side, should be wholehearted and provided in the spirit of comradeship. Support for the other side, the reactionary side, may be appropriate at times. On a specific and limited civil liberties issue, it may be correct for the ACLU and other forums to lend some legal support by way of amicus participation. However, support should be miserly and stingy—limited to the most proscribed of circumstances and focused upon the narrowest of issues. (quoted in Neier, 1979, p. 87)

"Single-issue" members were also blamed by Neier. It was assumed that the Nixon impeachment fight had drawn large numbers of single-issue individuals into the organization—individuals whose primary interests lay in removing Nixon from office, not in the more generalized defense of civil liberties. With Nixon's demise came a general decline in interest and hence in membership. Moreover, no issue emerged to fill the void left by the resolution of the Watergate crisis. Thus, not only were the single-issue members never properly socialized to more general civil liberties values, but there were also few salient issues to reinforce their initial libertarian impulses. Consequently, the Skokie-Nazi issue was especially effective at alienating these already rather weak members.

Another perspective on the ACLU posture vis-à-vis right-wing political minorities emerged in conjunction with the ACLU defense of the Klan in Mississippi. A prevalent critique is well exemplified in a memorandum of protest over the Klan defense by a member of the Mississippi ACLU board:

> I believe that the very existence of organizations like the Klan and the Nazi Party poses a clear and present danger to the physical safety and civil rights of minority people. The issue of defending the so-called free speech rights of fascist gangs, whose very purpose is to deprive minority people of free speech and other constitutional rights, could scarcely provide more graphic proof that many constitutional rights do not exist in a vacuum but that in many cases the rights of one group must be weighted against the rights of others. (quoted in Neier, 1979, p. 92)

Thus, Neier seems to believe that three categories of ACLU members formed the bulk of those abandoning the organization over the Skokie issue—the "Nixon era" members who were never properly educated by the ACLU; the progressives who believe in only limited assistance to right-wing organizations; and those who find Nazi ideology to be so reprehensible that their rights are subservient to the rights of those they seek to destroy. Further, it is believed that the leadership of the state affiliates of ACLU was consensually united in support of the organization's defense of the Nazi's rights. Each of these speculations can be addressed with the data at hand.

It is perhaps appropriate to begin by reporting member attributes *unrelated* to defecting. In the demographic attributes of defectors and non-defectors, no differences have been found that are related to gender, occupation, or education. For instance, there is only a weak relationship between race and quitting, with black and Hispanic members slightly more likely to have quit than whites. While approximately one-tenth of the black members defected over the Skokie issue, nearly one-third of the Hispanic members quit over this issue. Overall, however, there is little differentiation on the basis of race between quitters and non-quitters.

Neither is there much regional variation in defection rates. Only six states experienced defections at a rate more than ten percentage points higher than the national average, but these are mostly small affiliates (Maine, Mississippi, Idaho, and Alaska) for which our estimates are relatively unstable. The large-state exceptions are Tennessee and New Jersey (19 percent). The defection rates for California, New York, and Illinois, arguably the most important states for the ACLU, are 9, 11, and 16 percent, respectively. California and 11 other states had more defections over non-Skokie issues, however, than over Skokie. Caution should be exercised in interpreting these figures because state-level conclusions are statistically suspect, and none of the cross-state differences is very substantial.

There has been much speculation that reactions to the Skokie affair vary substantially depending upon the religious affiliation of the individual, and, in particular, that Jews—given the obvious significance of the Nazi issue for them—were more likely to have defected than non-Jews. There is some support for these speculations. Those claiming no religious affiliation defected at a very low rate (5 percent). Of the religions represented by at least 1,000 members (in the weighted sample), similarly low rates of defections were observed for Congregationalists, Quakers, Unitarians/Universalists, members of the United Church of Christ, Episcopalians, Catholics, non-denominational Protestants, Presbyterians, Baptists, and Methodists. Only two religions—Lutherans and Jews—have substantially higher defection rates. Reform Jews defected at a rate of 11 percent; Conservative Jews at 23 percent; and non-sectarian Jews at 11 percent. The defection rate for Lutherans was 9 percent. Though nearly one-half of the defectors were Jewish, the overall defection rate for Jews (14 percent) is not dramatically higher than that for non-Jews, and we therefore conclude that the direct effect of religion on defection is not great.

It might also be expected that those with experience as victims of Nazi crimes would be less willing to tolerate ACLU's defense of the party. Some tendency in this direction exists, but it is not strong.

In sum, none of the demographic attributes of the members is very useful in distinguishing between defectors and non-defectors. A demographic composite of the "average" defector could be drawn, but it would be quite similar to the non-defector composite. It seems more useful therefore to consider attitudinal and organizational determinants of defections.

As expected, there is a very strong relationship between attitudes toward the principle Skokie ordinances and defection—over one-third of those supporting both Skokie ordinances quit over the Nazi issue, while only 3 percent of those opposing the ordinances quit—but the strongest predictor of defection is the subjects' views of whether ACLU should have represented the Nazis. Table 4.6 demonstrates that a majority of those who "strongly disagreed" with the ACLU position quit the organization; at the other extreme, only a tiny fraction of those supporting the Union's action defected. Despite the strength of this relationship, it is remarkable that defections were not more widespread. A very large majority of the 11 percent of the membership who disagreed with the ACLU did *not* quit. Similarly, only a bare majority of the 7 percent who disagreed strongly with the ACLU position quit. At least 9 percent of the defectors *supported* ACLU's defense of the Nazis, even if they felt it impossible to be a member of such an organization. If we ignore recent joiners and those who quit for other reasons, we find that 82 percent of the membership supported the ACLU in both their attitudes and their behavior, 12 percent were behaviorally supportive, but attitudinally in opposition, and 5 percent expressed attitudinal and behavioral disagreement.

Though this relationship is strong, attitudes toward the organization do not completely determine changes in membership status so we also consider next the question of the general libertarian beliefs held by the defectors. Defection is modestly related to general support for freedom of speech (as measured by the items shown in Table 5.1, p. 111): 11 percent of those unwilling to offer constitutional protection to most types of speech quit ACLU over Skokie. A more significant relationship exists between defection and attitudes toward freedom of assembly. While those more supportive of the heckler's veto (see Table 5.2, p. 118) are only slightly more likely to have quit over Skokie, general attitudes toward the majority's right to prohibit obnoxious assemblies (see Table 5.3, p. 119) are strong predictors of defection. Only a tiny fraction of those generally supporting the right to assemble quit, whereas a large percentage of those generally not favorably predisposed toward

TABLE 4.6. Attitudes toward ACLU Defense of Nazi Rights and Defections—ACLU Members

ACLU Should Defend the Nazis	Percent Resigning Over Skokie
Agree Strongly	0.4
Agree	0.9
Neutral	8.6
Disagree	16.3
Disagree Strongly	54.9

Total N = 116,944

demonstrations in hostile territory quit. For example, 19 percent of the members willing to grant communities the right to veto demonstrations quit, whereas only 1 percent of those recognizing no such community right quit. Thus, though it is true that the context of Nazism strongly affected reactions on the Skokie issue, it appears that the controversy should be understood as a question of *free assembly* rather than of *free speech*. The specific content of a Nazi speech is irrelevant to most of the defectors. Nazis, *ipso facto*, should not be allowed to demonstrate.

But are these defectors generally weak libertarians? Table 4.7 reports the defection rates in relation to a number of general libertarian items (see Table 5.5, p. 124). These measures of general commitment to civil liberties are drawn from a "test" that ACLU advises potential members to take to determine whether they are likely to be satisfied members of the organization. Over one-fifth of those scoring poorly on the test (less than 7 libertarian responses) quit over Skokie, whereas less than one percent of the members with perfect scores quit. Thus, defectors were drawn from the portion of the membership with attitudes less supportive of civil liberties.

Similar results are produced when a different measure of general commitment to civil liberties is used. On the basis of responses to items typically used to measure political tolerance (see Table 5.7, p. 130), the subjects were classified on a four-category political tolerance scale. Only 1 percent of the strong libertarians defected, whereas 35 percent of the strong non-libertarians defected. The percentage for the moderate libertarians is 9; for the weak libertarians, it is 20 percent. Statistically, this is a very strong relationship. Thus, it appears that the defectors were primarily ACLU members with weak general commitments to civil liberties. Perhaps it was not the idiosyncratic aspects of the Skokie

TABLE 4.7. General Libertarianism and Defection Rates—ACLU Members

Number of Libertarian Responses	Percent Resigning Over Skokie
Less than 7	21.4
7	18.1
8	14.0
9	9.6
10	9.1
11	4.0
12	3.9
13	0.8

Total N = 117,105

dispute that drove these members to resign. Instead, any tough civil liberties issue that became salient to them may well have stimulated their resignations. This finding is generally compatible with ACLU's understanding of the defectors.

Are defectors drawn from any particular segment of the ideological spectrum? Table 4.8 suggests not. There is only a slight tendency for those identifying themselves as on the "radical left" to defect (too few members to analyze associated themselves with the radical right). The hypothesis that political ideology is related to reactions to Skokie receives little support from the survey data.

But perhaps this measure of ideology is not very useful because it is too subjective; it allows the subject to define the left-right continuum. It might be more instructive to consider, as best we can, the reasons why individuals joined ACLU as evidence of their ideological and libertarian commitments. That is, the motivations for joining may provide some indication of the ideological priorities of the members.

Table 4.9 reports the reasons respondents gave for joining ACLU and the defection rate for each group. It should first be noted that most members (70 percent) claim that no specific civil liberties cause stimulated them to join the organization. The defection rate for these individuals, as well as for those who joined over civil liberties in general, over unspecified specific causes, and who cannot remember why they joined, is very low. Second, only a tiny percentage of the subjects reported that they joined over the Nixon impeachment activity, and almost none of these members resigned. The Vietnam War motivated 2 percent of the current members to join and 11 percent of these members quit over Skokie. This rate is somewhat higher than the overall defection rate of 4.3 percent. Third, other important issues reported by members to have stimulated them to join the organization include women's rights and civil rights. The latter group is somewhat more likely to have quit over the defense of the Nazis, no doubt as a function of general revulsion toward right-wing extremist groups like the Nazis and Klan. Finally, high defection rates are observed for those joining ACLU over the death penalty issue, police issues, and poor people's and union rights. It is this latter group especially that Neier probably had in mind when he asserted that "progressives" defected at a higher than average rate, and it appears that he was correct. However, this is a fine illustration of a classical statistical error. It is true that nearly one-third of this group defected; however, the total number of people joining the organization for this reason is so small that they constitute only a tiny proportion *of the defectors*. In general, we conclude that there is a slight tendency for those somewhat less concerned specifically with First Amendment rights to have quit over Skokie. Thus, while ACLU is not completely accurate about the defectors' original motivations for joining the organization, the logic of the position—that specific-issue joiners are somewhat less likely to hold strong, generalized commitments to civil liberties—receives some support from the data.

A more general hypothesis is that those who are only peripherally involved in the organization were more likely to have defected. Irrespective of initial motivations for joining, greater organizational involvement

TABLE 4.8.   Ideology and Defection—ACLU Members

Ideological Self-Identification	Percent Resigning Over Skokie
Radical Left	9.7
Extremely liberal	4.0
Liberal	4.7
Slightly liberal	9.2
Moderate	9.3
Slightly Conservative	7.0
Conservative	1.8
Other	8.5
Don't know	7.7

Total N = 116,238

TABLE 4.9. Motivation for Joining ACLU and Defections Over Skokie—ACLU Members

Reason for Joining	Percent of Total Membership	Percent Defecting Over Skokie
Nazi Issue	0.1	—
Vietnam	2.0	11.3
Nixon—Watergate	0.8	0.0
Women's Rights	2.1	7.8
Gay Rights	1.6	0.4
Civil Rights	3.5	13.7
Red Scare	1.1	5.1
Criminal Justice	0.4	0.0
Death Penalty	0.3	18.9
Police	0.5	12.7
Political Dissidents	0.4	12.2
Poor People—Unions	0.3	31.8
Student Rights	0.5	1.0
General Civil Liberties	4.9	6.1
Other	0.2	24.4
Specific Cause—Unspecified	2.0	6.3
No Specific Cause	69.7	4.7
Don't Remember	9.4	8.5
	99.8	
	(117,124)	

results in more effective socialization and reinforcement of libertarian norms and values.

Organizational involvement can be measured in a variety of ways. At the simplest level, the greater the number of years of membership in ACLU, the greater the opportunity for involvement. However, defection rates do not vary significantly according to the number of years of membership. Nor is it the case that members who pay greater attention to ACLU publications are less likely to have quit. Those who have been active in ACLU affairs (e.g., who have attended ACLU meetings or functions) are quite unlikely to have quit (3 percent); those moderately involved are somewhat more likely to have quit (6 percent); and those uninvolved are even more likely to have quit (12 percent). These differences, though in the expected direction, are not great however, and generally we conclude that organizational involvement has little direct effect on libertarian commitments.

While there is little support for the belief that defectors are drawn from a somewhat less active segment of the organization, it is certainly true that the leadership was almost perfectly united in its defense of the organization's position. We have discovered only four members of the state affiliate boards of directors who resigned over the Skokie issue and each of these cited additional reasons for leaving the organization. While it is important to consider the caveat imposed by the response rate within the leadership sample, it appears that the understanding of the ACLU National Office on this point is correct.

Finally, only a small percentage of those defecting justify their anti-Nazi rights position through reference to the forfeiture of rights by the Nazis. Thus, the perceptions of membership reaction by the national leadership of ACLU are somewhat accurate, but in nearly every instance exaggerated. That is, the variables thought to be related to defection are not strongly related statistically.

A MULTIVARIATE ANALYSIS OF DEFECTION

In order to explore more complex and indirect effects of these variables on defection, a multivariate analysis is necessary. The analysis will focus on determining whether the relationship between libertarian attitudes and defection behavior is contingent upon levels of organizational involvement and religious affiliation.

It is first useful to construct a measure of the attitudinal predispositions of the members. This has been accomplished through regression analysis, using as predictor variables general tolerance attitudes and specific Skokie opinions. The details of the construction of this measure are given in note 5 to Chapter 7. Table 4.10 reports the strong bivariate relationship of this variable to defection. Generally, defection behavior is strongly related to attitudes. The predicted scores from the regression analysis can be treated as measures of attitudinal predispositions—specifically, propensities to behave—and, once collapsed into categories, allow the hypotheses to be tested.

Table 4.11 reports the multivariate analysis of defection, attitudes, and religious affiliation. Several aspects of this table are worthy of note. First, among Jews and non-Jews the relationship between attitudes and behavior is strong, although it is a little stronger for Jews. Second, Jews are somewhat less likely to hold strongly libertarian views than non-Jews: 56 percent of the non-Jews, but only 44 percent of the Jews are very

TABLE 4.10. Libertarian Predispositions and Defection Behavior—ACLU Members

Attitudinal Predisposition	Percent Resigning Over Skokie
Strong Libertarian	0.2
Moderate Libertarian	2.1
Weak Libertarian	18.5
Non-Libertarian	53.5

Total N = 118,339

strong libertarians. *Third, when attitudes are controlled, Jews are more likely to defect from the ACLU than non-Jews.* Non-libertarian non-Jews defected at a rate of 46 percent; the rate for Jews with similar attitudes was 60 percent. Among weak libertarians, the difference in defection rates was as substantial: for non-Jews, the rate was 14 percent; for Jews, it was 28 percent. When attitudinal predispositions are more libertarian, Jews and non-Jews differ little—they are both guided in their behavior by their values. But in the absence of substantial libertarianism, other factors—such as the perception of the degree of threat posed by the Nazis—become significant and lead Jews to defect at higher rates.

Nevertheless, an overwhelming proportion of those whose behavior is incorrectly predicted is drawn from nonlibertarians who failed to defect. In seeking an explanation for the behavior of this group it is useful to consider the conditional effect of organizational loyalty and involvement. It is hypothesized that high organizational involvement mitigates the linkage between nonlibertarian attitudes and behavior. Table 4.12 reports data relevant to this hypothesis.

TABLE 4.11. The Conditional Effect of Religious Affiliation on Defection Rates—ACLU Members

Attitudinal Predisposition	Percent Resigning Over Skokie	
	Non-Jews	Jews
Strong Libertarian	0.1 (51,084)	0.6 (11,574)
Moderate Libertarian	2.3 (27,863)	1.3 (6,447)
Weak Libertarian	13.9 (9,641)	28.2 (4,683)
Non-Libertarian	46.4(2,882)	60.2 (3,344)

NOTE: Figures in parentheses are numbers of cases.

The hypothesis is strongly supported. Although the level of organizational involvement has no effect on those with strong libertarian attitudes, this group being quite unlikely to defect under any circumstances, its effect on the other members is dramatic. Among those with strongly intolerant attitudes, the defection rate varies from 32 percent for those highly involved in ACLU activity, to 55 percent among those with medium involvement, and 87 percent among those with low involvement. The number of individuals in some of these categories is small (reflecting in part the relationship between involvement and civil liberties attitudes) but defectors are drawn quite disproportionately from the sector of the membership with weak civil liberties commitments *and* with marginal levels of involvement in the organization.

It is useful to consider these findings in the light of more general theories of the relationship between attitudes and behavior (see also Chapter 7). Attitudes do not always result in consistent behavior; instead, the behavioral impulse flowing from attitudes must be strong enough to overcome a variety of "hurdles" impeding behavior (see Campbell, 1963). Attitudes represent abstract generalizations, whereas behavior occurs within discrete and concrete situations. Situations emit stimuli that make it easier or more difficult to engage in consistent behavior. The classic illustration of this process involves interpersonal discrimination: despite prejudiced attitudes, discriminatory behavior frequently fails to materialize in face-to-face situations because norms governing interpersonal interactions discourage such behavior. In the case of ACLU members, the attitude-behavior relationship was mitigated by two important factors. First, the hurdle for defection was lowered for a particular segment—Jews—presumably because of the stimuli

TABLE 4.12. The Conditional Effect of Organizational Involvement on Defection Rates—ACLU Members

Attitudinal Predisposition	Percent Resigning Over Skokie Level of Organizational Involvement		
	Low	Moderate	High
Strong Libertarian	0.1 (3,126)	0.3 (41,505)	0.0 (19,010)
Moderate Libertarian	6.4 (2,062)	2.2 (26,233)	0.3 (6,389)
Weak Libertarian	12.7 (992)	18.3 (11,488)	21.4 (2,324)
Non-Libertarian	86.7 (626)	54.8 (4,502)	31.9 (1,291)

NOTE: Figures in parentheses are numbers of cases.

emitted by the Skokie case. It should be noted, however, that the situational stimuli do *not* play a role in the presence of strong commit-ments to civil liberties. Defections among libertarian Jews were negligible, just as they were among libertarian non-Jews. It is only in the presence of a preexisting tendency toward behavior that this notion of hurdles becomes useful.

On the other hand, the hurdle to behavior is raised for other groups, in particular, for those with a strong commitment to the ACLU. The effect of nonlibertarian attitudes is blocked for most of the members who are actively involved in ACLU affairs. As involvement declines, the hurdle becomes lower and behavioral predispositions materialize in actual behavior. Thus, because of organizational loyalty the ACLU lost fewer members than it should have based on the substantive issues involved.

In summary, the multivariate analysis reveals that:

1. The likelihood of defection is strongly related to civil liberties attitudes. Among those with strong commitments to civil liberties, defection is extremely rare.

2. Jews are somewhat less committed to civil liberties and thus defected at a somewhat higher rate than non-Jews.

3. However, when attitudes are held constant, Jews defected at a rate higher than non-Jews, suggesting that the situational constraints of the Skokie case made intolerant behavior easier.

4. Organizational loyalty and involvement strongly influenced defection rates (even with attitudes held constant). Greater organi-zational involvement mitigated the impact of nonlibertarian atti-tudes, thus reducing the negative impact of the issue on ACLU.

IMPLICATIONS FOR ACLU

Skokie presented an important controversy for ACLU. But was it unprecedented? ACLU had defended the rights of the radical right previously (including Nazis), and disputes over organizational priorities are not uncommon. How can the seemingly extreme reaction and counter-reaction to the issue be explained and what implications for the future of the Union can be suggested?

It must first be noted that other issues are potentially at least as divisive as was the Skokie issue. Table 4.13 reports responses to the ACLU test items, as well as Skokie opinions. It can be seen that the ACLU position on the death penalty arouses *more* opposition than Skokie aroused. Indeed, on a series of crime-related issues, a sizable anti-libertarian minority exists within the organization. There is obviously more than a single chink in the libertarian armor of the organization.[1]

It should also be noted that the issues likely to generate conflict do not necessarily involve the political right. For ACLU to take a more separationist or anti-church stance on the church and state issue would generate conflict. Similarly, it seems that issues of crime and justice cannot be extended much further without at least some membership reaction. The death penalty is a particularly salient issue as well. Generally, efforts to enlarge the issue domain either by movement to the left or right seem likely to run considerable risk of conflict within the organization.

Skokie was a relatively salient issue for the membership and it apparently generated quite a bit of reflection on the role and function of the Union. Because most ACLU members seem not to be comfortable with an idiosyncratic defense of their positions on Skokie, many searched for a principled umbrella under which they could shelter their beliefs. Table 4.14 shows the distribution of responses to a question asking about the proper function and priorities of the organization.

In contrast to many of the findings reported above, there is considerable dissensus within the membership on the proper role of the organization. A simple majority of the members (but two-thirds of those with an opinion) believe that the ACLU should defend all individuals and groups seeking assistance. The leadership is even more united in this view. Among those who would place restrictions on the types of groups receiving assistance, the predominant responses are to avoid defending advocates of violence and fascism, and those not respecting the First Amendment rights of others. The remaining responses are scattered, but at least some of the responses would justify refusing to defend Nazis (e.g., "don't defend tiny political minorities"). Generally, the ACLU should expect substantial dissent from its members any time it defends the rights of rightists.

It seems that member reaction to civil liberties conflicts can be understood in terms of utilitarian calculus. Opinions on issues reflect the calculation of the difference of costs and benefits. So long as costs are minimal, support for the civil liberty can be expected. However, as costs rise, benefits must also rise in order to avoid a negative balance. As few would quarrel with the proposition that the costs of the Skokie case

TABLE 4.13. Issue Consensus

Issue	ACLU Position Agree/Disagree	Percent Agreeing with ACLU Position	
		ACLU Members	ACLU Leaders
High school students are within their rights when they express political opinions, circulate petitions and handbills, or wear political insignia in school.	A	94.5	97.6
A woman has a private right to decide whether to have a child or undergo an abortion.	A	93.8	94.6
Police should be allowed to conduct a full search of any motorist arrested for an offense such as speeding.	D	92.6	97.1
A man should be denied unemployment compensation if fired from his job for growing a beard.	D	91.6	95.4
Court calendars are so crowded that the right to trial by jury should be restricted to persons accused of major crimes only.	D	87.0	94.5
Students who shout down speakers to achieve their aims subvert the principles of academic freedom.	D	86.2	87.4
The officials in Skokie passed a law in response to the Nazi application [for permission to demonstrate] that required anyone wanting to speak, parade, or demonstrate to apply for a permit. The permit would be denied if, in the opinion of the village officials, the proposed speech portrays "lack of virtue" in others or "incites hostility."...Do you favor or oppose such a law being passed?	*	86.0	97.3

Statement			
In the same city, anyone who wants to hold a public march must also post a $350,000 insurance bond (although this requirement can be waived by the City). This requirement applies to everyone, not only the Nazis, and since insurance companies rarely will write such insurance, few bonds have been posted.... Do you favor or oppose such a law being passed?	*	84.4	96.5
The C.I.A. should be able to prevent any former employees from writing about the agency without the C.I.A.'s prior approval.	D	82.4	92.8
Government consolidation of dossiers on individual citizens violates the right to privacy.	A	81.5	86.7
The ACLU is currently representing the right of the Nazis to march in Skokie. Do you agree or disagree with this action?	*	81.2	94.3
A radio station that permits the reading of an anti-Semitic poem over the air should have its F.C.C. license revoked.	D	80.1	88.2
In their fight against crime the police should be entitled to use wiretaps and other devices for listening in on private conversations.	D	78.9	89.1
In Skokie, the Nazis sought a permit to hold a public rally. If it were up to you to decide, would you grant the permit application or deny it?	*	78.7	95.4
Membership in the John Birch Society by itself is enough to bar an applicant from appointment to the police force.	D	78.5	90.0
The use of tax funds to support parochial schools involves compulsory taxation for religious purposes and thus violates the First Amendment.	A	77.2	87.9

TABLE 4.13. (*Continued*)

Issue	ACLU Position *Agree/ Disagree*	Percent Agreeing with ACLU Position	
		ACLU Members	*ACLU Leaders*
In light of present standards of justice and humanity, the death penalty has become "cruel and unusual punishment" in violation of the Eighth Amendment.	A	69.8	88.2
The "separation of church and state" clause of the First Amendment should be used to eliminate the tax-exempt status of religious institutions.	*	54.0	59.6
Countries that discriminate among their citizens on the basis of religion should be denied U.S. foreign aid.	*		

*These items were not taken from the ACLU pamphlet "Where Do You Stand on Civil Liberties."

Source: James L. Gibson and Richard D. Bingham, "On the Conceptualization and Measurement of Political Tolerance," *American Political Science Review*, Vol. 76, No. 3, September 1982, p. 613.

were high, the crisis must be viewed largely in terms of member inability to identify possible benefits of supporting the rights of Nazis to demonstrate.

Defections are primarily attributable to conflict over value priorities. For some, an expansive definition of fundamental civil liberties is the *sine qua non* of an acceptable society. Others seem to value public order and freedom from personal physical and intellectual assault more highly. Civil liberties conflicts are always played out within the context of "zero-sum" constraints. When rights are allocated to some interests, they are deducted from others. From some ACLU members the "net costs" of this controversy were too high.

Yet the stimuli—and values elicited—from a controversy are susceptible to manipulation. In the case of Skokie, the issue was only belatedly focused on the Skokie ordinances. Nearly all of the ACLU membership claimed to be at least somewhat familiar with the Skokie controversy, yet only 44 percent were aware of the group libel ordinance and only 39 percent were aware of the insurance bond requirement (approximately one-fourth of the leadership was unaware of these provisions). Moreover, the degree of exposure to ACLU's position is unrelated to views on the issue, possibly (but not necessarily) leading to

TABLE 4.14. Member Views of ACLU Functions and Priorities

Proper Function of ACLU	ACLU Members	ACLU Leaders
Defend constitutional rights for all people and/or groups	58.1%	72.8%
Don't defend fascists-racists/defend progressives only	4.2	4.0
Give fascists lower priority	2.4	1.3
Don't defend tiny political minorities	0.7	0.2
Don't defend those using violent means	10.0	5.5
Don't defend those who would deny rights	4.3	1.6
Dont defend those who can pay/want to defend themselves	3.0	2.7
Defend individuals not groups	1.1	0.9
Other	0.1	0.2
No Answer	14.4	10.8
	100.0	100.0
	(132,880)	(1281)

the conclusion that ACLU ineffectively presented its position. While awareness of the specific provisions of the Skokie ordinances does not itself predict the likelihood of defection, the more the dispute is characterized as a traditional First Amendment case, the greater is the support for the organization.

Perhaps because ACLU misunderstood the character and objectives of its members, or perhaps because the magnitude of the initial negative response to its position (especially from the media and other non-members of the organization) forced the leadership into a defensive posture, ACLU's crisis is best understood as stemming from its ineffectiveness at assisting its members in identifying benefits from defending the rights of Frank Collin and the Nazis (just as its recovery was a function of its offensive efforts to proselytize its members). As with all organizations, maintenance of internal support is at least as important as the policy and political efficacy of organizational activity. Now that the ACLU has learned its lesson, it is unlikely that future crises will be so debilitating.

NOTE

1.   Opinions on several of these issues are fairly intense. Using the percentage indicating that their intolerant beliefs on the items in Table 5.5 are "strongly" held as an indicator of issue salience, other issues stand out as salient and intense. Of those agreeing that "A man should be denied unemployment compensation if fired from his job for growing a beard," 40 percent agreed strongly. Abortion also generated strong feelings among anti-abortionists (37 percent "strong"), followed by the item on the political rights of high school students (28 percent). At first thought it seems nonsensical that the issue of unemployment compensation for bearded men would be so salient to those with intolerant general attitudes. But the similarity lies, no doubt, in the perception that both represent an extreme extension of principles that are, in the abstract, consensually supported. To the extent that a clearly articulated constitutional underpinning is not available to the members (or if the connection is too distant) conflict is likely to increase.

5　Conceptual and Operational Approaches to Political Tolerance

As typically defined by social scientists, political tolerance refers to a willingness to extend the rights of citizenship to all members of the polity, that is, to grant political freedoms to those who are politically different. For instance, according to Sullivan, Pierson, and Marcus, "tolerance implies a willingness to 'put up with' those things that one rejects. Politically, it implies a willingness to permit the expression of those ideas or interests that one opposes. A tolerant regime, then, like a tolerant individual, is one that allows a wide berth to those ideas that challenge its way of life..." (1979, p. 784). Others define tolerance similarly.

But what sort of activities must be given "wide berth?" The earliest effort to measure political tolerance focused not only on the rights of speech and assembly ("making a speech in your community"), but also on such rights as that of not being excluded on the basis of one's political affiliations from having one's book in a library, from working as a singer or entertainer, from teaching in a university or high school, or from working in a defense plant (Stouffer, 1955). More recent research operationally defined tolerance to include the right to be considered as a candidate for president of the country, to speak, to hold rallies, to exist as a legal group, to teach in public schools, to be free from wiretaps, and to socialize with people, that is, to live next door, come to dinner, and date daughters and sons (Sullivan et al., 1978–79). Others have attacked the problem more directly by attempting to define democracy. Prothro and Grigg (1960) postulated two essential elements of democracy: majority rule and minority rights, including the freedom to dissent. Stouffer (1955) focused upon tolerance for political non-conformists, and inquired about a wide variety of activities, including the buying of soap after it had been advertised on the radio by a communist entertainer. McClosky (1964, p. 363) has identified the most exhaustive list of key dimensions of democracy. The list includes:

consent; accountability; limited or constitutional government; representation; majority rule, minority rights; freedom of thought, speech, press, and assembly; equality of opportunity; religious toleration; equality before the law; the rights of juridical defense; and individual self-determination over a broad range of personal affairs (see also McClosky and Chong, 1980; McClosky and Brill, 1983). Thus, a panoply of actions has been identified that must be put up with, but there is remarkably little agreement on precisely which norms must be accepted and what activities must be allowed.

In addition, most tolerance researchers (excluding McClosky) do not offer rigorous conceptualizations or operationalizations of the *subdimensions* of political tolerance. For instance, support for free speech is a common element in measures of tolerance, but the continuum (support obviously not being a dichotomy) has not been conceptually or operationally specified. Certainly the Stouffer item on free speech cannot be defended as an adequate measure of willingness to protect the right; at best, it is only a measure of abstract commitment to the freedom. In general, current approaches fail to identify the theoretical subcomponents of the grand concept "political tolerance"; instead of treating tolerance as a syndrome of attitudes, a belief system, each dimension of which is conceptually and operationally specified, researchers have typically treated tolerance as a single unidimensional attitude.

Our research deviates from previous work in attempting a rigorous specification of the relevant subdimensions of tolerance. Rather than offering an exhaustive and global definition of tolerance, one that would nonetheless be incapable of satisfying a very large proportion of scholars, we focus upon support for institutional guarantees for opportunities for political opposition. *Specifically, political tolerance is opposition to state actions that limit opportunities for citizens, individually or in groups, to compete for political power* (cf. Dahl, 1971). Opportunities for political opposition include the right to vote, to participate in political parties, and to organize politically. Also essential are opportunities to engage in political persuasion, for example, to speak and to assemble and demonstrate. Treating tolerance in this fashion gives the concept obvious relevance to the competition and contestation necessary in democratic regimes (see Dahl, 1971, and Chapter 1, above). Although support for other norms may be necessary in order for democracies to exist—and certainly other norms help it to flourish—rights of political opposition are consensually recognized as the *sine qua non* of the democratic style of political organization. Thus, tolerance is opposition to state action that limits the content of, as well as the opportunities for, political communications among citizens. It is a propensity to extend guarantees of the rights to speak, to assemble, to form political associations, etc., to more groups, representing more ideas, under more circumstances.

Recognition that rights of political opposition are an essential element of political tolerance does not, however, resolve all operational and conceptual problems. Just which activities must be protected, and for whom, in order to insure that political minorities have an opportunity to become a political majority? Operationally, how are the relevant continua to be specified and calibrated? At the abstract level, all would agree that freedom of speech is fairly important to democratic polities; but exactly what sorts of speech must be protected, for instance, by freedom of speech? Before the concept of political tolerance is to have empirical and theoretical utility these difficult questions must be answered.

It is instructive to examine existing approaches to support for freedom of speech from this perspective. Generally researchers have been more concerned with the types of groups speaking than with the types of speech spoken. Typically, political tolerance has been measured by asking subjects whether unpopular (presumed or ascertained) minority political groups should be allowed to make speeches. In the absence of any specification of the content of the speech, the variance in these items is no doubt overwhelmed by affective attitudes toward the group. To ask whether a communist should be allowed to speak evokes responses much too strongly confounded by the wide variety of expectations and evaluations of what communists typically say in their speeches. Moreover, this approach leads to the mistaken impression that the public would support a universal ban on communists' speeches, rather than the more likely possibility that it would limit certain types of speeches regardless of the affiliation of the speaker. Although the efforts of Sullivan and others to develop measures that control group affect are certainly laudable, they do not resolve the more fundamental problem of developing and calibrating scales of support for oppositionist political *activity*.

Valid measures of support for civil-liberties activities must also specify a meaningful context in which the liberty is to be exercised. When the context is not specified, the stimulus is too vague to carry a common meaning for all respondents. For instance, Lawrence asked subjects to consider whether or not "people should be allowed to hold a peaceful demonstration to ask the government to act on some issue"

(Lawrence, 1976, p. 92). Rather than describing a range of circumstances under which demonstrations might occur, this item leaves it to the respondent to survey all possible scenarios and to conclude that demonstrations should "always," "sometimes," or "never" be allowed. This is a demanding task. It is not surprising that when a series of more concrete circumstances was put to the subjects, substantial slippage occurred. Nearly one-fourth of those responding "always" would prohibit a demonstration in favor of open housing; over a third of those giving a "never" response would allow demonstrations against pollution! What is the cause of this apparent inconsistency? Subjects simply failed to scrutinize comprehensively the domain of possibilities. Since such a task requires substantial thought (and Lawrence did observe a relationship between education and consistency), and since the greater the amount of thought given, the greater the likelihood of a "sometimes" response, a preferable approach is to have the analysts—rather than the respondent—specify, and thereby control, the contextual domain. Better control both of attitudes toward groups and of attitudes toward activities must be achieved.

Moreover, it must be recognized that the exercise of civil liberties generates conflict among values. Democracy may require free speech, but it also requires at least some social order, for instance, and the various requisites of democracy must be balanced. As the substantial gap between responses to abstract and concrete questionnaire items suggests, the exercise of most important civil liberties is a conflictual, zero-sum activity (and it is for this reason that there is so-called "inconsistency" in the application of abstract beliefs to concrete circumstances). In heterogeneous societies, the exercise of liberty by one group is usually costly to others. The history of disputes over freedom of speech in the United States vividly illustrates the highly conflictual, not infrequently violent, context of the exercise of rights. Attempts have been made to deny speech because it is too costly to those who abhor violence (*Terminiello v. City of Chicago*, 337 U.S. 1, 1949); who dislike profanity (*Cohen v. California*, 403 U.S. 15, 1971); who respect the authority of schools over political expression by students (*Tinker v. Des Moines Independent Community School District*, 393 U.S. 503, 1969); who believe in the legitimacy of war and conscription (*United States v. O'Brien*, 391 U.S. 367, 1968); who are members of ethnic or racial minority groups (*Beauharnais v. Illinois*, 343 U.S. 250, 1952); and, generally, who have a strong attachment to the political status quo. Speech rarely occurs in a value vacuum; the exercise of rights generates costs, and these costs are sometimes so substantial that conflict ensues.

Thus, inquiries about "a speech in my community" are inadequate because they fail to provide the subjects with information about the type of value conflict created within the particular context.

Thus, it is not useful to think of political tolerance as an attitude itself, but instead it should be treated as a hypothetical construct that characterizes the priorities assigned in the instance of value conflict. One who values the right to free assembly more heavily than social order will give responses to questionnaire items that can be designated as "tolerant." The necessity of value conflict is recognized by those requiring that their measures of tolerance be directed toward disfavored objects, but the value conflict must be sharpened considerably in order to control it by posing less obtuse "context-controlled" stimuli. The hierarchical structure of the subjects' beliefs can then be revealed through a series of concrete items posing value conflicts.

One context-sensitive approach to political tolerance might be to elicit opinions through detailed scenarios of civil-liberties disputes. Such an approach, however, makes it very difficult to disentangle the many beliefs contributing to the subject's opinion. A more useful approach is to separate out the various values involved in civil-liberties conflicts and to attempt to measure each with a context-sensitive measure. That is, the major components of tolerance must be rigorously and independently measured, and consideration must be given to the nature of the interrelationships among the components.

In this research, we identify several specific conceptual dimensions of political tolerance. These dimensions are suggested by Dahl's polyarchy concept. Specifically, tolerance of public political opposition is postulated to be composed of support for the following values:

    1. Freedom of speech: the breadth of types of speech given legal and constitutional protection.

    2. Freedom of assembly: (a) willingness to risk violent confrontations in order to insure demonstrators access to public places, and (b) willingness to allow nonviolent affronts to communities in order to insure access to public places.

    3. Freedom of political association: opposition to government restrictions on and surveillance of minority political groups.

So that we may assess the relationship of these measures to more traditional approaches, the generalized approach of Stouffer and the omnibus strategy of McClosky and his colleagues are also represented by items in the survey. The empirical indicators of these concepts can now be addressed.

MEASURES OF POLITICAL TOLERANCE

Support for Freedom of Speech

Stouffer used a single item to measure support for freedom of speech: "Should a _____ be allowed to speak in your community?" Obviously, such an item encompasses a wide variety of circumstances surrounding speeches, circumstances that are completely uncontrolled in the measure. What sort of speech is contemplated, where, and under what circumstances? It is not unreasonable to assume that a subject who conjures up the image of Nazis demonstrating in a Jewish community in favor of the extermination of Jews will respond differently from one who imagines a Nazi address to a private meeting of the local Bund on the matter of school desegregation. In order to impose control on the item, it is necessary to specify a freedom of speech continuum that is independent of any particular group and that reflects the sort of value conflict typically observed in actual free-speech disputes.

As simple as the proscription "Congress shall make no law... abridging the freedom of speech..." appears at first glance, as constitutional scholars know, the controversies generated by the exercise of free speech in a pluralistic society are many and complex. If support for freedom of speech is defined as the willingness to extend protection to various types of speech that evoke conflicts in values, a continuum based on *types of speech* can be constructed instead of one that seeks to measure support for free speech by focusing on the group seeking to speak. Although there may be some overlap between the type of speaker and the speech, under the assumption that it makes little difference which group is calling for the violent overthrow of the government, this strategy results in a measure with little contamination from group affect. The measure in not "group controlled" but, in a sense, the group stimulus is neutralized and can be assumed to contribute little to the observed variance in the responses. Further, the items are phrased specifically in terms of state constitutional policy on the various types of speech, not the respondent's own personal preference. Using actual controversies as a guide to calibrating the scale, we asked the subjects whether or not several types of speech should be constitutionally protected. The results are shown in Table 5.1.

TABLE 5.1. Support for Freedom of Speech[a]

Type of speech	Should this type of speech be protected by the First Amendment?				
	Definitely	*Probably*	*Probably not*	*Definitely not*	*No opinion*
	%	%	%	%	%
Speech extremely critical of the American system of government					
ACLU members	84.3	12.0	1.8	1.5	0.4
ACLU leaders	95.5	4.2	0.2	0	0.2
Common Cause & ACLU members	75.7	15.6	3.2	5.6	0.0
Common Cause only members	60.8	24.9	7.8	5.8	0.6
Speech extremely critical of the First Amendment to the U.S. Constitution					
ACLU members	77.4	16.0	3.0	2.6	1.1
ACLU leaders	92.8	6.5	0.3	0.2	0.2
Common Cause & ACLU members	72.6	16.0	4.1	6.3	1.0
Common Cause only members	55.8	27.1	7.8	8.1	1.1
Symbolic speech, such as burning one's draft card in protest of the war in Vietnam					
ACLU members	71.3	17.2	6.2	3.5	1.7
ACLU leaders	87.3	9.1	2.8	0.1	0.8
Common Cause & ACLU members	65.1	21.5	6.3	5.8	1.2
Common Cause only members	47.7	25.4	12.3	11.7	2.8

TABLE 5.1. (continued)

Type of speech	Should this type of speech be protected by the First Amendment?				
	Definitely	Probably	Probably not	Definitely not	No opinion
Speech extremely critical of particular minority groups					
ACLU members	61.3	25.1	7.6	5.3	0.7
ACLU leaders	84.6	13.6	0.8	0.8	0.2
Common Cause & ACLU members	58.4	26.0	7.5	7.5	0.5
Common Cause only members	42.4	31.2	14.2	11.5	0.6
Speech supportive of an enemy of the U.S.					
ACLU members	52.0	31.6	8.4	5.3	2.7
ACLU leaders	79.0	17.2	2.1	0.7	1.0
Common Cause & ACLU members	45.9	32.3	12.4	7.9	1.5
Common Cause only members	27.8	33.8	18.0	12.8	2.6
Obscene or profane speech					
ACLU members	43.6	30.5	15.9	7.0	3.0
ACLU leaders	69.6	21.2	5.5	2.0	1.7
Common Cause & ACLU members	36.2	31.5	17.4	12.7	2.2
Common Cause only members	21.9	25.4	23.8	25.9	2.9

	Definitely protected	Probably protected	Probably not protected	Definitely not protected	No opinion
Speech advocating the overthrow of the U.S. government					
ACLU members	48.3	26.2	12.9	10.9	1.7
ACLU leaders	76.8	15.2	4.6	2.9	0.4
Common Cause & ACLU members	41.0	24.3	13.5	20.4	0.7
Common Cause only members	24.2	23.1	19.0	32.8	0.9
Speech that *might* incite an audience to violence					
ACLU members	27.1	34.0	26.6	10.0	2.3
ACLU leaders	50.2	31.3	13.3	4.0	1.3
Common Cause & ACLU members	18.4	27.1	32.4	18.4	2.7
Common Cause only members	10.3	25.2	37.4	24.9	2.3
Speech *designed* to incite an audience to violence					
ACLU members	9.8	10.4	29.8	48.1	1.9
ACLU leaders	21.5	16.5	27.6	31.9	2.6
Common Cause & ACLU members	7.7	8.2	22.3	60.0	1.7
Common Cause only members	7.5	6.1	18.6	67.1	0.7

[a]The question read: "Different people have different ideas about what kinds of speech should be protected under the First Amendment to the U.S. Constitution. We are interested in getting your opinion about whether particular types of speech should be protected under the First Amendment. For each of the following types of speech, please indicate whether you believe it should definitely be protected, probably be protected, probably not be protected, or definitely not be protected by the First Amendment. That is, please mark the blank which comes closest to your opinion for each of the following types of speech."

Source: James L. Gibson and Richard D. Bingham, "On the Conceptualization and Measurement of Political Tolerance," *American Political Science Review* Vol. 76, No. 3, September 1982, p. 608.

Table 5.1 shows that the level of tolerance for different types of speech varies dramatically depending upon the content of the speech. Very few would prohibit speech "extremely critical of the American system of government," but not many would allow speech "designed to incite an audience to violence." Support for freedom of speech declines substantially as the speech becomes more threatening to the existing political system, and as the implications for action increase, although it is speech, not action itself, to which the items refer. A large majority of respondents would not protect speech designed to incite an audience to violence, although the intent of the speaker does have considerable impact on the willingness of the subjects to protect the speech. Generally, there is nearly always a democratic consensus among ACLU leaders; there is usually a democratic consensus among ACLU members; and only occasionally is there a consensus among Common Cause members. Overall, however, there are very few types of speech that are universally supported by members of ACLU and Common Cause.

These items were subjected to Guttman Scaling in order to determine if a single underlying dimension could account for the responses. Guttman Scaling was used on these free speech items because cumulativeness, rather than covariance, is the sort of constraint reflected in the relationships of the stimuli. That is, it is expected that the subjects will allow speeches only up to a certain degree of threat; any speech more threatening will not be allowed. The scaling analysis of the nine items in Table 5.1 suggests, however, only marginal scalability, owing largely to two items that are only weakly related to the primary construct. Responses on symbolic speech and obscene speech account for a major portion of the errors in the scale. Many subjects seem to feel that obscene speech should be evaluated differently from other, more politically-relevant types of speech. The item soliciting opinion on symbolic speech may actually be too concrete to serve as a reliable measure; that is, the draft card example (from *United States v. O'Brien*), a fairly extreme instance of symbolic speech, may have unduly influenced the responses. Moreover, symbolic speech has been problematic for the Supreme Court and constitutional scholars, so it would not be surprising that these subjects might have some difficulty as well. Thus, the variance in the responses to these two items is contaminated by additional dimensions, resulting in the poor scalability coefficients. When these two items are removed, the results are much improved. The coefficient of scalability for the seven-item scale for ACLU members is .61; for ACLU leaders, it is .81; and for Common Cause members it is .68. The nine-item coefficients are .45, .64 and .51, for the three groups, respectively. Further, factor analysis of the nine questions produced markedly lower communalities for these two items, despite the fact that they are not located at either extreme of the scale. Therefore, symbolic and obscene speech items have been excluded from further analysis. Scale scores were assigned to the respondents by assigning the rank of the most difficult approved item, plus .5 if a "definitely should be protected" response was given to the item.

It is obvious that support for freedom of speech varies considerably depending upon the type of speech, causing curiosity concerning the causes of reactions to the more typical item about "communists making a speech." Is there an anticipation that the communists would "incite an audience to violence," or that they might advocate "the overthrow of the U.S. government"? The responses of ACLU and Common Cause members suggest that great differences in the frequencies would be observed depending upon which of these two types of speech is anticipated. (Note also that over 90 percent of these subjects respond tolerantly to the Stouffer free-speech items for communists.) We cannot, of course, know the specific type of speech imagined by the respondent, but it seems likely that variability in responses to these items is a function of a concrete scenario manufactured by the subjects immediately prior to their responses. This does not mean that the responses are abstract; rather, they are too variable in specific content to be useful. This new scale controls the content much more effectively and rigorously.

Support for Freedom of Assembly

Conflict over freedom of speech typically involves freedom of assembly issues. Few would probably object if Stouffer's communists were to make a private speech. Difficulties arise when unpopular minority political groups seek access to streets and other public property in order to express their views. It is therefore essential that support for free assembly attitudes be considered as an explicit and separate subdimension of political tolerance.

Beyond the problem of the "regulation" of assemblies, two rationales are sometimes advanced to justify prohibition of public demonstrations. The first is the proposition that a substantial threat of an assembly becoming violent justifies its prohibition. (Most would agree that demonstrators seeking access to public property for the purpose of violent activity can be legitimately denied such access.) Public safety and order should not be threatened by demonstrations, it might be argued; the First Amendment guarantees only "the right of the people *peaceably* to assemble."

Yet even the question of violence is not as simple as it may seem. Most public demonstrations present some possibility of violence. And what of violence *perpetrated against*, not by, the demonstrators? Fear of violence from a hostile crowd—if allowed to serve as a justification for prohibiting assemblies—could effectively eliminate many public demonstrations. Thus, the problem of the heckler's veto is an extremely important component of support for freedom of assembly.

A second important element of free assembly concerns the location of the demonstration. Most would agree that the state can regulate demonstrations, but can communities prohibit demonstrations by groups solely because the majority considers the views of the group to be abhorrent? Is there a community right to privacy that supersedes the right to assembly? Must the nonviolent harm done to a community by a demonstration be subordinated to the right to assemble? These questions are of obvious importance, given the publicity gains that flow from marching through "enemy" territory. Failure to support assemblies because of tension between community and group ideology is a very substantial limitation on the rights of minority political groups.

We have measured attitudes on these two dimensions of freedom of assembly. Table 5.2 reports the item measuring support for the heckler's veto. The phrasing of the question deliberately attributes the threat of violence to the crowd, not to the demonstrators, following closely the factual circumstances attending many demonstrations (see, for example, *Edwards v. South Carolina*, 372 U.S. 229, and Walker, 1978). Nevertheless, substantial portions of ACLU and Common Cause members are willing to stop the demonstration at the first sign of actual violence (a rock is thrown), whereas nearly one-half of the Common Cause members would stop the assembly before any violence occurred. The leaders of ACLU are unwilling to allow the demonstration to be terminated short of a riot, believing, no doubt, that is is the obligation of the police to maintain an orderly audience for the demonstration. Thus, although there may be substantial support for freedom of assembly in the abstract, the freedom is for many subordinate to the value of public order.

So as to measure support for the local community's right to prohibit access to its streets to those expressing abhorrent views, the subjects were asked to evaluate four scenarios involving demonstrator-community conflict (see Table 5.3). The most acceptable of the situations involves the request of a black civil-rights group to march in a white southern community. Large majorities of all three of the groups would support the issuance of a permit to demonstrate. Somewhat less support exists for permits for members of the Palestine Liberation Organization to demonstrate in a Jewish community and for Nazis to demonstrate in a white Protestant community. The most difficult scenario is that of Ku Klux Klansmen marching in a black community. As we have consistently observed, the ACLU leadership is consensual in supporting the assembly rights of these unpopular groups. A large majority of the ACLU membership, but only a slight majority of the Common Cause membership, hold similar libertarian attitudes. Generally, though, the context of the demonstration has some impact upon support for freedom of assembly.

An index has been created that measures the intensity as well as the substance of beliefs on these four items. The index was computed by counting the number of instances in which the subject would allow a demonstration, multiplying that score by 2, adding .5 to the score for each "strong" support for the demonstrators, and subtracting .5 for each "strong" opposition. Thus, the index varies from –2.0 (four responses of "strongly oppose") to 10.0 (four responses of "strongly support"). It might also be noted that these four items scale in the Guttman sense.

Political Association and Government Oppression

A slightly different component of tolerance is one that emphasizes the freedom to engage in political activity without the interference of the government. Members of the Socialist Worker's Party may be allowed to hold public demonstrations, but if their offices are regularly burglarized by the government, as they have been in the United States, then their oppositionist rights are "chilled," to say the least. Citizens may be willing to support certain freedoms for groups while simultaneously supporting government action against the group and its members.

In order to measure support for government suppression of unpopular political minorities, we asked the subjects to express support or opposition to six types of government action against Communists, Nazis, and the members of the Ku Klux Klan. Responses to the items are shown in Table 5.4.

TABLE 5.2. Support for Freedom of Assembly: Heckler's Veto[a]

	ACLU Members %	ACLU Leaders %	Common Cause & ACLU Members %	Common Cause Only Members %
The police should be allowed to stop the demonstration when				
a crowd begins to form.	0.5	0	1.7	1.4
members of the crowd begin to taunt the group.	1.9	0.7	3.7	6.9
the crowd appears to be on the verge of a violent reaction.	22.6	6.8	28.6	40.2
a member of the crowd picks up a rock.	3.9	2.8	5.1	4.0
a rock is thrown in the direction of the demonstrators.	11.1	8.3	9.3	10.8
the demonstrators begin to fight with the crowd.	36.8	36.5	32.0	25.1
The police should not be allowed to stop the demonstration.	21.2	47.0	17.8	9.7
No opinion.	2.0	1.1	1.7	1.7

[a]The question read: "Many public demonstrations pose a threat of violent reactions from crowds. Consider a demonstration that is itself peaceful, but which attracts a hostile crowd. Should the police be allowed to stop the demonstration in order to avoid violent crowd reactions? If so, at what point should the demonstration be stopped?"

Source: James L. Gibson and Richard D. Bingham, "On the Conceptualization and Measurement of Political Tolerance," *American Political Science Review* Vol. 76, No. 3, September 1982, p. 610.

TABLE 5.3. Support for Freedom of Assembly: Majority Abhorrence

	Strongly support %	Support %	Oppose %	Strongly oppose %	No opinion %
What if a black civil-rights group asked to be allowed to hold a march in a white southern community—would you oppose or support granting a permit?					
ACLU members	58.0	36.6	3.4	0.9	1.1
ACLU leaders	82.9	15.2	1.0	0.6	0.4
Common Cause & ACLU members	51.2	43.8	3.4	0.5	1.2
Common Cause only members	33.7	49.4	10.7	3.0	3.3
Suppose the Palestine Liberation Organization (PLO) sought to march in a Jewish community. Should a permit be granted?					
ACLU members	39.6	42.5	10.1	5.6	2.1
ACLU leaders	70.0	25.0	2.2	1.8	0.9
Common Cause & ACLU members	33.0	45.2	12.9	6.5	2.4
Common Cause only members	16.3	40.4	25.7	13.5	4.0
Should the Ku Klux Klan be granted a permit to march in a black community?					
ACLU members	36.2	40.2	13.3	8.7	1.5
ACLU leaders	67.8	26.6	3.1	2.1	0.4
Common Cause & ACLU members	30.1	41.1	16.0	9.8	3.1
Common Cause only members	14.1	36.7	28.4	18.3	2.6

TABLE 5.3. (continued)

	Strongly support	Support	Oppose	Strongly oppose	No opinion
What if the Nazis asked to be allowed to hold a march in a white Protestant Community? Would you support or oppose granting a permit in such a circumstance?					
ACLU members	38.0	45.3	9.1	4.9	2.6
ACLU leaders	69.8	26.7	1.7	1.3	0.6
Common Cause & ACLU members	31.2	46.3	11.5	7.2	3.8
Common Cause only members	15.3	45.4	22.1	12.9	4.3

Source: James L. Gibson and Richard D. Bingham, "On the Conceptualization and Measurement of Political Tolerance," *American Political Science Review* Vol. 76, No. 3, September 1982, p. 610.

Something approaching unanimity on each of the items is observed among members of the ACLU. Very little support exists for suppression of the groups, although one-fourth of the ACLU members support some form of government action against some groups. The greatest amount of support is for banning the public display of the symbols of the Nazis (swastika) and of the Klan (burning cross), and for registration and covert surveillance (e.g., wiretapping) of these two groups. While the latter may be presumed to be justified by the subjects because of the occasionally violent nature of these two groups, it is more difficult to understand the rationale for accepting a ban on symbols.

Members of Common Cause are not nearly so united, however. Substantial minorities support registration, covert surveillance, and a ban on swastikas. Common Cause members are also more likely to support the repression of Communists than are members of the ACLU. Although support for any particular repressive governmental policy falls far short of a majority, one-half of the Common Cause membership would support some sort of repression against one of these political minorities. Of the three groups considered, only ACLU leaders consensually reject political repression of Communists, Nazis, and Klansmen.

These items tap a somewhat different dimension of political tolerance in that they refer to support for a more activist posture against political minorities on the part of the government. Rather than simply rejecting efforts at exercising political rights by minorities (e.g., speaking), these items go more directly to willingness to challenge the very existence of opposition groups. This is obviously a more menacing form of intolerance than is reflected in the measures of intolerance of assemblies and speeches.

Scale scores were assigned to each subject by means of factor analysis. In order to reduce the number of items subjected to the factor analysis, nine small indices were first created for each of the six actions by summing across the three groups. This results, for example, in an index of support for banning unpopular political groups, an index varying from 0 to 3. Similarly, three group-based measures were created by summing for each group across the six actions. The advantage of such a method is that relatively idiosyncratic opinions on a particular item are reduced in importance and the scaling results are consequently cleaner. The factor analyses were conducted on the complete pool of subjects (i.e., not differentiated by group), although the results differ little from those observed when the factor analysis was conducted on each group separately.

TABLE 5.4. Support for Government Repression

	Percentage Supporting Restriction[a] on		
	Communists	Nazis	Klansmen
Outlaw organized party			
ACLU members	1.7	6.0	7.0
ACLU leaders	0.4	1.3	2.0
Common Cause & ACLU members	3.8	12.1	10.5
Common Cause only members	7.8	17.3	16.6
Prohibit members from running for office			
ACLU members	2.2	6.4	6.2
ACLU leaders	0.5	1.3	1.0
Common Cause & ACLU members	5.7	10.2	9.5
Common Cause only members	10.8	19.8	16.2
Covert surveillance			
ACLU members	6.9	9.1	9.4
ACLU leaders	2.0	2.6	3.0
Common Cause & ACLU members	10.5	12.4	12.1
Common Cause only members	26.7	29.1	26.3
Governmental registration			
ACLU members	7.4	9.4	8.8
ACLU leaders	2.1	2.6	2.5
Common Cause & ACLU members	19.8	22.6	21.2
Common Cause only members	34.1	35.6	30.3
Ban public activities			
ACLU members	1.5	6.9	8.3
ACLU leaders	0.1	1.6	1.6
Common Cause & ACLU members	3.4[b]	10.5	12.6
Common Cause only members	7.5[b]	18.4	18.8
Ban display of symbols			
ACLU members	3.1	9.4	12.0
ACLU leaders	0.5	1.5	2.7
Common Cause & ACLU members	3.7[b]	16.0	19.3
Common Cause only members	10.5[b]	24.9	27.1
Favor no repressive acts			
ACLU members	84.7	75.9	74.5
ACLU leaders	95.6	93.8	92.9
Common Cause & ACLU members	71.8	61.7	60.7
Common Cause only members	49.1	40.7	42.1

[a]Respondents were asked to indicate all of the actions they would favor the government taking against these groups (e.g., favor outlawing any organized communist party).

[b]Because of a printer's error, a significant number (approximately 75 percent) of the questionnaires sent to members of Common Cause omitted these two items. The reported percentages are based only on those given an opportunity to respond to the question, a significant minority of the membership.

Source: James L. Gibson and Richard D. Bingham, "On the Conceptualization and Measurement of Political Tolerance," *American Political Science Review* Vol. 76, No. 3, September 1982, p. 611.

Miscellaneous Civil Liberties

The discussion to this point has focused on support for oppositionist rights (speech, assembly, and association) as indicators of political tolerance. Although these rights are essential to political communication and opposition, political tolerance is frequently considered to be broader in scope. Stouffer, for instance, posed questions of support for eclectic public library collections, and others—notably McClosky—have not confined their measures of tolerance to attitudes toward assembly, speech, and association. In order to consider the relationship of tolerance, as defined by these crucial oppositionist rights, to the more diffuse approach to tolerance, the subjects were asked to express agreement or disagreement with fourteen items representing a variety of civil-liberties conflicts. All of the items, except the one on the elimination of the tax-exemption status for churches, are drawn from the ACLU pamphlet "Where Do You Stand on Civil Liberties?," and most have to do with freedoms guaranteed in the Bill of Rights. The pamphlet represents a test that the ACLU encourages prospective members to take. It is asserted that those scoring 75 percent or more are likely to be satisfied members of the organization. The responses are shown in Table 5.5.

Several aspects of these data are noteworthy. First, only the ACLU leaders approach consensus in their responses. A number of issues generate a non-negligible intolerant minority within the ACLU membership, however. Common Cause members are even more split by these issues. Although these subjects are no doubt more supportive of civil liberties than the general public, a lack of consensus still exists.

The data also suggest the types of issues likely to generate conflict over civil liberties. The problem of the Eighth Amemdment and the death penalty; the definition of separateness in church–state relations; and the question of the rights of conservatives and racists are all issues that fail to evoke overwhelming libertarian majorities.

There are also some interesting instances of consensus among the subjects. The right of students to overt political expressions—recognized by the U.S. Supreme Court in *Tinker v. Des Moines*— is nearly unanimously supported. Abortion is not nearly as controversial among members of these groups as it is among the mass public in general. There is only a single item on which Common Cause members are more tolerant than ACLU members and leaders—the issue of students who heckle public speakers into silence. Presumably this follows from the greater ideological intensity of a segment of the ACLU membership and

TABLE 5.5. Miscellaneous Civil Liberties

	ACLU Position	Percent "Libertarian"			
	Agree/ Disagree	ACLU Members	ACLU Leaders	Common Cause & ACLU Members	Common Cause Only Members
		%	%	%	%
High school students are within their rights when they express political opinions, circulate petitions and handbills, or wear political insignia in school.	A	94.5	97.6	92.2	86.0
A woman has a private right to decide whether to have a child or undergo an abortion.	A	93.8	94.6	94.5	87.1
Police should be allowed to conduct a full search of any motorist arrested for an offense such as speeding.	D	92.6	97.1	85.3	75.7
A man should be denied unemployment compensation if fired from his job for growing a beard.	D	91.6	95.4	91.7	84.9
Court calendars are so crowded that the right to trial by jury should be restricted to persons accused of major crimes only.	D	87.0	94.5	77.8	73.1
Students who shout down speakers to achieve their aims subvert the principles of academic freedom.	D	86.2	87.4	89.3	90.4
The C.I.A. should be able to prevent any former employees from writing about the agency without the C.I.A.'s prior approval.	D	82.4	92.8	80.4	61.5

124

Statement					
Government consolidation of dossiers on individual citizens violates the right to privacy.	A	81.5	86.7	82.0	69.9
A radio station that permits the reading of an anti-Semitic poem over the air should have its F.C.C. license revoked.	D	80.1	88.2	74.6	67.3
In their fight against crime the police should be entitled to use wiretaps and other devices for listening in on private conversations.	D	78.9	89.1	78.3	57.7
Membership in the John Birch Society by itself is enough to bar an applicant from appointment to the police force.	D	78.5	90.0	69.5	66.2
The use of tax funds to support parochial schools involves compulsory taxation for religious purposes and thus violates the First Amendment.	A	77.2	87.9	81.5	71.0
In light of present standards of justice and humanity, the death penalty has become "cruel and unusual punishment" in violation of the Eighth Amendment.	A	69.8	88.2	70.4	44.9
The "separation of church and state" clause of the First Amendment should be used to eliminate the tax-exempt status of religious institutions.	*	54.0	59.6	55.2	46.5

Source: James L. Gibson and Richard D. Bingham, "On the Conceptualization and Measurement of Political Tolerance," *American Political Science Review* Vol. 76, No. 3, September 1982, p. 613.

*ACLU has taken no position on this issue.

leadership. On every other item the rank order is the same: ACLU leaders are most tolerant, followed by ACLU members and then by Common Cause members. For the 13 ACLU test items, nearly all of the leaders, over 85 percent of the ACLU members, but only two-thirds of the Common Cause members, agree with the ACLU position on 75 percent or more of the items.

The 14 items in Table 5.5 were subjected to a factor analysis in order to assess their dimensionality. The solution from common factor analysis with oblique biquartimin rotation is shown in Table 5.6. Orthogonal rotation was inappropriate, inasmuch as no *a priori* assumption about the independence of possible subdimensions was warranted. Three relatively distinct factors emerged from the analysis. The first rotated factor is strongly dominated by items relating to police and the order and security of society. Most of the items specifically concern the tension between order and liberty, a tension focused on the degree of legitimate intrusiveness of order-maintenance forces. The two items with relatively small coefficients—concerning high school students and unemployment compensation—probably are related to social order through their implication of nonconformity and defiance of legitimate authority. In general, the first factor seems to measure the degree of support for constraints on liberty for the purpose of maintaining order.

The second factor is also easily interpreted. The two strongly related items refer to liberties of the political right. The final factor is primarily related to religious freedom and separation of church and state. Abortion may be associated with this factor because it is seen as an issue with connotations of religious freedom.

Scores on the three factors are fairly strongly interrelated, suggesting that the responses to the items stem from a common attitude or belief. Rather than performing a higher order factor analysis on the three factor scores, however, the interrelatedness of the various tolerance beliefs will be considered below.

Tolerance à la Stouffer

In order to explore the relationship of these measures to the typical Stouffer items, questions measuring tolerance for four types of activity by five unpopular minority political groups were included in the questionnaire. Instead of the two-stage Guttman Scaling process used by Stouffer and others (see Nunn, Crockett, and Williams, 1978, pp.

TABLE 5.6. Common Factor Analysis of Miscellaneous Civil Liberties Items

Item	Pattern Factor Loading (Oblique Rotation)[a]		
	Factor 1	Factor 2	Factor 3
In their fight against crime the police should be entitled to use wiretaps and other devices for listening in on private conversations.	.80[b]		
The C.I.A. should be able to prevent any former employees from writing about the agency without the C.I.A.'s prior approval.	.70		
Government consolidation of dossiers on individual citizens violates the right to privacy.	.64		
In light of present standards of justice and humanity, the death penalty has become "cruel and unusual punishment" in violation of the Eighth Amendment.	.62		
Police should be allowed to conduct a full search of any motorist arrested for an offense such as speeding.	.62		
A man should be denied unemployment compensation if fired from his job for growing a beard.	(.37)		
High school students are within their rights when they express political opinions, circulate petitions and handbills, or wear political insignia in school.	(.37)		
Membership in the John Birch Society by itself is enough to bar an applicant from appointment to the police force.		-.76	
A radio station that permits the reading of an anti-Semitic poem over the air should have its F.C.C. license revoked.		-.63	

127

TABLE 5.6. (continued)

Item	Pattern Factor Loading (Oblique Rotation[a])		
	Factor 1	Factor 2	Factor 3
Court calendars are so crowded that the right to trial by jury should be restricted to persons accused of major crimes only.		(-.36)	
The use of tax funds to support parochial schools involves compulsory taxation for religious purposes and thus violates the First Amendment.			.72
The "separation of church and state" clause of the First Amendment should be used to eliminate the tax-exempt status of religious institutions.			.53
A woman has a private right to decide whether to have a child or undergo an abortion.			.46
Students who shout down speakers to achieve their aims subvert the principles of academic freedom			(.26)
Eigenvalue (unrotated solution)[c]	3.36	1.54	1.31
Percentage of variance explained	24.0	11.0	9.4

[a]Oblique, biquartimin rotation. The correlations of the factors are: $r_{12} = -.56$; $r_{13} = .53$; $r_{23} = -.53$.

[b]Loadings are pattern loadings. Only loadings greater than or equal to .4 are shown (except when the maximum coefficient for an item is less than .4). Items have been reflected where necessary so that low scores always indicate support for the liberty.

[c]The eigenvalue of the fourth factor is .98.

Source: James L. Gibson and Richard D. Bingham, "On the Conceptualization and Measurement of Political Tolerance," *American Political Science Review* Vol. 76, No. 3, September 1982, p. 614.

180–85), we have developed a somewhat more sophisticated method for creating an index. First, a generalized group-based measure of tolerance was created by summing the tolerant responses for each of the five groups across the four different activities. This resulted in the creation of five group-specific indices. Second, an activity-based measure of tolerance was created by summing the tolerant responses for activities across groups. Thus, the original pool of 20 items was reduced to 9 indices measuring support for the civil liberties of unpopular political groups and activities. Descriptive data are shown in Table 5.7. (Substantive discussion of these results can be found in Chapter 3.)

These indices were also subjected to factor analysis. The analysis clearly indicated a unidimensional structure (and as such, no rotation was performed), with a single, strongly dominant factor. The items contribute approximately equally to the factor, with a slightly smaller contribution from the index of opposition to censorship of library books. Generally, the responses to the items appear to be dominated by a single attitude.

CONSTRAINT IN TOLERANCE BELIEF SYSTEMS

Those who study public opinion must constantly be sensitive to the possibility that the object of inquiry may have no palpable existence—meaningful opinions on salient political issues frequently do not exist in members of the mass public. At least since Converse's seminal article in 1964, it has been clear that many of the great issues that stir scholars to research cause barely a ripple within the mass public. Public opinion is sometimes fickle, but it is also frequently unconstrained, unstable over time, and heavily influenced by extraneous stimuli. Moreover, even when opinions do exist, they are usually connected in ways unfamiliar to logicians and social scientists. The problem of "non-attitudes" and belief system constraint are central to much contemporary inquiry into public opinion.

It is surprising that research on political tolerance has so rarely concerned itself with such problems as belief system constraint and the temporal stability of attitudes—especially given the relevance of these areas of inquiry to the "abstract-concrete" problem in tolerance research (Prothro and Grigg, 1960; Jackman, 1978; Margolis and Haque, 1981; Jackman, 1981)—while research on public opinion has rarely referred to tolerance beliefs (but see Nie and Rabjohn, 1979, and the attending critique of Sullivan et al., 1979), and more rarely still has focused upon

TABLE 5.7. Tolerance as Measured by Stouffer Items

			Percentage "Perfectly" Tolerant	
	ACLU Members	ACLU Leaders	Common Cause & ACLU Members	Common Cause Only Members
Group-based tolerance				
Atheists	85.3	95.4	79.1	60.6
Communists	79.6	72.4	65.1	46.4
Militarists	71.6	87.1	61.2	44.0
Nazis	68.2	87.5	58.2	41.1
Klansmen	63.5	83.3	55.8	37.9
Activity-based tolerance[a]				
Speaking	88.6	97.8	84.8	72.8
Publishing	88.4	92.9	85.3	77.6
Demonstrating	70.1	91.2	64.6	45.8
Teaching	65.1	65.4	49.9	36.9

[a]For each group, four activities were considered:

"If such a person wanted to make a speech in your community against/in favor of _____, should he/she be allowed to speak?"

"Should such a person be allowed to organize a march against/in favor of _____ in your community?"

"Should such a person be allowed to teach in a college or university?"

"If some people in your community suggested that a book he/she wrote against/in favor of _____ should be taken out of your public library, would you favor removing the book?"

Source: James L. Gibson and Richard D. Bingham, "On the Conceptualization and Measurement of Political Tolerance," American Political Science Review Vol. 76, No. 3, September 1982, p. 615.

elites. Two bodies of theory that have much to say to each other have been developed largely independently.

Constraint involves predictability. Beliefs within a common substantive domain are constrained if they are "inter-predictable." If they are organized in a logical, ideological, near-ideological, or even "group benefits" or "nature of the times" fashion (Campbell et al., 1960), beliefs on issue i should predict, at least to some degree, beliefs on issue j. Within the context of political tolerance, constraint implies that beliefs on one dimension of tolerance—for instance, free speech—are related to beliefs on other dimensions of tolerance—for example, free assembly. If assembly and speech beliefs are drawn from the same abstract commitment to tolerance, then they ought to be related empirically.

Much attention has been given to the level of constraint of the elements of liberal–conservative belief systems, and the initial unhappy findings of Converse and *The American Voter* have been hotly disputed. Arguments have recently been made that beliefs may be connected by relatively idiosyncratic constraining principles (e.g., Lane, 1962; Marcus, Tabb, and Sullivan, 1974); that constraint may vary greatly depending upon the degree of order in the external stimuli about which beliefs are directed, and consequently that it should not be expected to find ordered political beliefs connected to and shaped by disordered American political reality (e.g., Field and Anderson, 1969; Pierce, 1970; Bennett, 1973; and Nie with Andersen, 1974); that beliefs are quite sensitive to the specific indicators employed, making constraint difficult to judge and also rendering hazardous the comparison of items not worded extremely similarly (e.g., Sullivan, Piereson, and Marcus, 1978; Bishop, Tuchfarber, and Oldendick, 1978; Sullivan et al., 1979; Bishop et al., 1979); and that the dominant scaling techniques are insensitive to some forms of constraint, focusing almost exclusively on covariation, and ignoring, for instance, cumulativeness. However, a careful examination of the evidence of even the most optimistic of the participants in the debate reveals that: a) belief connectedness within members of the mass public is at best only adequate for the masses to perform limited democratic functions; b) in no sense can constraint be considered to be high or substantial; and c) the amount of constraint within members of the elite is surely higher than that of the mass public.

There is not much debate over the supposition that constraint is more evident within the belief systems of elites, largely because little inquiry has been conducted (thus making it difficult to observe anomalies and contradictions). The initial examination of elite belief systems was undertaken by Converse (1964), who concluded that greater constraint existed among elites (defined as congressional candidates). Some contrary evidence from other studies can be found (e.g., Luttbeg, 1968; Brown, 1970; and Herzon, 1980), and an attack has been launched on Converse's analysis (Pierce and Rose, 1974; Wray, 1979), but in fact very little evidence exists to support or refute Converse's argument. Is there variability in constraint across different elite groups and across varying issue domains? What is is about the elite experience that contributes to greater constraint? In operational terms, what does a highly constrained belief system look like? What are the empirical maxima of the inter-item correlations in a perfectly constrained system? These questions remain unanswered because of the paucity of data on elites.

One suspects that the willingness to assume that elite belief systems are more highly constrained than mass belief systems flows in part from other research on elites that depicts them as more sophisticated, knowledgeable, concerned, and as more democratic. But even though more research has been conducted on elite tolerance than on elite belief systems, the major elite studies can be easily listed:

1. Stouffer's (1955) analysis of local influentials (leaders of 14 organizations in towns with populations between 10,000 and 150,000);

2. the Nunn, Crockett, and Williams (1978) replication of Stouffer's survey;

3. McClosky's (1964) research on delegates to the 1956 Democratic and Republican national conventions;

4. McClosky and Brill's (1983) analysis of community leaders and activists, and organizational elites; and,

5. this analysis of leaders and members of the American Civil Liberties Union and members of Common Cause.

While the few data sources available are fairly consensual in their finding that elites are more committed to the "rules of the game," little of this research considers the manner in which tolerance beliefs are organized.

One reason why constraint has received so little attention in the tolerance literature is that tolerance is rarely conceptualized as a syndrome or system of beliefs. Investigation of constraint relies upon a multidimensional conceptualization of abstract beliefs. That is, like those who are willing to distinguish materialist and post-materialist components of liberalism (Inglehart, 1977), we are willing to admit the possibility that tolerance belief systems may be multidimensional *and constrained.* Especially as belief systems become sophisticated and complex—for instance, belief systems pertaining to the rights of political opposition in a heterogeneous, democratic society—there may emerge internal subdimensions that are themselves more strongly constrained internally (within–subdimensions) than externally (inter–subdimension). Even the "belief systems" of U.S. Supreme Court justices have been shown to be multidimensional (Schubert, 1974). However, the predominant conceptualization of tolerance forecloses much inquiry into constraint because tolerance is treated as a unidimensional attitude. While the attitude may be measured by multiple indicators (e.g., support for speeches by communists, atheists, and socialists), inter-item correlations are not indicators of constraint (and are rarely treated as such) but rather are indicators of reliability and scalability. Because of the poverty of the unidimensional conceptualization of political tolerance, constraint has rarely been considered (but see Nie and Rabjohn, 1979; Sullivan et al., 1979).

Multiple tolerance attitudes, each measured by multiple indicators, can be analyzed to determine the level of constraint. Table 5.8 reports the Pearson correlation coefficient matrix resulting from our eight tolerance scales (each of which employed multiple indicators).

There are several interesting aspects to these data. First, as revealed by separate factor analyses, the structure of beliefs is very similar for ACLU members, leaders, and Common Cause members. The correlation matrices for the ACLU leaders are very similar, although in general the restricted variation in their responses attenuates the coefficients slightly. The similarity between Common Cause and ACLU members in the way beliefs are interrelated is somewhat surprising, as it was expected that ACLU members would exhibit more evidence of ideological order-ing of beliefs than the members of Common Cause. Generally, though, the three groups can be collapsed in the analysis of constraint.

Second, attitudes toward speech, assembly, and political association are moderately interrelated. Those favoring the protection of many types of speech tend to be willing to support demonstrations despite community opposition ($r = .45$), or the threat of violence ($r = .42$). However, the largest observed correlation among these four measures is only –.56 (abhorrent demonstrations—government oppression), sug-

TABLE 5.8. Correlations among Multiple Indicators of Tolerance[a]

	1	2	3	4	5	6	7	8
1. General tolerance (Stouffer)	1.00							
2. Rights of the right	.48	1.00						
3. Abhorrent demonstrations	.66	.46	1.00					
4. Liberty v. order	-.37	-.66	-.37	1.00				
5. Government oppression	-.67	-.43	-.56	.36	1.00			
6. Free speech	.48	.39	.45	-.35	-.42	1.00		
7. Church and state	-.28	-.57	-.29	.63	.22	-.26	1.00	
8. Heckler's veto	.37	.34	.40	-.34	-.34	.38	-.25	1.00

[a]Combined ACLU and Common Cause samples.

Source: James L. Gibson and Richard D. Bingham, "On the Conceptualization and Measurement of Political Tolerance," American Political Science Review Vol. 76, No. 3, September 1982, p. 616.

gesting that although these attitudes may belong to a common belief system, they are empirically distinct. Even the two measures of assembly attitudes are not strongly correlated ($r = .40$). The absence of stronger correlations suggests that conflict may be seen among the various rights of political opposition; some of those strongly supporting freedom of speech would limit access to a public forum in order to make that speech (a position reminiscent of the judicial philosophy of Justice Hugo Black). At the very least, these items do not tap identical attitudes. Political tolerance is a syndrome of attitudes; beliefs on various dimensions of the concept are distinguishable, even among elites.

In comparison to Converse's congressional candidates, the tolerance beliefs of ACLU and Common Cause members are somewhat more constrained than the candidates' foreign policy beliefs, and somewhat less constrained than their domestic policy beliefs (although Converse used gammas to represent correlations among his categorical items so the strict comparability of coefficients is omitted). Generally, though, these findings are consistent with our treatment of political tolerance as a *syndrome* of connected beliefs. And these correlations most likely represent very nearly the maximum correlation that can be expected to be observed when the analysis is conducted on multiple beliefs rather than multiple indicators of a single belief.

It should also be noted that the scale based on the Stouffer items (general tolerance) performs surprisingly well. It is at least moderately related to all of the other measures except church and state attitudes. However, the correlation between the Stouffer items scale and support for freedom of speech is only .48, although the Stouffer items are more strongly related to community privacy attitudes ($r = .66$) and opposition to political oppression ($r = .67$). (It must be remembered that the Stouffer set of activities was supplemented with an item on demonstration—see Table 5.7.) Regressing the Stouffer scale on the other seven tolerance measures results in an R^2 of .59, with the major independent contribution being made by attitudes toward government oppression and freedom of assembly. Thus, nearly one-half of the scale's variance cannot be accounted for by the other activity-based measures of tolerance.

The three factor scores from the miscellaneous civil-liberties items are themselves moderately interrelated, but they are not strongly related to the other measures. Attitudes toward church and state correlate very weakly with support of civil liberties, whereas the other two scales are weakly to moderately associated. Generally, these attitudes must be considered distinct components of tolerance.

When the eight variables are subjected to factor analysis (with biquartimin rotation), a two-dimensional structure emerges. However, the two dimensions are very strongly related ($r = .76$). The pattern coefficients reveal a second dimension that is composed almost exclusively of the three factors from the miscellaneous civil-liberties items. Although this may be at least partially a methodological artifact, support for rights of political opposition seems to hold a distinct position within civil-liberties belief systems. Since the first unrotated factor accounts for less than 50 percent of the variance among the items, it is reasonable to conclude that these beliefs are all part of a common system, but also that they are empirically distinct.

This analysis suggests that is may be useful to distinguish between two types of civil liberties: rights regarding political opposition and rights related to freedom from government intervention in certain aspects of the private lives of citizens. Opposition rights include rights to political speech, assembly, and association. These rights frequently conflict with the desire of individuals and communities to be insulated from political conflict and insult. Privacy rights have little to do with political opposition; rather, they represent more individualistic, human rights. Religious freedom, protection against the abuse of discretion by criminal justice authorities, and equal opportunity are examples of this rather broad category. Indeed, this distinction may even account for the peculiar performance of the obscenity item in the analysis of the free speech items above. Although attitudes toward the two categories of civil liberties are strongly related, they are analytically and empirically distinct.[1]

Summary

The measures presented here are context controlled. They focus upon specific activities, use multiple indicators, and present subjects with stimuli that are located on a dimension calibrated by actual civil-liberties disputes. Attitudes are thus measured by posing circumstances that increase the level of conflict among various values. When little or no conflict is present (e.g., the Stouffer items), the political tolerance of these subjects is relatively high. As the conflict heightens, tolerance declines predictably. The data presented strongly support the thesis that political tolerance is context sensitive and that context must therefore be controlled. Finally, attitudes toward the various subdimensions of political tolerance are interrelated, but not so strongly as to justify the conclusion that the attitudes are unidimensional. Instead, political tolerance represents a syndrome of beliefs, or a belief system.

DISCUSSION

Most actual conflicts over the civil liberties of minority political groups stimulate several beliefs and varying subdimensions of particular beliefs. When the multidimensionality of political tolerance is recognized, it becomes obvious that a particular dispute may stimulate more than a single civil-liberties attitude. These attitudes may conflict, even though in the abstract there is no logical inconsistency among them, and even though they may be derived from a common source (such as personality attributes). For instance, because support for civil liberties is never absolute, attitude scores for respondents indicate the breadth of types of speeches that would be granted legal protection and the breadth of types of assemblies that would be legally allowed. Beliefs on these two dimensions may conflict, and more importantly, the context of the dispute—perhaps the identity of the group involved, the content of the speech, the feelings of the local community toward the speakers—interacts with the beliefs, as shown in Figure 5.1. As with judges deciding cases, citizen reactions to civil-liberties conflicts represent the evaluation of the stimulus or controversy on the continua defining each of the subdimensions of the tolerance belief system, as well as on dimensions independent of tolerance (e.g., social order). If the decisions derived independently from each subdimension are not in conflict, then a position on the issue is easily reached. If conflict exists, then positions represent some process of reconciling the beliefs, either through the reclassification of the stimulus or the direct reconciliation of competing beliefs.

Further, statistical relationships between generalized political tolerance and specific opinions or actions are likely to be attenuated because of contextual factors. The context affects the translation of more general and abstract beliefs into more specific and concrete beliefs and actions. The observed correlation between generalized political tolerance and specific political action thus may not be great, when in fact the causal effect is substantial. We are unclear about precisely how this process works. However, predictions of behavior from a syndrome of attitudes measured by items incorporating context will be much more successful than predictions derived from unidimensional, context-insensitive items.

Substantively, the most surprising finding of this chapter is the breadth of items on which a not insignificant intolerant minority exists within these elite interest groups. ACLU leaders are consensual in their support of nearly all of the civil-liberties questions; the ACLU members frequently deviate from consensus; and Common Cause members only infrequently exhibit even a solid majority. Table 5.7 provides a clear illustration of this finding. It is obvious that members of ACLU are more willing than most to allow dissidents to engage in political activities—and thus they may legitimately be considered carriers of the creed—but there are also clear circumstances in which sizable intolerant minorities emerge. Fear that violence may result as a consequence of the exercise of civil liberties gives pause to some; others are wary of the extension of civil liberties to seriously antisystem groups. But the threat of violence, especially from "outside agitators" and other malcontents, is an intimate part of the struggle over civil liberties. If support for the rights of political opposition is limited to circumstances that minimize the likelihood that the activity will be effective, then political tolerance is suspect. If the maintenance and expansion of civil liberties are indeed contingent upon a strongly united libertarian elite, then these data give rise to concern.

Recent research on attitudes toward civil liberties makes clear the complexity of libertarian attitudes. This research adds an additional component to that complexity in demonstrating the dimensionality of political tolerance. It is of course not surprising that these beliefs are complex; rarely is social and political conflict over civil liberties simple, and beliefs bear at least some relationship to reality. As more sensitive

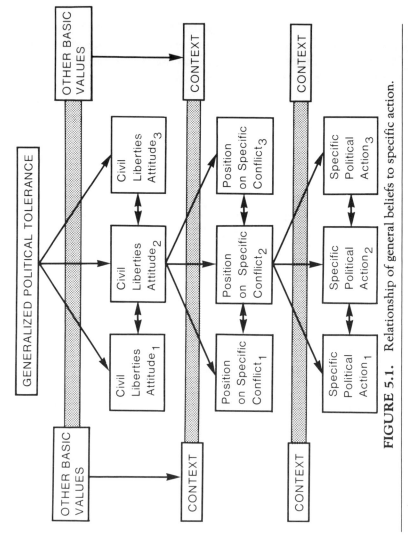

FIGURE 5.1. Relationship of general beliefs to specific action.

Source: James L. Gibson and Richard D. Bingham, "On the Conceptualization and Measurement of Political Tolerance," *American Political Science Review* Vol. 76, No. 3, September 1982, pp. 617.

measures are constructed, progress on more important research, such as explaining reactions within specific instances of civil liberties conflicts, can then be made. It is to the question of the relationship between these general attitudes and specific reactions to the Skokie controversy that we therefore turn next.

NOTE

1.   Much of the initial concern over the nature of belief systems focused upon the temporal stability of attitudes, as well as their cross-sectional interrelatedness (Converse, 1964, 1970). Nearly all of the research which followed was directed toward constraint alone, however, for obvious reasons of data availability. As the Survey Research Center panel data have become more heavily analyzed, the problem of temporal stability, at least among mass subjects, has received more attention (e.g., Converse and Marcus, 1979; Marcus, 1979). Investigations of the temporal stability of elite attitudes are exceedingly rare, however (Campbell et al., 1960, Converse, 1964, 1970, 1975; Brown, 1970, Madsen and Sheth, 1977).

Attitude stability is important for the same reasons as constraint. Responses stable over time are indicative of beliefs that are embedded in a matrix. Such beliefs are difficult to change because of the many adjustments necessary to restructure the entire belief system. At the least, great instability in responses suggests that the particular stimulus generating the response may actually have *created* the response (Converse, 1970). Investigations of attitude stability provide further evidence on the nature of belief systems.

As for beliefs about "fundamental" rules of the democratic game, it is unlikely that much change would occur over relatively short periods of time in political tolerance attitudes. Tolerance beliefs probably stem in significant degree from personality attributes (Sniderman, 1975; Sullivan et al., 1981) and early childhood socialization (Patterson, 1979), and therefore are resistant to the influence of short-term stimuli. Moreover, such beliefs *should not* be easily alterable if citizen support for democracy is to serve as a reservoir of support, to be drawn upon in times of political crisis. As in the case of diffuse support (Easton, 1965), the implications of political tolerance for regime maintenance are dependent upon attitudinal stability.

There is little empirical evidence to suggest that tolerance attitudes are stable. Certainly there has been change over the last few decades, particularly in attitudes toward repressing communists (Nunn, Crockett, and Williams, 1978; Davis, 1975; Cutler and Kaufman, 1979). But if tolerance attitudes are at all similar to other attitudes held by members of the mass public, there is little reason to expect stability. Indeed, as existing measures of political tolerance are so heavily influenced by group affect, which of course does not demonstrate great stability, observed tolerance may be quite unstable. On the other hand, if treated as attitudes about symbolic phenomena, it might be expected that tolerance would be more stable than concrete opinions (Bennett, 1977). No panel data on political tolerance exist, however, so the issue is subject only to speculation.

6 The Application of General Tolerance Attitudes: Reactions to the Skokie-Nazi Dispute

Despite the acknowledged importance of elite attitudes for the maintenance of democracy, minimal research has gone beyond the description of these beliefs to inquire into their political consequences. For instance, we know little of the behavioral implications of attitudinal support for the democratic rules of the game. How often do citizens—elite or mass—take action on the basis of their attitudes? Is abstract commitment to democratic rights of any use in predicting reactions—in either opinions or behavior—in concrete disputes? To what degree are responses to questionnaire items on the civil liberties of minority groups "non-attitudes," that is, beliefs that had no existence or meaning to the subjects before they were asked to respond to the survey questions? Moreover, the implicit linkage model of much of this research is so simplistic that its utility is questionable. Few would be willing to defend explicitly the model that:

attitudes$\rightarrow$ behaviors$\rightarrow$ public policy$\rightarrow$ ability of minorities to exercise rights,

but it nevertheless guides much of the current research effort in the field. Each of these linkages is so complex and so heavily qualified by conditional relationships that the "model" can hardly be said to provide a theoretical justification for the study of tolerance attitudes.

This linkage model is particularly suspect because of its failure to take into consideration the "slippage" that occurs in the translation of general attitudes into reactions to specific situations. Such slippage has been well documented in existing literature. For instance, Lawrence asked subjects to consider whether "people should be allowed to hold a peaceful demonstration to ask the government to act on some issue" and whether demonstrations in general should "always," "sometimes," or "never" be allowed (Lawrence, 1976, p. 92). Nearly one-fourth of those responding "always" to the general question would prohibit a demonstration in favor of open housing; over a third of those responding "never" would allow demonstrations against pollution! It is difficult to ascribe much importance to the responses given to survey items of this sort. Those wishing to draw conclusions about the *systemic* consequences of these tolerance beliefs are confronted with the great difficulty of judging which, if any, of the measures of tolerance—abstract or concrete—have behavioral implications. This has led some to the conclusion that mass opinion—as measured by social scientists—is nearly irrelevant to the maintenance of liberal democracy.

While this slippage between abstract and applied beliefs is characteristic of the mass public, elites or opinion leaders and political activists are typically thought to be more consistent in translating general attitudes in specific situations (and Lawrence did observe a relationship between education and consistency). This is fortunate for those who subscribe to the elitist theory of democracy because elites are generally more committed to democratic values. Thus, those with the strongest democratic attitudes are also those who are most capable of linking their specific opinions and behavior to their more abstract attitudes, presumably insuring democratic responses in actual civil liberties controversies, and, ultimately, democratic public policy.

Yet data and systematic tests of hypotheses relevant to the above propositions are rare. Few elite studies have been conducted, so much more is known of the structure of mass opinion than of elite opinion. Moreover, because none of the extant research focuses upon *actual* civil liberties disputes, relying instead on disputes contrived through questionnaire items, the processes of incorporating both abstract attitudes and contextual perceptions into specific opinions is little understood. Given the presumed importance of the processes for the maintenance of democracy, this is a research question of no minor consequence.

In this chapter we assess the extent and causes of inconsistency in the opinions and beliefs of elites, based on the Skokie-Nazi conflict. The degree of congruence between abstract civil liberties attitudes and specific opinions on the Skokie dispute is examined. We conclude that among the members of these elite groups, abstract commitments to democratic norms played a very significant role in structuring responses to the conflict. Thus, this analysis suggests that the attitudes of the democratic elite may be vitally important to the protection of the civil liberties of minority political groups. Before turning to this analysis, however, we must first consider existing approaches to the problem.

THE "IRRATIONALITY" OF APPLIED BELIEFS

Following Prothro and Grigg (1960), researchers have usually assumed that those who would deny civil liberties to a particular group or under a particular circumstance are irrational, logically inconsistent, or "unprincipled." For instance, a logical implication of the principle of minority rights is said to be the position allowing a communist to make speeches favoring communism. For Prothro and Grigg, "the logical connection of the specific proposition with the general proposition is virtually self evident" (Prothro and Grigg, 1960, p. 292).

But there are those to whom the logic is not quite so evident, and, indeed, a qualification to the major premise could well render the specific response perfectly logical (cf. Luttbeg, 1968). It is not particularly fruitful, however, to pursue the *logic* of beliefs; rather, the problem should be reconceptualized as one of the empirical interrelationships of the elements within the tolerance belief system.

The difficulty of "applying" abstract beliefs on freedom of speech illustrates this process well. At the outset, it is doubtful that anyone subscribes to all of the logical implications of this principle. Few, for instance, who support freedom of speech in the abstract would react "rationally" to the prospect of a false cry of "Fire!" in a crowded cinema, despite the fact that such a cry is clearly subsumed within most definitions of "speech." This specific application that flows from the more general principle would generate considerable evidence of slippage between abstract and applied beliefs. Therefore it is useful to consider support for freedom of speech from a more realistic perspective, and to treat the concept from the perspective of the types of actual conflict found in American politics over the meaning and implications of the general principle "Congress shall make no law abridging freedom of speech."

Nor is this an isolated and aberrant example of the difficulty of application (and deduction in general). As even a cursory overview of American political and constitutional history reveals, the application of general principles is replete with ambivalence and ambiguity. Would the social scientist hold the mass public to a standard of "rationality" far higher than that exhibited by members of the United States Supreme Court, in particular, and the United States political system in general? Certainly it must be admitted that the logic of application is somewhat less than compelling.

The difficulty of connecting abstract and applied beliefs stems from the fact that there is frequently competition and conflict among equally "fundamental" beliefs. Different rank orderings of principles, though strictly speaking unnecessary within a perfectly logical system, account for the apparent illogic of the masses. Let us consider the process in greater detail.

Three types of beliefs may be distinguished: fundamental beliefs, middle-range beliefs, and opinions. In a perfectly rational belief system, fundamental beliefs would not be logically inconsistent (but they would not necessarily be logically connected, just as premises are not necessarily logically connected), middle range beliefs would be deducible from fundamental beliefs (with no inconsistency among middle-range beliefs), and opinions would follow logically from the middle-range beliefs (again, without conflict).

Fundamental beliefs, representing abstract principles, are by their very nature highly generalized. As generalizations, they are insensitive to contextual factors and therefore are assumed to be relevant to *all* possible situations. A particular context—such as a communist speaking in the community—is typically assumed to stimulate only a single belief, and the belief is thought to be consistent with only one kind of substantive response to the situation. Less universal beliefs are also logically consistent with only a single more universal belief. If these assumptions are valid, it is not possible to reach an anti-democratic conclusion within a specific context from general democratic beliefs. Individuals doing so must be engaging in faulty reasoning. For instance, a position opposing the right of Ku Klux Klansmen to speak that is based on the justification that "The Ku Klux Klan is against certain races and religions and letting a member of this organization speak might lead to prejudice against these groups" (Sarat, 1975, Table 1, pp. 252–53) is assumed to be derivable from no abstract democratic beliefs. Thus, anti-democratic beliefs can be explained by asserting that people do not engage in "principled thinking" (Sarat, 1975).

Very few people, even including political philosophers, have such highly articulated belief systems, and it is the work of a lifetime even to attempt to impose such structure. Indeed, the highest form of development and sophistication that can be observed with any frequency is probably the attempt to reconcile subsets (most likely in pairs) of the middle-range beliefs. Attempts to reconcile opinions with middle-range beliefs are probably far more common that is usually thought. To limit the freedom of speech to those who would respect the freedom of speech of others, for instance through some commitment to reciprocity, might therefore be completely logical.

The problem for the analyst is that middle-range beliefs are frequently *rank ordered* rather than logically connected. Freedom of speech is supported; but so too is social order. Therefore, whether a speech that represents a threat to order is to be protected is a function of the relative weights of the two middle-range preferences.[1]

Individuals may hold conflicting beliefs, with conflict among beliefs resolved through prioritization or compartmentalization. The particular non-tolerance beliefs that are activated depend on the context. Inconsistency among beliefs and opinion and behavior can thus be hypothesized to be contingent upon the situational constraints associated with efforts to exercise rights within particular contexts. If a concrete civil liberties dispute elicits conflicting beliefs, an anti-democratic response can result from principled thinking.

Typically, we observe that people will allow some forms of speech, by some groups, under some conditions, but not other forms. Support for one form but opposition to another is sometimes considered "inconsistent." The first belief does not co-vary with the second (unless of course there is a negative relationship, a circumstance that must be interpreted as constraint). Nonetheless, the subject may be consistently (from the perspective of the cumulative scaling model) applying an abstract attitude, an ideal point, to a particular stimulus. Indeed, it is intuitively satisfying to posit a model in which opinions on specific issues are partially a function of the strength or difficulty of the stimulus. "Costless" expressions of ideas naturally are tolerated—everyone would grant communists the right to speak in private. As the cost of the speech increases, the potential for conflict with other principles also increases, until a threshold is reached at which the second principle dominates the generalized belief in freedom of speech. At that point, the speech becomes too difficult to support.[2]

Concrete disputes over civil liberties almost certainly elicit these additional abstract beliefs. The issue of a Ku Klux Klan speech probably evokes attitudes toward freedom of speech and assembly, attitudes toward social order (under the assumption that a potential for violence exists if the speech were allowed), and attitudes toward the rights of minority groups to be free from insults. An anti-Klan position may be logically derivable from abstract principles (other than those of freedom of speech and assembly) that are essential to the effective functioning of democracies. It cannot be assumed that the tenets of civil liberties are perfectly compatible with all principles that contribute to the effective functioning of democracies.

Thus, a contextual explanation of civil liberties attitudes is essential. Though the thought process generating opinions on specific civil liberties conflicts may not be, strictly speaking, deductive in nature, the important theoretical question is to understand how the contextual aspects of the specific issue impede the derivation of specific opinions from attitudes toward generalized democratic principles. Empirically, this means that the research question is not one of logical consistency but is instead one of the degree of relationship or correlation between various abstract positions and opinions on specific issues.[3] It is to this issue that we next turn.

APPLYING ABSTRACT BELIEFS TO THE SKOKIE CONFLICT

To some extent the Skokie dispute is surprising in that it seems to be an example of a breakdown of consistency between abstract and concrete civil liberties beliefs on the part of the educated middle class, precisely the group *least* expected (according to the elitist theory of democracy) to be willing to support the oppression of political minorities. One therefore wonders about the degree to which positions on the Skokie conflict reflect more general attitudes toward civil liberties and democratic norms. Consequently, we consider the degree to which the opinions of ACLU members and leaders and Common Cause members reflect more generalized attitudes toward the rights of political minorities.

The analysis will focus upon two dependent variables: whether the subject would permit the demonstration, and an index of support for the two provisions of the Skokie ordinances. At the center of the conflict over the right of the Nazis to hold public demonstrations are the Skokie ordinances. The ACLU and Common Cause members were questioned on their reactions to the insurance bond and "group libel" provisions of the Skokie ordinances, with the results shown in Table 6.1.[4] While it is inaccurate to characterize the opponents of the ACLU position on Skokie as representing a "massive" segment of the organization, they do comprise a substantial minority. Within the ACLU, 21 percent of the members and 5 percent of the leaders failed to oppose *both* ordinances; the percentage within Common Cause is much greater—46 percent. There is similar variation in the responses to whether a permit to demonstrate should be issued to the Nazis. One-fifth of the ACLU members would deny a permit, but the leaders are virtually unanimous in their view that the demonstration should be

TABLE 6.1. Attitudes toward Skokie Ordinances on Nazi
Demonstrations

	ACLU Members	ACLU Leaders	Common Cause Members
Ordinance to deny demonstration permits if "group libel" would occur			
Strongly favor	2.6	0.7	7.5
Favor	8.7	1.3	24.8
No opinion	2.7	0.7	4.9
Oppose	36.9	15.3	37.4
Strongly oppose	49.1	82.1	25.4
	100.0	100.0	100.0
	(129,258)	(1,272)	(192,500)
Ordinance requiring insurance bond			
Strongly favor	1.7	0.3	5.0
Favor	8.0	1.4	18.7
No opinion	5.8	1.7	9.2
Oppose	37.9	18.2	43.5
Strongly oppose	46.6	78.3	23.5
	100.0	100.0	100.0
	(129,292)	(1,270)	(195,020)
Should the permit be granted?			
Yes, grant	78.7	95.4	59.2
No opinion	2.8	0.9	4.8
No, deny	18.5	3.8	36.0
	100.0	100.0	100.0
	(129,129)	(1,275)	(194,600)

NOTE: Ns have been weighted to reflect probabilities of selection and response rates. Details on the weighting may be found in Chapter 3.

Source: James L. Gibson and Richard D. Bingham, "Elite Tolerance of Nazi Rights," *American Politics Quarterly* Vol. II, No. 4, October 1983, pp. 409–418. Copyright © 1983 by Sage Publications, Inc. Reprinted by permission of Sage Publications, Inc.

allowed. A slight majority of Common Cause members would allow the demonstration.

The index of support for these provisions of the Skokie ordinances takes into account the substance and intensity of opinion on the group libel and insurance bond ordinances. The minimum score is 1 (strong support for both ordinances); the maximum is 4 (strong opposition to both ordinances); and the midpoint is 2.5 (no opinion on both ordinances, or mixed, balanced opinions). The means (and standard deviations) for the ACLU members, leaders and Common Cause members, respectively, are: 3.3 (.67); 3.8 (.46); and 2.9 (.77).

In Chapter 5, we provided evidence that eight scales of political tolerance attitudes are particularly useful:

    1. willingness to extend constitutional protection to threatening speech;

    2. opposition to the "heckler's veto";

    3. willingness to allow demonstrations by groups abhorrent to the community;

    4. opposition to government oppression of political groups;

    5. support for liberty versus social order;

    6. support for the rights of the right wing;

    7. support for separation of church and state; and

    8. general political tolerance as measured by a variant of the traditional Stouffer items.

These scales measure tolerance not in the sense of "abstract" commitments, but rather in the sense of generalized attitudes.

The first issue to be considered is that of the relationship between the measure of ordinance opinion and opinion on whether the demonstration should be allowed to take place. The associations within the three groups are shown in Table 6.2. As expected, there is a moderate, but not overwhelming, relationship between the two variables. For instance, among members of the ACLU, 72 percent of those supporting the ordinances would deny a permit to march, whereas 88 percent of those opposing the ordinances would issue the permit. While most of the subjects hold opinions on the march that are consistent with their views of the Skokie ordinances, a surprising number do not (13, 4, and 18 percent, for the three groups respectively). Nor are the statistical relationships strong—attitudes toward the ordinances explain little more than a quarter of the variance in the permit variable (although some curvilinearity is apparent). Generally, those adopting an intolerant position on the ordinances are more likely to permit the march (perhaps in the belief, for instance, that the Nazis would not libel any ethnic

TABLE 6.2. Ordinance Opinion and Willingness to Allow a Nazi Demonstration

Ordinance Opinion	Percentage Willing to Grant a Permit		
	ACLU Members	ACLU Leaders	Common Cause Members
Strong support, both ordinances			
1.0	15.3	—	22.7
1.5	17.4	—	17.4
2.0	20.8	—	25.9
2.125	21.5	—	23.7
2.25	36.7	—	38.5
2.5	48.2	75.0	33.0
2.75	73.7	90.5	62.5
2.875	68.2	—	64.5
3.0	78.3	87.2	75.1
3.5	87.4	96.0	84.5
4.0	95.7	98.6	93.1
Strong opposition, both ordinances			

Source: James L. Gibson and Richard D. Bingham, "Elite Tolerance of Nazi Rights," *American Politics Quarterly* Vol. II, No. 4, October 1983, pp. 409–418. Copyright © 1983 by Sage Publications, Inc. Reprinted by permission of Sage Publications, Inc.

groups) than those opposing the ordinances are to ban it. To the extent that there is "slippage," it is largely in the failure to apply generally intolerant attitudes in an intolerant fashion.

To what degree do positions on this particular conflict reflect more generalized attitudes toward civil liberties issues? Which of the dimensions of civil liberties attitudes best predict opinion on Skokie? These questions are addressed by the data in Table 6.3.

Several of the attitudinal variables exhibit strong relationships to unwillingness to deny the Nazis a permit to demonstrate. The strongest correlation is with the measure of willingness to allow demonstrations by groups representing abhorrent political beliefs, but general political tolerance, attitudes toward government oppression, and ordinance attitudes are also moderately strong predictors. Somewhat surprisingly, support for freedom of speech and opposition to the heckler's veto are only weakly related to permit opinions. The other variables are also only weakly related.

Most of the variance in permit opinion can be explained by attitudes toward abhorrent demonstrations (as revealed by the betas from the

TABLE 6.3. Determinants of Willingness to Deny Nazis a Permit to Demonstrate

	ACLU Members		ACLU Leaders		Common Cause Members	
	r	Beta	r	Beta	r	Beta
Ordinance attitudes	-.49	-.14	-.40	-.16	-.51	-.16
Freedom of speech attitudes	-.34	.02	-.24	.03	-.33	.01
Heckler's veto attitudes	-.27	-.01	-.20	.03	-.28	.03
Attitudes toward abhorrent group demonstrations	-.71	-.52	-.60	-.47	-.71	-.53
Government oppression attitudes	-.51	-.11	-.44	-.08	-.50	-.10
Liberty v. order attitudes	-.19	.05	-.15	-.07	-.25	.04
Attitudes toward rightist rights	-.31	.05	-.19	.09	-.33	.04
Church & state attitudes	-.17	-.02	-.05	.06	-.17	-.01
General political tolerance	-.57	-.15	-.43	-.16	-.55	-.12
R^2	.554		.427		.540	

Source: James L. Gibson and Richard D. Bingham, "Elite Tolerance of Nazi Rights," *American Politics Quarterly* Vol. II, No. 4, October 1983, pp. 409–418. Copyright © 1983 by Sage Publications, Inc. Reprinted by permission of Sage Publications, Inc.

multivariate regression analysis). For most, opinion on Skokie is a
direct extrapolation of opinion toward communities' "right" not to be
invaded by alien and abhorrent demonstrators. Indeed, the relationship
is so strong that none of the other variables has a substantial independent
impact (although the presence of multicollinearity requires caution in
this interpretation). It should also be noted that predictability of permit
positions is reasonably strong and remarkably consistent across all
three groups (as shown by the R^2 values). Moreover, when dichotomized
opinions (grant-deny) are subjected to discriminant analysis predictability is high: the opinions of 91 percent of the ACLU members, 98
percent of the ACLU leaders and 86 percent of Common Cause members
are predictable from the general attitude variables. Remarkably little
"slippage" is apparent.

It is also fruitful to consider the correlates of support for the
Skokie ordinances. These data are shown in Table 6.4.

Once more, the measure of attitudes toward abhorrent group
demonstrations is the best predictor, although its superiority over the
other independent variables is somewhat diminished. Ordinance opinions also reflect attitudes toward free speech, general political tolerance,
and attitudes toward government oppression. The multivariate results
again indicate that the variable measuring support for communities'

TABLE 6.4. Determinants of Attitudes toward Skokie Ordinances

	ACLU Members		ACLU Leaders		Common Cause Members	
	r	Beta	r	Beta	r	Beta
Freedom of speech attitudes	.43	.13	.40	.15	.39	.09
Heckler's veto attitudes	.36	.13	.31	.08	.39	.13
Attitudes toward abhorrent group demonstrations	.55	.33	.42	.17	.55	.27
Government oppression attitudes	.38	.03	.43	.18	.48	.13
Liberty v. order attitudes	.36	.08	.28	.01	.39	.07
Attitudes toward rightist rights	.45	.15	.37	.11	.49	.21
Church & state attitudes	.27	-.01	.26	.06	.25	-.15
General political tolerance	.43	.02	.39	.09	.49	.04
R^2	.403		.328		.433	

Source: James L. Gibson and Richard D. Bingham, "Elite Tolerance of Nazi Rights,"
American Politics Quarterly Vol. II, No. 4, October 1983, pp. 409–418. Copyright © 1983 by
Sage Publications, Inc. Reprinted by permission of Sage Publications, Inc.

privacy rights has the strongest independent impact. Regardless of the other issues involved, those supporting communities' discretion to control access to their streets are likely to support the Skokie ordinances, a completely logical finding. It must be noted that the utility of these variables for predicting ordinance opinions is somewhat less than their utility for predicting permit opinions.

In that the variable measuring support for community privacy is such a powerful predictor of the other opinions it is important to consider how these attitudes are interrelated. These data are shown in Table 6.5.

Support for communities' right to prohibit demonstrations is strongly related to the general political tolerance scale. Those generally more tolerant are more likely to deny local communities the right to prohibit demonstrations. Attitudes toward government oppression have a modest impact on these attitudes, but none of the other variables has much independent influence.

A sizable proportion of the variance in this measure is not explicable in terms of general civil liberties attitudes, perhaps reflecting an unwillingness or uneasiness on the part of civil libertarians to impose repugnant ideologies upon communities. That is, it may be that much of the "misprediction" (unexplained variance) is attributable to tolerant individuals who are less willing to support the rights of repugnant groups than favored groups. There may also be variability in consistency that is related to the degree of conflict between the community and the group. Table 6.6 reports the results of an analysis conducted to shed some light on this question. Using discriminant functions incorporating the seven predictor variables shown in Table 6.5, predictions were made of opinions (dichotomized) on the four scenarios that comprise the "abhorrent group demonstrations" measure. The predictions are dichotomized as "tolerant" (allow the demonstration) or "intolerant" (prohibit the demonstration). The table also reports actual opinion so that the nature of mispredictions can be investigated (see Table 6.6).

It should first be noted that those with tolerant general attitudes (predictably tolerant individuals) quite effectively translate their general views into specific opinions. Only very small proportions of the ACLU members and leaders who are generally disposed toward tolerance would prohibit the various demonstrations. The figure is somewhat higher for Common Cause members, approaching one-fifth in the case of a proposed Klan demonstration in a black community. Some variation is observed across the scenarios. The dissonance created by a proposed

TABLE 6.5.   Determinants of Attitudes toward Abhorrent Group Demonstrations

	ACLU Members		ACLU Leaders		Common Cause Members	
	r	Beta	r	Beta	r	Beta
Freedom of speech attitudes	.43	.12	.35	.11	.40	.09
Heckler's veto attitudes	.32	.08	.32	.14	.37	.13
Government oppression attitudes	.55	.22	.48	.27	.53	.17
Liberty v. order attitudes	.29	.00	.21	.01	.34	.01
Attitudes toward rightist rights	.43	.10	.33	.25	.42	.08
Church & state attitudes	.24	.03	.10	-.19	.24	.02
General political tolerance	.65	.39	.43	.15	.62	.38
R^2	.500		.341		.457	

Source: James L. Gibson and Richard D. Bingham, "Elite Tolerance of Nazi Rights," American Politics Quarterly Vol. II, No. 4, October 1983, pp. 409–418. Copyright © 1983 by Sage Publications, Inc. Reprinted by permission of Sage Publications, Inc.

TABLE 6.6. Predictability of Opinions on Demonstrations and Communities' Right to Privacy

	Predicted Opinion					
	Tolerant			Intolerant		
	ACLU Members	ACLU Leaders	Common Cause Members	ACLU Members	ACLU Leaders	Common Cause Members
Actual Opinion:[a] Civil Rights Group						
Tolerant	98.1[b]	99.4	94.2	84.1	79.7	73.6
Intolerant	1.9	0.6	5.8	15.9	20.3	26.4
Actual Opinion: Palestine Liberation Organization						
Tolerant	93.4	97.7	82.4	49.4	76.0	34.2
Intolerant	6.6	2.3	17.6	50.6	24.0	65.8

Actual Opinion: Klansmen					
Tolerant	91.3	98.1	80.6	34.1	56.3	25.2
Intolerant	8.7	1.9	19.4	65.9	43.8	74.8
Actual Opinion: Nazis					
Tolerant	95.0	99.3	88.1	40.3	85.2	27.5
Intolerant	5.0	0.7	11.9	59.7	14.8	72.4

[a]The items asked the subjects to indicate whether a permit to demonstrate should be issued to a black civil rights group seeking to demonstrate in a white Southern community; to the PLO seeking to demonstrate in a Jewish community; to the Ku Klux Klan seeking to demonstrate in a black community; and to Nazis seeking to demonstrate in a white protestant community.

[b]Entries for tolerant and intolerant actual opinion total to 100 percent (except for rounding error).

Source: James L. Gibson and Richard D. Bingham, "Elite Tolerance of Nazi Rights," American Politics Quarterly Vol. II, No. 4, October 1983, pp. 409–418. Copyright © 1983 by Sage Publications, Inc. Reprinted by permission of Sage Publications, Inc.

civil rights demonstration in a white southern community is not sufficiently high to dissuade those with tolerant attitudes from supporting
the march, but, for many more, the dissonance reaches a peak in the
instance of Klan demonstrations. Generally though, "slippage" between
more abstract attitudes and the more specific opinions is slight for these
subjects.

The data on those with intolerant general attitudes reveal a different
pattern. In the case of a southern civil rights demonstration, large
majorities in all three groups defect from their general intolerant position.
In the other three instances, substantial "inconsistent" libertarian
minorities are observed (majorities in the case of ACLU leaders). Even
in the most extreme instance of demonstrator-community conflict—
Klansmen in black communities—one-third of the ACLU members,
one-half of the leaders, and one-quarter of Common Cause members
would allow the demonstration. *To the extent that slippage is occurring it is
in the failure of those with intolerant attitudes to adopt intolerant positions in
specific conflicts.* Since it is difficult to imagine a more severe conflict
between demonstrators and communities than those portrayed in these
four questions, it must be concluded that a sizable proportion of those
with intolerant attitudes would very rarely oppose groups' efforts to
demonstrate.

Similar results are observed when opinions on whether to grant the
Nazis a permit to demonstrate in Skokie are analyzed. Using the nine
predictor variables shown in Table 6.3, 96, 99, and 91 percent of the
predicted tolerant ACLU members, leaders, and Common Cause
members, respectively, would issue the permit. Among those with
intolerant attitudes in these three groups, 27, 42, and 23 percent would
allow the demonstration. To the extent that these subjects fail to base
specific opinions on more general attitudes, it is those with intolerant
attitudes, not those with tolerant attitudes, who are inconsistent.

These findings demonstrate just how important the context of
particular disputes is for understanding the linkages between generalized
attitudes and specific opinions. For those with intolerant attitudes,
certain of these disputes apparently do not stimulate abstract civil
liberties attitudes. When the scenario postulates an action or group
with which the respondent (presumably) agrees, the tolerance belief
system is not even activated. In a sense, then, this is a reconfirmation of
the point made by Sullivan, Pierson, and Marcus (1982), and others
that one cannot be tolerant of something that one favors. But it is worth

emphasizing that the opposite is also true—that one cannot be intolerant of something one favors.

The variability in the predictability of opinions (especially among those who hold intolerant general attitudes) no doubt reflects the interactive nature of specific contextual stimuli with generalized preferences. Specific opinions reflect not only generalized attitudes, but also a host of other factors associated with the particular context of the dispute. Civil liberties disputes vary in intensity, in the degree to which the effort to exercise the liberty imposes costs on others in the community. Those with generally intolerant attitudes are those who are willing to accept little of the associated costs of the exercise of civil liberties. It may be hypothesized that the variability in predictability of opinions across the four scenarios is a function of perceptions of whether the costs imposed on the community by the demonstration are excessive. "Inconsistency" in opinion—as represented for instance by the 49 percent of the intolerant ACLU members who would nonetheless allow a PLO demonstration in a Jewish community—illustrates that costs are perceived to be insufficient to cross even the relatively low civil liberties attitudinal hurdle. Tolerance simply indicates the height of the hurdle that must be overcome in order for the right to be extended; specific opinions also reflect perceptions of the severity of the particular dispute as well.

CONCLUSIONS

The reactions of members of the ACLU and Common Cause to the Skokie dispute were quite predictable from their general civil liberties attitudes. However, three important qualifications and extensions of this finding emerge. First, those opposing the rights of Nazis seem to rely most heavily on their general position on the rights of communities to control access to public property for the purposes of political demonstrations. Attitudes toward the "protectability" of various types of speech are much less useful predictors of opinions on the Skokie conflict. Skokie was foremost a freedom of assembly dispute. This of course is compatible with the "post-diction" that opposition to a Nazi demonstration in a different community would be diminished, as in fact was the case when the Nazis finally demonstrated in Chicago. While the presumed content of the Nazi speech no doubt made the assembly question more urgent, the content of the Nazi demonstration (which was actually to be focused upon the Nazi right to freedom of assembly) was irrelevant (and certainly the "prior restraint" barrier in free speech cases made that avenue of attack less likely to succeed).

A second, somewhat surprising finding is that such a small proportion of those with generally tolerant attitudes failed to adopt a tolerant point of view on this dispute. Popularly, Skokie was frequently viewed as the "typical" liberal reaction to threats to their own self-interests, and perhaps this is so. But unless Skokie caused an adjustment in more general attitudes (as they were reported on the questionnaires), those with tolerant attitudes, if not liberals, adopted a tolerant position on the dispute. Generally, it is those who hold less tolerant general attitudes who failed to act consistently; that is, who failed to support the Village government.

These findings lead in turn to the conclusion that despite all of the publicity and conflict, the controversy was not perceived as being very "extreme." That is, Skokie was not perceived as a limiting case, as a "fire in a crowded theater" case, on the civil liberties continuum. Libertarians took the case in stride—it was unnecessary to invoke idiosyncratic or extraordinary justifications for their positions. Similarly, many who were intolerant, who may be thought of as people with a lower threshold for prohibiting political speech and assemblies, apparently perceived the Skokie case as *not* extreme enough to cross even their much lower threshold. Indeed, these people were *less* likely to adopt an intolerant position on Skokie than they were in other scenarios. For all the publicity attached to the Skokie case, there are many instances in which more severe conflict over civil liberties might arise. With respect to their opinions, the members of ACLU and Common Cause reacted predictably to the civil liberties issues involved in the Skokie case.

Thus, in spite of the popular perception that Skokie represented a case in which a substantial portion of the libertarian elite was inconsistent in translating general libertarian beliefs into the Skokie situation, we found little evidence of such slippage. It is the least tolerant segment of the elite population that experienced the most difficulty in translating abstract beliefs into concrete opinion.

NOTES

1. This conceptualization implies a somewhat atypical approach to operationalizing "constraint." Usually constraint is assessed by a correlation

coefficient such as gamma. These coefficients assess the predictability of belief$_1$ from belief$_2$. In its somewhat more sophisticated manifestation, a model of the following type is posited.

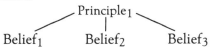

Observed relationships among belief$_1$, belief$_2$, and belief$_3$ are taken as evidence of the existence of principle$_1$, and hence of constraint (see, for examples, Bishop, et al., 1978, 1979; Nie and Rabjohn, 1979; and Sullivan, Piereson, and Marcus, 1978; and Sullivan, et al., 1979).

The predictability—or better, covariance—approach is quite useful in a variety of contexts, and we would agree that it represents one form of constraint. However, it is not the only form. Indeed, the covariance approach is insensitive to a higher, and more common, form of constraint: cumulativeness.

Cumulativeness implies predictability, not between each item pair, but rather predictability between the generalized preference of the individual (the "i" point) and the response to the particular stimulus (the "j" point). Certainly such predictability is evidence of a quite high level of constraint.

2.   Obviously, this model has been applied repeatedly and profitably to the behavior of members of the United States Supreme Court (e.g., Schubert, 1965, 1974).

3.   It should be noted that we have not adequately anticipated this point in our own research. The proper research design is one that seeks to account for specific opinion with reference to tolerance attitudes *and* any other attitudes or contextual perceptions that might contribute to the explanation of the opinions. We did not adequately conceptualize the alternative explanations—such as toleration of social disorder—and consequently do not have proper measures of the concepts to consider in the analysis. Thus, we can determine the degree to which specific opinions reflect generalized attitudes, but we cannot offer a full-blown theory of opinion formation.

4.   The insurance bond ordinance required demonstrators to get a permit at least thirty days in advance of the demonstration and to post liability insurance of $300,000 and property damage insurance of $50,000. The group libel ordinance made it a crime to disseminate any material promoting or inciting hatred against persons by reason of their race, religion, or national origin. For the text of these ordinances see Appendix A.

7   The Behavioral Consequences of Political Tolerance

The foregoing analysis of tolerance attitudes has not addressed the question of just why citizen attitudes toward democratic norms, and their opinions in specific disputes, are so crucial. A partial answer can be found by scrutinizing the model implicit in research on this problem. Democracy is typically defined as some set of institutional, constitutional, and policy arrangements facilitating majority rule, but not at the expense of guaranteed opportunities for the minority to create or become a majority (e.g., Dahl, 1971). The threat to democracy, as a responsive form of government, is that the majority will, in attempting to solidify its position, alter democratic institutions, constitutions, and policies in order to constrain the rights of opponents. Without the constraints of the democratic rules of the game, majority rule easily becomes majority tyranny. Thus, research on citizen attitudes toward democratic norms is justified implicitly by some sort of assumed behavioral and linkage processes: citizen attitudes have consequences for their political behavior, and, in turn, for public policy.

Linkage processes have been investigated in many contexts (e.g., Miller and Stokes, 1964; Page and Shapiro, 1983), but research on citizen support for democratic values has rarely moved beyond the mere description of levels of support to investigation of the important behavioral and linkage hypotheses. Indeed, the only work directly examining the behavioral implications of citizen attitudes derives from a quite distinct tradition focusing on unconventional political behavior (e.g., Muller, 1979; Muller, Jukam, and Seligson, 1982). This is understandable because, apart, perhaps, from inactivity as "behavior," political actions do not have the continuous existence of attitudes. That is, attitudes can be measured at any point in time; behavior must be measured in proximity to the stimuli evoking the action.[1] When behavioral stimuli occur periodically, as in voting, research is more easily conducted. However, opportunities to deprive citizens of their civil liberties occur with less regularity. The ordinary citizen simply does not get many formal opportunities to support or oppose the oppression of minorities.[2] Thus, this form of political participation has been rarely studied.

Moreover, the presumption that attitudes are important because they predict behavior when the circumstances or opportunities arise, should provide only little solace. Generally, the simple, direct relationship between attitudes and behavior is rather weak (e.g., Wicker, 1969), largely (but not exclusively) because it is mediated by a host of situational factors (e.g., Zanna, Higgins, and Herman, 1982). Thus, it is not surprising that Prothro and Grigg reported that 42 percent of the residents of Tallahassee told interviewers that they agreed with the statement that "a Negro should not be allowed to run for mayor of this city," but "a few months before the survey a Negro actually did conduct an active campaign for that office without any efforts being made by the 'white' people to obstruct his candidacy" (1960, p. 294). The behavioral and policy consequences of attitudes toward democracy are far from obvious, simple, and direct.

In this chapter we assess the relationship between tolerance attitudes and behavior. More specifically, we attempt to determine the conditions under which attitudinal support for the democratic rules of the game has consequences for political behavior, and ultimately for the authoritative allocation of rights. We begin with a simple hypothesis relating attitudes and behavior, but then proceed to test a more complex model of "contingent consistency." Many member of the ACLU and of Common Cause took various overt actions to prohibit the Nazis from demonstrating, thus providing an interesting context within which to analyze the attitude-behavior problem. Because we are interested in trying to understand the role of contextual variables in moderating the attitude-behavior relationship, the dispute provides an ideal context for testing contextual hypotheses. Thus, this chapter reports an analysis of the Skokie-Nazi conflict from the perspective of micro-level behavioral theory.

CONCEPTUALIZING THE ATTITUDE-BEHAVIOR RELATIONSHIP

Attitudes may be thought of as "acquired behavioral predispositions" (Campbell, 1963, p. 92). As such, they are a residue of previous experience, a residue that produces a patterned tendency to respond to stimuli in a certain way. Thus, an attitude is a *tendency*, a propensity. Attitudes do not necessarily produce behavior, but rather they represent a tendency to behave in a certain fashion. Further, this tendency may be more or less strong; for some, the probability of behaving in a manner consistent with the attitude is very high, given a set of circumstances, while for others it might be very low. Attitude-behavior consistency thus is dependent in part upon the strength of the behavioral impulse.

The strength of the propensity interacts with the nature of the specific circumstances to produce behavior. Situations vary in accordance with the cost imposed upon the behaver of performing the behavior. That is, situations present varying hurdles or thresholds to behavior. Whether a given propensity will result in behavior therefore is determined in part by the "difficulty" of performing the act. Strong propensities will only be blocked by high hurdles, whereas weak propensities may be blocked by relatively low hurdles. The strength of the propensity interacts with the situational context in producing behavior.

Research on racist attitudes illustrates this process nicely. Individuals with racist attitudes have a propensity to behave in a discriminatory fashion. However, whether discriminatory behavior occurs depends substantially upon the context of the potential behavior. Situations in which the individual can remain anonymous are more likely to result in discriminatory behavior than situations in which the behavior is public and the individual is personally accountable (DeFleur and Westie, 1958). The former circumstance presents a very low threshold—even weak racist propensities may generate discriminatory behavior. The latter circumstance represents a high threshold—only very strong racist attitudes will generate discriminatory behavior. Individuals' attitudes must therefore be understood within the context of the situation in order to predict behavior (LaPiere, 1934).

This notion of threshold has considerable utility for understanding the linkage between civil liberties attitudes and behaviors. In addition to individuals' attitudes toward civil liberties, perceptions of the context in which the liberties are to be exercised must be incorporated into the model. In particular, general attitudes interact with evaluations of the particular group seeking the liberty, the nature of the specific liberty, and the effect of the exercise of the liberty (see Lawrence, 1976, on the first two of these variables). Even the most tolerant attitudes will not result in libertarian behavior under all possible circumstances. Each of these conditions affecting the attitude-behavior linkage must be considered in more detail.

It is well established that levels of support for civil liberties depend upon the group asserting the liberties. The Stouffer measures of commitment to civil liberties demonstrate variability in tolerance when respondents are queried about various groups, for instance. Some of this variation is attributable to attitudes toward the groups; the greater the threat to the individual posed by the group, the greater the willingness to withdraw civil liberties (Stouffer, 1955; Lawrence, 1976). Not everyone is threatened by the same groups, but it is unusual for individuals to be willing to grant civil liberties to the group most threatening to them (Sullivan, Pierceson, and Marcus, 1982). Only the strongest libertarian attitudes can overcome the hurdle presented by a threatening political minority.

Variation exists by type of group, but also by type of activity. At the extreme, few would deny any political minority the right to correspond privately with their elected representatives, while most would deny the right to demonstrate daily anywhere they chose. Of the activities referred to in the Stouffer items, for instance, the most difficult action to gain mass acceptance for is teaching in college. Many would grant para-militarists the right to make speeches, but only a few would grant them the right to teach in a university. Presumably, even fewer would allow them to teach in a high school. The type of activity is obviously of considerable importance to the attitude-behavior linkage.

Finally, and relatedly, the consequences of the exercise of the liberty influence the degree to which libertarian attitudes direct behavior. For example, few would sanction the false cry of "Fire!" in a crowded cinema because of the consequences of the speech. It is not the group doing the shouting, nor the activity itself, but rather the context and consequences of the activity that determine reactions to the situation. The speech is not inherently unprotected, but is unprotected within the circumstances.

Any understanding of civil liberties attitudes and behaviors must take these contextual factors into account. Attitudes are only contingently related to behavior and the contingency is defined with respect to the group, the activity, and the consequences of the activity. For certain groups and activities, within certain circumstances, the hurdles to behavior are too high for attitudes to overcome. If we are to understand this process, civil liberties attitudes and behaviors must be examined within a fully defined context. The implication is that much can be gained from an analysis of civil liberties attitudes and behaviors within the context of an actual conflict over the rights of a minority political group. Investigations of abstract beliefs, or even concrete beliefs referring to very general hypothetical contexts, contribute little to understanding the linkage problem. As Zellman (1975: pp. 34–35) asserted: "The hypothetical concrete situations which elicit civil liberties attitudes lack the actor specificity, articulated context, and threat salience that is present in real-life situations involving dissents." The Skokie-Nazi conflict lacks none of these and is thus ideally suited for an investigation of the linkage process.

SIMPLE MODELS OF THE ATTITUDE-BEHAVIOR RELATIONSHIP

Attitudinal Support for Civil Liberties: The Independent Variables

In addition to the generalized tolerance attitudes reported in Chapter 5, we have measured opinion on the specific issues in the Skokie dispute (see Chapter 6). An indicator of opinion toward the ordinances was constructed from evaluations of the insurance bond requirement and the "group libel" provisions of the Skokie laws. Of the ACLU members, 79 percent opposed both ordinances, while comparable figures for ACLU leaders and Common Cause members are 95 and 54 percent, respectively. Consequently, it is not surprising that fairly large percentages of ACLU members and leaders (79 and 95 percent, respectively) would issue a permit for the demonstration; 59 percent of the Common Cause members are of a similar opinion. While strongly related, opinions toward the ordinances do not completely determine positions on whether to allow the demonstration. Finally, the subjects were queried about their evaluation of the ACLU's involvement in the dispute; 81, 94, and 64 percent of the three groups agreed or agreed strongly with the ACLU's stance. Thus, in addition to the five scales of generalized political tolerance, three measures of opinion on the issues are included as independent variables.

Behavioral Support for Civil Liberties: The Dependent Variable

The controversy in Skokie motivated a substantial number of individuals to engage in action either supportive of or opposed to the right of the Nazis to demonstrate. A large portion of the citizens of the Village mobilized in defense of their community (see Barnum, 1982). Those opposing the Nazis were quite active, expressing their views to and making demands of their political and religious leaders, and, on occasion, taking to the streets. Supporters of the rights of the Nazis were somewhat more restrained but nevertheless engaged in a variety of types of action. Action was not, however, limited to these direct participants in the dispute—both elites and masses across the country hotly contested the issues, resulting in an assortment of direct and indirect efforts to shape public policy.

The subjects were queried about actions they took on the issue (see Table 7.1). In all, approximately 20 percent of the members, 40 percent

TABLE 7.1. Intolerant and Tolerant Behaviors

	Percent Engaging in Activity		
	ACLU Members	ACLU Leaders	Common Cause Members
Intolerant Behaviors[a]			
Demonstrate	0.7	0.9	0.5
Join group	0.8	1.0	0.6
Financial contributions	1.7	1.7	2.8
Contact government	1.3	1.3	1.8
Organize people	0.6	0.9	0.5
Total engaging in intolerant behaviors[b]	6.4	0.7	3.4
Tolerant Behaviors			
Demonstrate	0.7	3.6	0.4
Join group	4.0	4.8	1.9
Financial contributions	18.0	33.0	8.4
Contact government	1.8	10.7	1.4
Organize people	0.8	8.6	0.6
Total engaging in tolerant behavior[b]	20.1	39.9	9.6

[a]The question read:

"Returning to the Nazis, have you taken any of the following actions in the last year with regard to whether the First Amendment guarantees the Nazis the right to hold public marches? (Please answer not in terms of your actions concerning Nazi *ideas* but rather in terms of your actions concerning the *First Amendment* issue.)"

[b]Because subjects could engage in multiple behaviors, the totals are not the sums of the individual activity percentages.

of the leaders and 10 percent of the Common Cause members did something in support of the rights of the Nazis, while 6, 1, and 3 percent, respectively, of the three groups engaged in some behavior in opposition to Nazi rights. Thus, although behavior is skewed somewhat toward action supporting the rights of this political minority, substantial proportions of these subjects acted on the controversy. If resignation from ACLU over Skokie is counted as an intolerant behavior, the proportions of each group engaging in some form of action are 27, 41, and 13 percent for ACLU members, leaders and Common Cause members, respectively.

The Attitude-Behavior Relationship

The simplest hypothesis relating attitudes and behavior is that those taking some action to deny the Nazis the right to speak and to assemble did so because of their intolerant attitudes, while those acting to extend the rights of Nazis did so because of their tolerant attitudes. Thus, the first hypothesis to be tested is that tolerant behavior is a direct function of tolerant attitudes.

Table 7.2 reports the simple correlations between the attitudinal variables considered above and three different indicators of behavior: an intolerant behavior–no behavior–tolerant behavior trichotomy, an intolerant–no behavior dichotomy, and a no behavior–tolerant behavior dichotomy. Several aspects of this table are worth noting. First, in general, there is little difference among the three groups in the magnitude and direction of the relationships. The attitudes associated with action are similar for ACLU members and leaders and Common Cause members. Second, those who took some action to block the exercise of Nazi rights are more attitudinally distinctive than those who took some action in support of Nazi rights. It is easier to predict intolerant behavior than tolerant behavior. Third, there is substantial variability in the degree to which the various attitudes predict behavior. Somewhat surprisingly, attitudes toward freedom of speech are only weakly related to action. Those viewing nearly all speech as constitutionally protected are only slightly more likely to have taken action in the controversy. On the other hand, free assembly attitudes are moderately related to action, especially in terms of differentiating those who behaved in an intolerant fashion from those acting tolerantly or not at all. More precisely, attitudes toward communities' rights to limit demonstrations by abhorrent groups, rather than willingness to prohibit demonstrations for fear

TABLE 7.2. The Direct, Bivariate Relationship of Libertarian Attitudes and Behavior

	No Behavior v. Tolerant Behavior			Intolerant Behavior v. No Behavior			Intolerant Behavior v. No Behavior v. Tolerant Behavior		
	ACLU Members	ACLU Leaders	Common Cause Members	ACLU Members	ACLU Leaders	Common Cause Members	ACLU Members	ACLU Leaders	Common Cause Members
Evaluation of ACLU involvement in Skokie	.29	.25	.32	.46	.29	.25	.46	.30	.39
Evaluation of Skokie ordinances	.27	.23	.28	.30	.26	.17	.36	.27	.32
Allow the demonstration	.21	.16	.23	.39	.40	.20	.37	.22	.29
Support for freedom of assembly:									
Abhorrent demonstrators	.24	.19	.25	.36	.29	.19	.37	.23	.30
Heckler's veto	.14	.19	.21	.10	.07	.06	.16	.20	.21
Support for freedom of speech	.13	.20	.10	.15	.09	.06	.18	.21	.11
Support for freedom of political association	.12	.13	.17	.28	.56	.21	.24	.22	.24
General tolerance (Stouffer)	.19	.17	.21	.35	.36	.19	.32	.23	.28

NOTE: Entries are Pearson correlation coefficients.

of violent hecklers, predict action. Thus, the Skokie issue, at least for those supportive of the Village's position, was primarily an issue of the location of the demonstration. Some relationship to Stouffer's tolerance measures is also observed, although it must be remembered that the traditional Stouffer activities were supplemented by an item referring to marches by unpopular political minorities. Those supporting government efforts to curtail political association are also somewhat more likely to have engaged in intolerant behavior.

Not surprisingly, attitudes more directly focused on the issue or opinions, are better predictors of behavior than more general tolerance. Generally, the best predictor is the respondent's evaluation of ACLU's involvement in the controversy. Similarly, evaluations of the ordinances and specific opinion on whether the demonstration should be allowed are moderately related to behavior. That the relationships are not stronger is not a function of the attitudes of the "behavers" but is rather attributable to the fact that many subjects with strongly tolerant attitudes took no action.

The various attitudinal variables are fairly strongly interrelated so a multivariate analysis of the attitude-behavior relationship must be considered. In this analysis, the general political tolerance measures are treated as exogenous variables, under the assumption that more abstract attitudes are antecedents to specific opinions. We assume that the opinion variable most proximate to behavior is the respondent's evaluation of the role of the ACLU (justified in part by the finding that this variable has the strongest bivariate relationship with behavior and by

TABLE 7.3. Explained Variance[a] in the Path Analysis of Tolerance Attitudes and Behavior

Dependent Variable	ACLU Members	ACLU Leaders	Common Cause Members
Behavior (trichotomized)	23.7	13.0	17.1
Evaluation of ACLU involvement in Skokie	56.9	37.4	62.6
Allow the demonstration	54.4	40.2	56.7
Evaluation of Skokie ordinances	36.5	29.9	41.6

[a]Entries are percentage of variance explained (R^2).

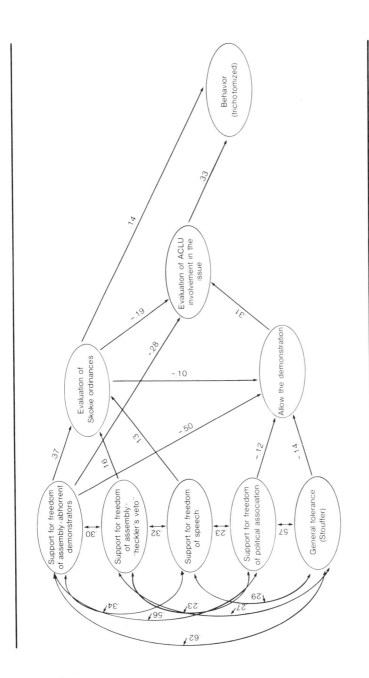

FIGURE 7.1. Path analysis[a] of libertarian attitudes and behavior—ACLU members.

[a] Paths less than .10 are not shown.

the assumption that evaluations of ACLU involvement flow from general tolerance attitudes and from evaluations of the ordinances and proposed demonstration). The path model is shown in Figure 7.1. Only paths with an absolute value exceeding .1 are shown and the data are presented only for the ACLU members. The results for Common Cause members are quite similar. For leaders of ACLU there are important differences, although they are most likely statistical artifacts associated with the skewed distribution of the behavior variable. In order to allow comparison of the results across the three groups Table 7.3 reports the amount of variance explained for each of the endogenous variables.

Almost one-fourth of the variance in the behavior trichotomy can be explained by the attitudinal model. Similar analysis of the dichotomous variables reveals that the model best discriminates those who engaged in intolerant behavior from all others. For instance, 25 percent of the variance in intolerant behavior can be explained, whereas only 10 percent of the variance in tolerant behavior can be accounted for. The strongest predictor of behavior is the respondent's evaluation of ACLU's role in the controversy (a finding also characterizing the Common Cause members: $p = -.29$), no doubt reflecting the fact that some who opposed the ACLU's involvement directed their intolerant behavior against the ACLU itself (i.e., the defectors). For others, however, this variable probably reflects the summary opinion resulting from the reconciliation of beliefs and values on the host of issues involved in the dispute—from organizational priorities to specific constitutional doctrine. This interpretation is supported by the remainder of the path model: over one-half of the variance in this opinion variable is explained by the other variables in the model. The strongest predictors are general support for freedom of assembly and specific opinion on whether the demonstration ought to be permitted, and, to a lesser degree, attitudes toward the specific provisions of the Skokie ordinances. Thus, evaluations of the ACLU's involvement in Skokie seem to reflect more general beliefs as well as specific opinions.[3]

The other endogenous variables are also uncommonly well predicted. Over one-half of the variance in opinion on whether the march should be allowed is explained. Even one-third of the variance in opinions toward the ordinances themselves is associated with general political tolerance. The very strong and widespread, direct and indirect, impact of attitudes toward freedom of assembly, as well as the negligible impact of free speech attitudes, should also be noted. This variable, reflecting assembly views within the context of demonstrator-community conflict, not only predicts specific opinions but is also moderately to strongly related to the other tolerance indicators.

A remarkably high percentage of the variance in behavior can be explained when we consider only those who took some form of action (i.e., omitting those engaging in no behavior). *For ACLU members, 75 percent of the variance is explained by the attitude and opinion variables. The comparable figure for the ACLU leaders is 89 percent, and for Common Cause members it is 83 percent.* Thus, among those taking action on the issue, attitudes are extremely useful predictors of behavior.

In general, behavior does reflect attitudes, although other attitudes are better predicted by attitudes than is behavior. Those who took action for or against Nazi rights behaved consistently with their attitudes. Largely as a result of the failure of many respondents to mobilize their attitudes into action, much unexplained variance remains. Perhaps a more sophisticated model of the relationship will be successful in further accounting for this unexplained variance.

CONDITIONAL MODELS OF THE ATTITUDE-BEHAVIOR RELATIONSHIP

Not for many years have social psychologists believed the impact of attitudes on behavior to be unmitigated by contextual forces. Instead, the nearly consensual view is that the relationship is one of "contingent consistency" (but see McGuire, 1976; Kahle and Berman, 1979). Attitude-behavior consistency is contingent upon the character of the attitudes themselves (e.g., Bem, 1972; Bagozzi and Burnkrant, 1979; Fazio and Zanna, 1978; Schlegel and DiTecco, 1982); the nature of the behavior and behavioral intentions (e.g., Fishbein and Ajzen, 1975, but see Bentler and Speckart, 1979); and, most importantly, the context within which the behavior takes place (e.g., Wicker, 1969; Frideres, 1971; Frideres, Warner, and Albrecht, 1971; Bem and Funder, 1978; Gibson, 1978; Abelson, 1982; Bordiga and Campbell, 1982; and Oskamp, 1977). If we are to predict behavior it is therefore necessary to know more than scores on simple attitude indicators.

In order to understand contextual moderators of the attitude-behavior relationship, it is useful to think of attitudes as behavioral impulses, or as "acquired behavioral dispositions" (Campbell, 1963). That is, all attitudes include an action, or action-potential component.

The strength of this behavioral impulse is highly variable across attitudes, although it is rarely negligible (it is almost always possible, for instance, to stimulate survey respondents to engage in "responding" behavior). The strength of the impulse is a function of many factors, such as the strength of the attitude, its salience, and centrality. Thus, the preceding section of this chapter was a test of the simple proposition that the more extreme and intensely-held the attitude, the more likely the subject is to behave. The hypothesis, "behavior, if it occurs, will be compatible with attitudes," has received considerable support.

Further efforts to account for variance in the measures for behavior must focus on factors contributing to the mobilization of attitudes into behavior. Behavior, of any type, always imposes some costs on the behaver, and therefore the utilitarian individual must anticipate some benefit before action is emitted. The costs of behaving are not invariant across situations, but rather are contextually determined. Indeed, it is useful to think of the situationally-defined costs of behavior as representing a "hurdle" that must be overcome before action is emitted. Attitudes do not routinely elicit behavior because behavioral impulses are blocked by highly variable, but rarely negligible hurdles. The hurdles that must be overcome may be raised in a particular situation owing to increased costs; they may also, however, be lowered by increasing benefits of behaving. The degree to which attitudes are mobilized into behavior is a function of the height of the hurdle associated with the context.

Hurdles to behavior may be imposed by any of a variety of factors, but in many civil liberties disputes, the salient contextual variables have something to do with perceptions of the demonstrator-community conflict. In the case of Skokie, two contextual factors will be considered as possible mediators of the attitude-behavior relationships: (1) expectations of violence and conflict in the event of a Nazi demonstration in Skokie; (2) particular abhorrence of the Nazis. Each of these may be conceptualized as costs that the respondent expects to be borne if the Nazis were to be allowed to exercise their civil liberties, and thus as contextual influences on the attitude-behavior relationship.

One of the most severe potential costs of public demonstrations is that the demonstration will become uncontrollable and that violence will erupt. This fear was especially salient in Skokie because of a variety of threats of confrontational counter-demonstrations by militant Jews and others. We hypothesize that those who are tolerant, but who expected violence, are less likely to have engaged in tolerant behavior.

Similarly, expectations of violence are expected to lower the hurdle to intolerant behavior among those with intolerant attitudes.[5] The perceived costs of allowing the Nazis to demonstrate in Skokie thus interact with tolerance attitudes, requiring one value—liberty—to be balanced against another—in this case, order.

The hypotheses receive little support: perceptions of greater costs to the community from the Nazi demonstration, measured through an open-ended item asking the subjects to indicate what they expected would happen if the demonstration were to take place in Skokie, do not increase the probability of those with intolerant attitudes behaving in an intolerant fashion (see Table 7.4). Regressing the cell percentages on

TABLE 7.4. The Conditional Impact of Expectations of Violence on the Attitude-Behavior Relationship

Attitudinal Tolerance[a]	Costs of the Demonstration-Expectations			
	Nothing	Verbal Confrontation	Possible Violence	Violence
	Percent Engaging in Intolerant Behavior			
0	100.0	—	100.0	71.3
1	100.0	—	49.3	94.4
2	100.0	—	75.1	43.3
3	54.5	100.0	68.1	87.0
4	53.1	100.0	34.7	45.3
5	55.2	9.8	29.0	30.6
6	82.9	97.7	14.5	34.8
7	69.6	34.7	46.3	56.4
8	5.3	4.1	21.4	19.5
9	32.7	21.3	16.0	9.6
10	0.0	50.0	1.0	1.5
11	20.1	0.0	0.5	1.6
	Percent Engaging in Tolerant Behavior			
12	0.5	0.0	1.0	0.7
13	2.4	2.0	14.1	3.7
14	8.3	11.7	11.3	6.8
15	22.2	17.4	16.8	11.7
16	11.8	7.6	13.1	13.3
17	22.8	17.8	26.5	23.2
18	24.3	19.5	28.3	39.5
19	37.1	31.6	33.5	39.9
20	30.6	39.2	43.6	27.6
21	34.8	37.6	41.2	40.8
22	—	—	100.0	0.0

[a]See note 9 for the specific measure.

the attitude scores allows the calculation of expected proportions of behavers for various combinations of attitudes and perceptions of the context. The predicted percentages for those with fairly intolerant attitudes (attitude score =5) are 56 percent for those expecting nothing to happen in the event of a Nazi demonstration; 66 percent for those expecting verbal confrontations; 39 percent for those expecting possible violence; and 43 percent for those expecting actual violence. Thus, the perception of increased costs to the local community *reduces* the likelihood of those with intolerant attitudes engaging in intolerant behavior. We can only speculate that this finding reflects the fact that the perception variable is poorly measured, and/or that those with intolerant attitudes perceive the very *idea* of the demonstration—apart from the expected actual consequences—to be sufficiently costly to mobilize them to action.

Nor is there evidence that those with more tolerant attitudes found it more difficult to behave when they perceived a high likelihood of violence. The expected rate of tolerant behavior for those with moderately strong tolerant attitudes (score = 20) and who expected nothing to happen is 23 percent; for those expecting a verbal confrontation it is 33 percent; for those expecting possible violence it is 49 percent; and for those expecting actual violence it is 26 percent. Thus, the hypothesis is not supported.

The hurdle to behavior may well be raised significantly for those who feel particularly threatened by the Nazis. The most salient aspect of the Skokie dispute was the confrontation between Nazis and Jews, and it would therefore be reasonable to hypothesize that religious and ethnic Judaism significantly affects perceptions of the context. For Jews—even tolerant Jews—to allow the exercise of civil liberties by Nazis in a Jewish community inhabited by Holocaust survivors, requires quite strong commitments to libertarian values. Thus, it may be hypothesized that tolerant Jews are less likely to act than non-Jews, and that intolerant Jews are more likely to act than non-Jews. Because those who are secular—in contrast to religious—Jews may be less threatened by the Nazis by virtue of their weaker ties to the Jewish community, we divide Jews into two groups. Table 7.5 reports the results of the contextual analysis.

There is little effect of religious affiliation in predicting behavior *in support of* the right of the Nazis to demonstrate. This is amply documented in Table 7.5, in which it can be seen that tolerant Jews are *neither* more nor less likely than non-Jews to have acted in a tolerant manner. The

TABLE 7.5. The Conditional Impact of Religious Affiliation on the Attitude-Behavior Relationship

Attitudinal Tolerance[a]	Religious Affiliation		
	Non-Jews	Secular Jews	Religious Jews
	Percent Engaging in Intolerant Behavior		
0	41.9	100.0	87.0
1	22.4	100.0	99.0
2	56.1	100.0	65.3
3	42.9	100.0	98.7
4	47.3	94.1	54.3
5	22.4	67.8	37.2
6	26.7	40.0	56.2
7	23.1	97.2	66.8
8	17.9	32.2	13.0
9	13.2	2.5	16.1
10	3.6	1.0	15.3
11	4.7	12.5	1.2
	Percent Engaging in Tolerant Behavior		
12	0.7	0.0	0.7
13	3.8	7.7	15.9
14	9.8	15.9	4.5
15	18.3	2.6	8.9
16	10.4	1.4	19.8
17	20.3	38.9	32.8
18	28.0	4.6	27.3
19	40.0	25.9	18.0
20	34.1	33.8	49.3
21	38.5	31.9	34.8
22	47.6	—	—

[a]See note 9 for the specific measure.

percentages predicted to act tolerantly for relatively tolerant non-Jews, secular Jews, and religious Jews are 36 percent, 27 percent, and 35 percent, respectively. Thus, this portion of the hypothesis receives little support; situational impediments to behavior are not higher for tolerant Jews than for tolerant non-Jews.

On the other hand, it is easier for intolerant Jews to act in a intolerant fashion than it is for intolerant non-Jews. As depicted in Figure 7.2, the differences in the intercepts and slopes are substantial for those with intolerant attitudes, although they converge at approximately the point of moderate tolerance, the point at which intolerant behavior ceases to occur with any frequency. Predicted rates of behavior make clear this effect: only 27 percent of the relatively intolerant non-Jews are expected to have engaged in intolerant behavior, whereas the comparable figures for secular and religious Jews are 62 and 51 percent, respectively.[6] Relatively intolerant Jews—secular and religious alike—were more likely to mobilize their attitudes into behavior than were non-Jews who were equally intolerant. In short, for Jews the hurdle that had to be overcome was less substantial.

Jews may perceive the costs and benefits of Nazis marching in Skokie differently from non-Jews. But if the process linking intolerant attitudes to intolerant behavior among Jews is *not* connected with perceptions of the costs to be imposed on the residents of the Village of Skokie, as suggested (but not demonstrated) by the analysis above of the perceptual variable, then through what process is the effect wrought? Moreover, the behavior of tolerant Jews seems not to be more sensitive to contextual influences than that of non-Jews. If Jewishness colors perceptions of the context it must do so in interaction with substantive attitudes.

While Jews differ little from non-Jews in their levels of general political tolerance and specific opinions, they did perceive the consequences of the potential Nazi demonstration as more serious than non-Jews. Among ACLU members, 29 percent of the non-Jews expected violence to erupt in Skokie, whereas 42 percent of the secular Jews and 48 percent of the religious Jews had the same perception. Comparable figures for Common Cause members are 38, 36, and 58 percent, respectively. No such relationship exists among the ACLU leaders, perhaps because of their greater awareness of the facts of the dispute. But the impact of religion on contextual perceptions is itself conditional, with moderate associations observed only among those with relatively intolerant attitudes. That is, among those with intolerant attitudes, Jews were more likely to expect violence; among those with tolerant attitudes Jews and non-Jews differed little. Thus, it seems that there are a series of interactions involved. Relatively intolerant non-Jews are little affected by the perceived costs of the demonstration, possibly because their perceptions differ from Jews qualitatively in ways not tapped by our crude measures. When Jews report that they expect violence to occur they may have perceptions of more serious and widespread violence than non-Jews.[7] Thus, the hurdle to behavior is lowered for intolerant Jews, in general, but especially for those expecting dire consequences from the demonstration.

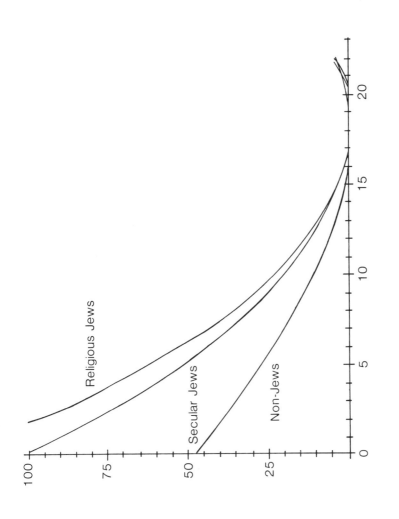

FIGURE 7.2. The conditional impact of religion on the attitude-behavior relationship.

177

Among the more tolerant segments of our samples, these interactions seem not to occur. Jews and non-Jews differ little; perceptions of the context have no interpretable influence. For these subjects, behavior followed directly from attitudes, with little influence from the context of the dispute. Generally, it seems that despite the superficially unusual nature of the Skokie-Nazi dispute, the civil liberties issues for those favorably predisposed toward civil liberties were fairly simple and the conflict was taken in stride by most.

Of course it is possible that those with tolerant attitudes were affected by different contextual factors. For ACLU members, loyalty to the organization may be important, inasmuch as the survival of ACLU itself became a direct issue in the Nazi-Skokie dispute. However, we have been unable to discover much statistical effect of organizational involvement or satisfaction with the organization.[8]

Thus, there is evidence that the relationship between attitudes and behavior is in part conditional upon perceptions of the context of the exercise of civil liberties. However, the effect is limited to those attitudinally predisposed not to be supportive of the exercise of civil liberties by unpopular political minorities.

CONCLUSIONS

The first conclusion from the analysis reported in this chapter is that it is apparent that this sort of atypical political behavior can be subjected to systematic inquiry. The logistics of such research are onerous to be sure, and, as a case study, the degree to which the findings can be generalized is unknown. But perhaps the generalizability of theories based upon conventional, largely electoral political participation is also suspect. As a legacy of the 1960s, many citizens engage in a variety of non-electoral political behaviors about which much too little is known. Political participation other than voting and direct involvement in electoral politics has important consequences; it can and should be studied.

Perhaps our most important micro-level finding is that attitudes concerning tolerance have behavioral consequences. Using a simple linear model of the attitude-behavior relationship, nearly one-fourth of the variance in the behavior measure can be explained. Such a finding is startling only when it is noted that existing literature reports weak direct relationships between attitudes and behavior. If research on political tolerance attitudes requires justification primarily in the presumed behavioral consequences of attitudes, then this research provides some support for continued attention to such attitudes.

To the extent that the attitude-behavior relationship reported in the analysis is less than perfect, it is because of the failure of a great many of our subjects to engage in *any* relevant behavior. Within the context of experimental research, of course, non-behavior is rarely a permissible option. Among ACLU and Common Cause members engaging in behavior, attitudes are quite strong predictors, accounting for over *three-fourths* of the variance in behavior. Non-behavior may be common, but misbehavior is rare.

This analysis shows some limited success in accounting for the process of mobilizing attitudes into behavior. Quite apart from substantive attitudes, it appears that contextual stimuli associated with the specific dispute make it easier for some to behave, while making it more difficult for others to behave. The evidence on this point is not nearly as strong as we expected, and considerable research in the future must be devoted to unraveling these complex, contextual relationships.

There are a number of factors that no doubt facilitate the translation of attitudes into behavior. First, those favorably predisposed toward action may require less stimulation in order to engage in political behavior. Since interest-group membership is surprisingly rare in American politics, simply by virtue of their membership in these groups, these subjects may be predisposed to act on political issues. We might hypothesize that a generalized propensity to act (a propensity that may even be more general than just behavior within political contexts) exists and that it greatly affects the relationship between attitudes and behavior.

Certainly elements of the context of action must be better specified in future research. Issue salience surely influences the mobilization of attitudes into behavior (even if we could find no direct effect of levels of information on the relationship). Though it is trivial to assert that before people will act on an issue it must be perceived as salient, we have virtually no clues as to how issues penetrate the consciousness of citizens (even if we understand something about issue formation at the macro-level). Perhaps opinion leaders, the media, and organized interest groups like the ACLU are especially crucial here, but maybe only as a necessary but not sufficient condition for issue awareness. Those who make even the most modest contributions to interest groups soon find themselves bombarded with requests for money and for action, but no existing theory considers how and they these various stimuli have such a greatly varied ability to generate a behavioral response. Generally, though, it seems that for many, political participation is far more issue-specific than is suggested by the general modes of participation perspective that is commonly accepted among those who study political participation.

Opportunities for action must also moderate the attitude-behavior relationship. Knowing how to act is not terribly easy once participation other than voting is attempted. Information costs—the names and addresses of elected representatives—may also paralyze behavior. Many of those motivated to act may simply be unable to overcome the logistical barriers to action.

Finally, this analysis suggests that attitudes may have consequences for public policy. It is on this important issue that we conclude this book.

NOTES

1. We do not mean to beg the question of whether attitudes have any real existence in the first place. Our argument is equally cogent in asserting that attitudes are more easily created than behavior at the point of measurement (cf. Converse, 1970).

2. Not all citizens of the countries of the world have so few opportunities, as the recent Egyptian referendum on the rights of Moslem fundamentalists, Coptic Christians, and other miscellaneous malcontents reveals.

3. There is some direct effect of knowledge on behavior. For instance, gamma for self-reports of the amount of information about Skokie and the likelihood of ACLU members engaging in tolerant behavior is .38; for intolerant behavior, gamma is .26. However, omitting those with low familiarity from the analysis changes the results shown in Figure 7.1 and Table 7.3 very little.

Another 2 to 5 percent of the variance can be explained by weighting the opinion variables by reports on the amount of information held on the dispute in general, the ordinances, and on ACLU's role, suggesting that "salience weights" may be somewhat useful in predicting behavior.

4. Much of the experimental literature on the attitude-behavior relationship focuses upon behavior that is "forced" (for an exception see Bentler and Speckart, 1979). That is, the subjects are required, usually within an experimental situation, to emit some behavior. Appropriately then, the research problem is concerned with attitude-behavior consistency. In this research, and in the real-world in general, non-behavior is a completely viable and well-used option. Thus, any understanding of the attitude-behavior relationship must also incorporate some explanation of the factor's influencing the mobilization of attitudes into behavior.

5. Creating a summary measure of tolerance is essential in order to make the fairly complex analysis of contextual effects manageable. The most useful such measure is derived from the regression analysis reported in Figure 7.1 and Table 7.3 above. If we assume that an attitude is a behavioral propensity, a propensity that must interact with contextual factors in order to produce actual behavior, we can then use the predicted value (Y hat) from the multivariate regression of the trichotomized behavior variable on the eight attitude and opinion measures. These predicted values represent the behavior expected on the basis of the particular configuration of civil liberties attitudes held by the subject, and will be referred to as attitudinal tolerance. The continuous predicted values were collapsed into categories that are .1 standard deviation in width to facilitate presentation of the results of the analysis. (Correlations of this variable with the factor score resulting from a factor analysis of the eight attitude and opinion variables exceed .9 for each of the three groups.) For ACLU members, the correlations of the variable with the three behavior indicators reported in Table 7.2 above are: .49, .32, and .47. With the tolerant-intolerant behavior dichotomy, the correlation is .85. The correlations for members of Common Cause are similar; those for ACLU leaders are somewhat weaker, probably as a result of attenuated variance because few engaged in intolerant behavior.

6. It should be noted that these curves fit the cell percentages quite well, explaining 82, 86, and 87 percent of the variance among non-Jews, secular Jews and religious Jews, respectively.

7. We have no direct evidence of this, but some inferential support can be adduced. For instance, Jews are much more likely to report World War II experience with the Nazis. They also claim in significantly greater numbers to have watched the television program "Holocaust." Both of these factors probably increased the perceived degree of threat from the Nazis. Nazis and the Skokie-Nazi controversy are undoubtedly more salient to Jews than to non-Jews. The data also reveal a relationship between religion and general and specific knowledge about the Skokie dispute. For instance, 61 percent of the Jewish ACLU members claimed to be "very familiar" with the Skokie-Nazi dispute, while only 38 percent of the non-Jews claimed a similar level of familiarity.

Although the differences are not great, Jews seem to be somewhat more threatened by the Nazis than non-Jews. They are more likely to believe that if the Nazis were in power in the United States they "would create a totally different and much worse system of government." For example, among ACLU members 79 percent of the non-Jews but 91 percent of the religious Jews gave this response. On the other hand, Jews are little more likely to perceive a higher probability of Nazis achieving political power. For example, 72 percent of the non-Jews and 69 percent of the religious Jews think it extremely or very unlikely that the Nazis will have any impact upon the American political system in the foreseeable future. The implication of these data is fairly obvious: Jews are as realistic as non-Jews in assessing the political efficacy of American Nazis, but, because of their historical experiences, are somewhat more likely to appreciate the catastrophic consequences of Nazis achieving power.

8. Several other conditional relationships were considered using the basic model $Y = a + bX + bC + bXC$, where $X =$ the attitude variable and $C =$ the conditional variable. Conditional variables evaluated include: (1) experience with the Nazis during World War II; (2) reports of having viewed the television showing of "Holocaust"; (3) organizational involvement; and (4) general satisfaction and agreement with the organization. None of these is a significant predictor of tolerant or intolerant behavior.

8   Conclusions and Implications

A number of previous studies have investigated political tolerance. Research has been conducted on the degree of tolerance in mass and elite opinion, on the degree of tolerance of public policy, including constitutional policy, and on the level of political freedom in society. But no single research project has pursued a complete model of political tolerance in the way in which we have. We began by conceptualizing political tolerance as generalized attitudes and have traced the consequences of these attitudes for opinion on a specific civil liberties conflict. We have then examined the linkages among attitudes, opinions, and political behavior. The effect of that behavior on organizational policy and action has also been considered. Finally, after describing public policy on the matter, we have considered the effect of the actions of an interest group on the allocation of rights and freedom by the political system. All of this has been presented within the context of a broader *micro-level* theory of the relationship between attitudes and behavior and within the context of a broader *macro-level* theory of the role of citizens, elites, groups, and institutions in the construction of public policy. Thus, this research is truly cross-level in focus.

It remains in this chapter to take a step away from the data and to consider more fully the macro- and micro-level implications of the findings. We shall begin at the micro-level.

MICRO-LEVEL IMPLICATIONS

In this research we have reported a new approach to the conceptualization and measurement of the political tolerance concept. Adopting an approach quite different from that used in previous research, we conceptualize tolerance as a multidimensional syndrome of beliefs. Each of these beliefs—in our case, support for freedom of speech, support for freedom of assembly, and support for freedom of political association—has been measured through multiple indicators, with the application of appropriate scaling techniques. Moreover, the specific measures are not abstract; nor are they devoid of specific content. Instead, the items reflect some of the conflict associated with actual civil liberties disputes. We have presented scales that are more reliable and valid measures of political tolerance.

We have also shown that the individual elements within the tolerance belief system are interrelated and constrained. The degree of association among the items is not extraordinary, but we have argued that, unless correlations are calculated among multiple indicators of a single tolerance dimension, very high correlations are not to be expected among the politically sophisticated. Though we have not been able to pursue the question of tolerance belief systems too thoroughly—we do not have, for instance, data on the temporal stability of the responses to these items—the analysis reported here represents a more sophisticated attempt at applying theories of belief-system structure to political tolerance attitudes.

It has also been shown that these generalized attitudes have implications for opinions on specific civil liberties conflicts. The "abstract-concrete" problem, we argue, has been misconstrued as a matter of logical consistency, when in fact it ought to be treated as a matter of empirical relationship between generalized attitudes and specific opinions. Obviously, opinion on a specific dispute reflects far more than generalized attitudes; a variety of variables associated with perceptions of the particular context of the dispute are important. Thus, our finding that approximately one-half of the variance in opinions on the Skokie-Nazi dispute can be explained by more generalized attitudes is about what should be expected. Opinion formation represents a process of adjudicating conflict among conflicting general attitudes far more than it represents the deductive application of principles to specific cases.

Most importantly, we have shown that these tolerance attitudes and opinions have substantial consequences for actual political behavior. The relationships are not simple; although we should not forget that, among those who acted, over *three-fourths* of the variance in behavior can be accounted for through a simple attitude-opinion model. Generally, when behavior occurs it is consistent with attitudes, but it is not always possible to predict when action will take place. The model we propose is one that posits that contextual stimuli—perceptions of actual civil liberties conflicts—raise and lower hurdles to engaging in behavior. Some contexts make it easier to engage in behavior; others make it more difficult. Our analysis has uncovered some limited support for this model, although it is perhaps not as strong as we initially expected. At least we have shown that tolerance attitudes are important for substantive political behavior, even if we are still somewhat unclear as to the precise pathways of influence.

In substantive terms, our analysis has discovered several somewhat unexpected conclusions. First, as with previous research, we find substantial differences in political tolerance between elites and masses, with elites being more tolerant than masses. But, using more valid measures of political tolerance, we see that a democratic consensus among political influentials does not always exist. The leaders of the ACLU are virtually unanimous on most tolerance issues and within the ACLU membership an extraordinary democratic majority frequently materializes. But Common Cause members, perhaps more representative of general opinion leaders and political influentials, are rarely united in support of democratic rights. This finding, as well as several others, had led us to a reconceptualization of the elitist theory of democracy (see the macro-level section below).

Secondly, the Skokie-Nazi conflict should be perceived as a free assembly, not free speech conflict. And while it appeared that the dispute made quite difficult demands on civil libertarians wishing to be true to their philosophies, in fact the Skokie-Nazi conflict was not nearly so difficult a case for most. More inconsistency was observed among those who were expected on the basis of their general attitudes to *support* the Village than was observed among those with more tolerant attitudes. For most ACLU and Common Cause members, the free speech/free assembly issues raised in the Skokie-Nazi affair were relatively easily subsumed under more general theories of the rights of political minorities.

A great deal of additional work on the micro-level model we have employed is necessary. In particular, it is important to determine how substantive attitudes influence perceptions of particular contexts and the precise manner in which perceptions and attitudes interact in shaping behavior. This is an onerous task, in part because it is so difficult to anticipate the manner in which disputes will be perceived. We have shown, for example, that the Skokie-Nazi dispute was perceived primarily in free assembly, not free speech, terms. More specifically, opinions and actions were shaped not so much by a fear of violence were the Nazis to demonstrate in Skokie—although these fears had an important indirect effect on the relationships—as by the belief that communities have the right to be free from demonstrations by "outsiders." Chicago was a more acceptable locale for the Nazi demonstration, not so much because of its heterogeneity or because it was not inhabited by hundreds of Holocaust survivors, but because *the Nazis lived there.* In order to understand how citizens react to disputes of this nature it is essential that future research focus on this problem of the formation of perceptions. Our research is largely inadequate on this question—we know little about how the various stimuli emanating from the dispute penetrated or failed to penetrate perceptual screens.

Perhaps the most important limitation of this research is its inability to account for the processes leading to the mobilization of attitudes into political behavior. There are countless instances in which some of those with seemingly identical attitudes acted while others did not. Certainly, interest groups play a vital role here, but even the processes of individual-group interaction are little understood. We simply have not made much progress in identifying the factors that catalyze behavior. We believe this to be an important priority for future research.

A host of other issues concerning political participation has not been addressed at all in this research. To what degree is political behavior simply a function of habit? To what degree does it reflect a more general propensity to act, a sort of personal dynamism? Is political behavior modality specific; that is, are there modes of political action that are favored by some but not by others? Outside the realm of voting, we have few rigorous models that are capable of predicting political activism. These and many other questions must be addressed in future micro-level research on behavioral intolerance.

MACRO-LEVEL IMPLICATIONS

The controversy in Skokie has been variously interpreted. Some believed that the ACLU was perilously harmed by its position on the issue, but they were clearly wrong, especially in the long-term consequences. More sophisticated analysts have seen in Skokie evidence that a tolerant elite consensus is *not* essential to the maintenance of civil liberties; that is, that the elitist theory of democracy is in need of major revision. David Barnum is the major proponent of this last view so we will give more detailed consideration to his position.

Barnum's analysis of the role of local elites in the Skokie-Nazi controversy drew several major conclusions. First, an *anti-democratic* consensus existed in Skokie:

> ...the consensus itself was essentially unanimous among public officials and community leaders in Skokie. It endorsed the propriety of committing all of the available resources of the Village of Skokie to the battle to prevent the Nazis from marching in the community. (Barnum, 1982, p. 498)

Local elites may have initially supported the rights of the Nazis but quickly succumbed to anti-democratic pressure.

> In the Skokie case, the general public, spearheaded by a vocal minority of citizens who felt particularly strongly that the Nazis should not be allowed to come to Skokie, was able to force the political elites to abandon any pretense of support for the right of the Nazis to march or even for the position that the Nazis should be allowed to come to Skokie but be ignored. Moreover, the general public, spearheaded by a vocal minority, was able to pressure the political elites to explore every possible avenue to action to prevent the Nazis from coming to Skokie. (Barnum, 1982, pp. 502–03)

Second, however, few argued in favor of illegal means of oppressing the Nazis:

> At the same time, however, the consensus did not endorse the use of all possible *means* to prevent the Nazis from marching in Skokie. In fact, it endorsed only the use of legal means.... Therefore, the consensus, while it was unapologetically 'antidemocratic' on the free speech issues involved, it was scrupulously 'democratic' on the remaining constitutional and political issues in the case. (Barnum, 1982, p. 498)

But legal avenues for oppressing the Nazis were unlikely to be successful, largely because of the power of the courts:

> What is clear is that the structural characteristics of the American democracy [non-accountable courts] permit elected officials and other public officials to withhold consensual support for a democratic norm such as the right of unpopular groups to hold peaceful demonstrations—indeed to join in a popular challenge to such a norm—without necessarily jeopardizing the prospect that the norm itself will be duly applied to a specific situation. (Barnum, 1982, p. 501)

Barnum concludes his analysis with the suggestion that the elitist theory of democracy be modified:

The assumption that consensual support, or at least majority support, for a democratic norm among the political elites is a prerequisite to its application must be replaced by a new set of tentative hypotheses. The first would seem to be that politically insulated institutions such as courts must be available to assume responsibility for the resolution of civil liberties issues and that without such politically insulated institutions, the application of democratic norms to specific situations cannot be guaranteed. The second hypothesis would seem to be that the existence of judicial mechanisms for resolving civil liberties disputes must be accompanied by something like consensual support among the political elites for the propriety of resorting to the courts and the necessity of accepting, without question, the policy determinations of the courts. Thus, it may be that in excep-tionally tense and intractable civil liberties controversies—of which the Skokie case was certainly an example—it will not be the inter-vention of the political elites, as such, but rather the mutually beneficial interplay of the political elites and the courts, to which the successful application of a democratic norm must be attributed. (Barnum, 1982, p. 504)

Barnum's analysis is an excellent contribution to our understanding of how democracies maintain democracy. The elitist theory of democracy actually proposes a relatively simple-minded process to protect demo-cracy. Barnum complicates the model considerably, especially in pointing to four major considerations that lead to democratic outcomes in disputes of the rights of political minorities. These are:

the relatively widespread support for the application of democratic norms to specific situations among the political elites, the tendency of the public to refrain from translating its attitudes into actions, the arcane and arduous character of the policy-making process, and the residual support for democratic norms in the abstract among the general public.... (Barnum, 1982, p. 506)

Thus, much more than elite support for civil liberties is necessary.

Nonetheless, Barnum is insufficiently sensitive to several factors. First, the traditional elitist view of the masses was supported to some degree by the Skokie controversy. The initial reaction of the majority in Skokie was anti-democratic; it was to determine a way in which the rights of the Nazis could be circumscribed. The initial response of the elites was democratic; it was to determine a way to minimize the damage of allowing the Nazis to demonstrate. It is only the extreme degree of arousal of the mass public that led to pressure on the elite to adopt anti-democratic proposals. Thus the traditional hypothesis of the elitist theory of democracy to the effect that aroused masses contribute to anti-democratic demands on the political system receives some support from the events in Skokie.

It is possible that local elites in Skokie acted in as democratic a fashion as was possible under the circumstances. Failure to respond to the demands of the residents of Skokie would have been politically suicidal, and, more importantly, would not have been effective in achieving a democratic outcome to the dispute. A cagey democrat might well have done just what the Skokie officials did—draft legislation that was patently unconstitutional, urge the citizens of Skokie to allow the issue to be submitted to the courts, and demand of citizens that they accept the decision of the courts, even though, in the end, there was such a high probability that courts would overturn the ordinances and allow the demonstration. *The elitist theory of democracy does not assert that elites will always be successful in insuring a democratic outcome. Instead, it asserts that elites will attempt to mold public policy to as democratic a position as is possible under the circumstances.*

Barnum is also too insensitive to the function of non-local elites in civil liberties disputes. Elitism relies to a considerable degree on some form of pluralism; that is, it postulates that the anti-democratic tendencies of the elite, which are, after all, less than the masses but not zero, will be checked by other elites, preventing tyranny through elite hegemony. Sullivan, Piereson, and Marcus are strong proponents of this point of view. However plural the national elites in the United States may be, few would argue that local elites represent such a diversity of viewpoints. Clearly, they did not in Skokie. Thus, it is not clear that the elitist theory of democracy predicts that *local* disputes will be resolved in a democratic fashion.

It is at this point that our research makes an empirical contribution. Two important conclusions follow from our analysis:

1. While the citizens and leaders of Skokie may have been consensual *in their opposition to* extending the rights of free speech and assembly to the Nazis, the national elite, at least the segment of the elite represented by members and leaders of the ACLU, was consensual *in support of* the rights (even if it is not always consensual on all issues).

2. The ACLU received considerable (indeed, consensual) support from its membership on the question of whether to defend the rights of the Nazis.

In general, in research of this sort it is important that the specific elite be clearly identified, since it is not at all uncommon for national and local elites to differ on issues involving the application of democratic principles. At least since the early 1960s, the national elite has been more supportive than local elites of the rights of political minorities. Both in terms of the elite resocialization hypothesis (i.e., socialization to a predominantly democratic national elite subculture—e.g., Key, 1961) and in terms of the acquisition of experience with democratic processes and procedures (e.g., negotiation, compromise, exposure to and tolerance of diversity), the national elite ought to be more tolerant and democratic. Indeed, a reasonable hypothesis is that local rights conflicts are most likely to reach a democratic conclusion when they become salient enough to attract national attention. Skokie was a case that supports this hypothesis.

But it is wrong to assume that a unified national elite is always available to enforce the rights of political minorities. It is not difficult to find instances of national elites engaging in and supporting political repression. For instance, who was responsible for the repressive legislation and other activity so infamously associated with the "red menace" of the late 1940s and early 1950s? It is true that a majority of mass citizens would not tolerate communists in the 1950s. But the "menace" was *not* salient to the masses. Stouffer (1955, p. 85) reports that 30 percent of his mass sample could not come up with a single correct name, not even Senator McCarthy's name, when asked to identify "any of the Senators or Congressmen who have been taking a leading part in [the congressional committees investigating Communism]"—so it can hardly be said that the repression represented the preferences of a mobilized mass public. He also reports that local influentials were strongly supportive of extending political rights to Communists. Most likely, then, it was the national elite, *acting without stimulation from a mobilized mass public,* that was responsible. Indeed, recent analyses of the era document the widespread agreement on the part of liberal and conservative leaders on the desirability of oppressing leftists (e.g., Navasky, 1980 and Caute, 1978). While it may be generally true that the national elite is more supportive than the local elite of the rights of political minorities, there are frequent and well-documented instances of substantial portions of the national elite failing to support democratic norms. Elite self-interest generates general support for minority rights, but minorities that challenge elite hegemony rarely are the beneficiaries of elite support.

Two dimensions to the dispute deserve mention as a possible corollary to the elitist theory of democracy. First, a democratic resolution to rights conflicts necessitates the availability of powerful political institutions accessible to the minority and insulated from the majority. It is no wonder that the state trial courts, the least insulated of the judicial institutions involved in the dispute, were the most receptive to the appeals of the Village. Yet the courts alone were insufficient to insure a democratic outcome. Instead, the role of the national elite in supporting political tolerance was crucial. As Barnum notes, the most democratic action of the Skokie elites was to urge that the issue be submitted to the courts and that the decision of the courts be obeyed. But how can civil liberties disputes reach the courts in the first place? Since political minorities rarely command the resources necessary to take advantage of even the minoritarian arenas, the role of active interest groups with resources is critical. The judiciary is accessible to minorities, but not to impoverished minorities. Without the ACLU's involvement in Skokie, the ordinances might still exist, and certainly Frank Collin would not have been permitted to hold his demonstration in either Skokie or Chicago. This in turn suggests that it is not elite *consensus* that is important to the maintenance of democratic rights, but rather that it is necessary that there be some resourceful democratic segment of the elite, even if only a minority.

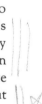

The democratic outcome in Skokie was obviously abetted by the existence of a non-accountable judiciary and some of the other factors that Barnum identifies. But perhaps the most significant factor was the willingness of the American Civil Liberties Union to pursue Frank Collin's case. This required not only a strong commitment to civil liberties on the part of the ACLU elites, but also a strong commitment on the part of the leaders of the Union *not* to respond to what they viewed as (even if viewed erroneously) the anti-democratic demands of at least a large portion, if not a majority, of their members. *If the internal politics of the ACLU had been more democratic, the outcome in the Skokie case would have been less democratic.*

Thus, the structure of organizations themselves may contribute to the maintenance of democratic rights. The "iron law of oligarchy" suggests that interest groups will not necessarily adopt positions consistent with the desires of a majority of the members of the group. Our data reveal that ACLU leaders were nearly unanimous on the Skokie dispute, while a significant minority of ACLU members opposed the position of the organization. The implications of one-fifth of the leaders dissenting from the organization's position are more substantial than those of dissent by one-fifth of the members. However, the very processes associated with the leadership of groups may contribute to greater tolerance and support for democratic rights. Thus, more representative groups may be less effective at mobilizing organizational resources in defense of the rights of unpopular minorities.

The maintenance of democracy may not depend upon a democratic local elite; nor may it require a *consensus* among the national elite. Instead, the existence of a resourceful and democratic segment of the national elite may be sufficient, so long as local disputes are capable of capturing the attention of this elite.

It is interesting that the elitist theory of democracy postulates the necessity of elite *consensus* over the rules of the democratic game. Certainly, elitism does not argue that in other areas of public policy the elite must be consensual before action is taken, or, perhaps more importantly, not taken. And obviously, there is a great deal of diversity in the democratic commitments of various segments of the elite (e.g., McClosky and Brill, 1983). Just as public policy is generally responsive to the preferences of minorities, it is easy to imagine that policy on the rights of political opposition are also responsive to the preferences of a minority of the elite.

The Skokie incident and these data provide nothing more than a limited empirical base for speculation about the prerequisites of democracy. However, the elitist theory of democracy is far more widely accepted than its scientific support would suggest. Before the theory is to achieve any scientific status it is necessary that it be subjected to much more extensive and rigorous testing.

In many respects the dispute in Skokie, Illinois, over the rights of a handful of Nazis seems insignificant. Though perhaps unimportant in itself, the dispute is theoretically fecund because it crystallizes many of the most relevant and difficult issues of politics and democracy. As we begin to understand the processes of rights conflicts, perhaps new insights into the oldest questions of political science will emerge. We hope that our analysis of the Skokie-Nazi conflict contributes to that understanding.

References

Abelson, Robert P. 1982. "Three Modes of Attitude-Behavior Consistency." In *Consistency in Social Behavior. The Ontario Symposium.* Volume 2. Edited by Mark P. Zanna, E. Tory Higgins, and C. Peter Herman. Hillsdale, N.J.: Lawrence Erlbaum Associates, Publishers, pp. 131–46.

Bagehot, Walter. 1966. *The English Constitution.* (With an Introduction by R. H. S. Crossman.) Ithaca, N.Y.: Cornell University Press. (Originally published in 1867.)

Bagozzi, Richard P., and Robert E. Burnkrant. 1979. "Attitude organization and the attitude-behavior relationship," *Journal of Personality and Social Psychology* 37:913–29.

Barnum, David G. 1982. "Decision making in a constitutional democracy: policy formation in the Skokie free speech controversy." *Journal of Politics* 44:480–508.

Bell, Leland V. 1973. *In Hitler's Shadow: The Anatomy of American Nazism.* Port Washington, N.Y.: Kennikat.

Bem, Daryl J. 1972. "Self-perception theory." In L. Berkowitz (ed.), *Advances in experimental social psychology.* Vol. 6. New York: Academic Press.

Bem, Daryl J., and David C. Funder. 1978. "Predicting more of the people more of the time: assessing the personality of situations." *Psychological Review* 85:485–501.

Bennett, Stephen Earl. 1973. "Consistency among the public's social welfare policy attitudes during the 1960s," *American Journal of Political Science* 17:544–70.

Bennett, W. Lance. 1977. "The growth of knowledge in mass belief studies: an epistemological critique," *American Journal of Political Science* 3:465–500.

Bentler, P. M., and George Speckart. 1979. "Models of attitude-behavior relations," *Psychological Review* 86:452–64.

Bishop, George F., Alfred J. Tuchfarber, and Robert W. Oldendick. 1978. "Change in the structure of American political attitudes: the nagging question of question wording," *American Journal of Political Science* 22:250–69.

Bishop, George F., Alfred J. Tuchfarber, Robert W. Oldendick, and Stephen E. Bennett. 1979. "Questions about question wording: a rejoinder to revisiting mass belief systems revisited," *American Journal of Political Science* 23:187–92.

Borgida, Eugene, and Bruce Campbell. 1982. "Belief Relevance and Attitude-Behavior Consistency," *Journal of Personality and Social Psychology* 1982:239–47.

Brown, Steven R. 1970. "Consistency and the persistence of ideology: some experimental results." *Public Opinion Quarterly* 34:60–68.

Campbell, Angus, Philip E. Converse, Warren E. Miller, and Donald E. Stokes. 1960. *The American Voter.* New York: John Wiley and Sons.

Campbell, Donald T. 1963. "Social attitudes and other acquired behavioral dispositions," in *Psychology: A Study of a Science. Study II. Empirical Substructure and Relations with Other Sciences. Vol. 6. Investigations of Man as Socius: Their Place in Psychology and the Social Sciences,* edited by Sigmund J. Koch. New York: McGraw-Hill Book Company.

Caute, David. 1978. *The Great Fear: The Anti-Communist Purge Under Truman and Eisenhower.* New York: Simon and Schuster.

Chicagoland's Community Guide. 1970. Chicago: Law Bulletin Publishing Co.

Converse, Philip E. 1964. "The nature of belief systems in mass publics." In *Ideology and Discontent,* edited by David Apter. New York: The Free Press.

Converse, Philip E. 1970. "Attitudes and non-attitudes: continuation of a dialogue." In *The Quantitative Analysis of Social Problems,* edited by Edward Tufte. Reading, Mass.: Addison-Wesley, pp. 165–89.

Converse, Philip E. 1975. "Public opinion and voting behavior." In *Handbook of Political Science,* Volume 4, edited by Nelson W. Polsby. Reading, Mass.: Addison-Wesley, pp. 75–169.

Converse, Philip E., and Gregory B. Marcus. 1979. "Plus ça change...: the new CPS election study," *American Political Science Review* 73:32–49.

Cutler, Stephen J., and Robert L. Kaufman. 1975. "Cohort changes in political attitudes: tolerance of ideological nonconformity," *Public Opinion Quarterly* 39:69–81.

Dahl, Robert A. 1961. *Who governs?.* New Haven: Yale University Press.

Dahl, Robert A. 1971. *Polyarchy: participation and opposition.* New Haven: Yale University Press.

Davis, James A. 1975. "Communism, conformity, cohorts, and categories: American tolerance in 1954 and 1972–73," *American Journal of Sociology* 81:491-513.

DeFleur, Melvin L., and Frank R. Westie. 1958. "Verbal Attitudes and Overt Actions: An Experiment on the Salience of Attitudes." *American Sociological Review* 23:667–73.

Easton, David. 1965. *A Systems Analysis of Political Life.* New York: John Wiley and Sons.

Fazio, R., and M. Zanna. 1978. "Attitudinal qualities relating to the strength of the attitude-behavior relationship." *Journal of Experimental Social Psychology* 14:398–408.

Field, John O., and Ronald E. Anderson. 1969. "Ideology in the public's conceptualization of the 1964 election." *Public Opinion Quarterly* 33:380-98

Fishbein, M., and I. Ajzen. 1975. *Belief, attitude, intention and behavior: an introduction to theory and research.* Reading, Mass.: Addison-Wesley.

Frideres, James. 1971. "Situational and personality variables as influencing the relationship between attitudes and overt behavior. *Canadian Review of Sociology and Anthropology* 8:91-105.

Frideres, James, Lyle G. Warner and Stan L. Albrecht. 1971. "The impact of social constraints on the relationship between attitudes and behavior." *Social Forces* 50:102-12.

Gibson, James L. 1978. "Judges' role orientations, attitudes, and decisions: an interactive model. *American Political Science Review* 72:911-24.

Hamlin, David. 1978. "Swastikas & survivors: inside the Skokie-Nazi free speech case." *The Civil Liberties Review* 4:8-33.

Hamlin, David. 1980. *The Nazi/Skokie conflict: a civil liberties battle.* Boston: Beacon Press.

Hand, Learned. 1959. *The Spirit of Liberty: Papers and Addresses.* (Collected with an Introduction and Notes by Irving Dilliard.) New York: Knopf.

Herzon, Frederick D. 1980. "Ideology, constraint, and public opinion: the case of lawyers," *American Journal of Political Science* 24:233-58.

Inglehart, Ronald. 1977. *The silent revolution: changing values and political styles among western publics.* Princeton: Princeton University Press.

————.1980. "Post-Materialism in an Environment of Insecurity." *American Political Science Review* 75:880-900.

Jackman, Robert W. 1972. "Political elites, mass publics, and support for democratic principles." *Journal of Politics* 34:753-73.

Jackman, Mary R. 1978. "General and Applied Tolerance: Does Education Increase Commitment to Racial Integration?" *American Journal of Political Science* 22:302-24.

Jackman, Mary R. 1981. "Education and Policy Commitment to Racial Integration," *American Journal of Political Science* 25:256-269.

Jennings, M. Kent, and Richard G. Niemi. 1981. *Generations and Politics: A Panel Study of Young Adults and Their Parents.* Princeton, N.J.: Princeton University Press.

Kahle, Lynn R., and John J. Berman. 1979. "Attitudes Cause Behaviors: A Cross-Lagged Panel Analysis," *Journal of Personality and Social Psychology* 37:315-21.

Key, V.O., Jr., 1961. *Public Opinion and American Democracy.* New York: Alfred A. Knopf.

Kish, Leslie. 1965. *Survey Sampling.* New York: John Wiley.

Lane, Robert E. 1962. *Political Ideology.* New York: The Free Press.

LaPiere, R.T. 1934. "Attitudes vs. Actions." *Social Forces* 13:230–34.

Lawrence, David G. 1976. "Procedural Norms and Tolerance: A Reassessment," *American Political Science Review* 70:80–100.

League of Women Voters, 1959. *This is Skokie.* Skokie, Ill.: League of Women Voters.

Lipset, Seymour Martin. 1960. *Political Man.* New York: Doubleday.

Lucas, J. Anthony. 1978. "The ACLU Against Itself." *New York Times Magazine* (July 9), pp. 9–11, 18, 20, 26–28, 30–31.

Luttbeg, Norman. 1968. "The Structure of Beliefs Among Leaders and the Public," *Public Opinion Quarterly* 32:398–409.

Madsen, Douglas and D.L. Sheth. 1977. "Non-Attitudes among Political Leaders: Some Evidence from a Panel Study." *Political Methodology* 4:119–37.

Mann, Jim. 1978. "Hard Times for the ACLU," *The New Republic* (April 15), 12–15.

Marcus, George, David Tabb, and John L. Sullivan. 1974. "The Application of Individual Differences Scaling to the Measurement of Political Ideologies," *American Journal of Political Science* 18:405–20.

Marcus, Gregory B. 1979. "The Political Environment and the Dynamics of Public Attitudes: A Panel Study," *American Journal of Political Science* 23:338–59.

Margolis, Michael, and Khondaker E. Haque. 1981. "Applied Tolerance or Fear of Government? An Alternative Interpretation of Jackman's Findings," *American Journal of Political Science* 25:241–55.

Maslow, A.H. 1954. *Motivation and Personality.* New York: Harper and Row.

McClosky, Herbert. 1964. "Consensus and ideology in American politics." *American Political Science Review* 58:361–82.

McClosky, Herbert, and Alida Brill. 1983. *Dimensions of tolerance: what Americans believe about civil liberties.* New York: Russell Sage Foundation.

McClosky, Herbert, and Dennis Chong. 1980. "The Learning of Civil Libertarian Norms Among Elites and the Mass Public." Paper delivered at the 1980 Annual meeting of the Western Political Science Association.

McGuire, William J. 1976. The concept of attitudes and their relations to behaviors. In H.W. Sinaiko and L.A. Broedling (eds.), *Perspectives on attitude assessment: surveys and their alternatives.* Champaign, Ill.: Pendleton.

Mill, John Stuart. 1956. *On Liberty.* Edited, with an introduction, by Currin V. Shields. Indianapolis: The Bobbs-Merrill Company, Inc. (Originally published in 1859).

Miller, Warren E., and Donald E. Stokes. 1964. "Constituency influence in congress." *American Political Science Review* 57:45–56.

Muller, Edward N. 1979. *Aggressive political participation.* Princeton: Princeton University Press.

Muller, Edward N., and Mitchell A. Seligson. 1982. "Support for Liberal and Civil Libertarian Conceptions of Democracy." Paper delivered at the 1982 Annual Meeting of the Western Political Science Association.

Muller, Edward N., Thomas O. Jukam and Mitchell A. Seligson. 1982. "Diffuse political support and antisystem political behavior: a comparative analysis." *American Journal of Political Science* 26:240-64.

Navasky, Victor S. 1980. *Naming Names.* New York: The Viking Press.

Neier, Aryeh. 1979. *Defending My Enemy: American Nazis, the Skokie Case, and the Risks of Freedom.* New York: E.P. Dutton.

Nie, Norman, with Christi Andersen. 1974. "Mass Belief Systems Revisited: Political Change and Attitude Structure." *Journal of Politics* 36:540-91.

Nie, Norman H. and James N. Rabjohn. 1979. "Revisiting Mass Belief Systems Revisited: Or, Doing Research Is Like Watching a Tennis Match," *American Journal of Political Science* 23:139-75.

Nunn, Clyde Z., Harry J. Crockett, Jr., and J. Allen Williams, Jr. 1978. *Tolerance for Nonconformity.* San Francisco: Jossey-Bass Publishers.

Oskamp, Stuart. 1977. *Attitudes and Opinions.* Englewood Cliffs, N.J.: Prentice Hall.

Page, Benjamin I., and Robert Y. Shapiro. 1983. "Effects of public opinion on public policy." *American Political Science Review* 77:175-90.

Pierce, John C. 1970. "Party Identification and the Changing Role of Ideology in American Politics," *Midwest Journal of Political Science* 16:25-42.

Pierce, John C., and Douglas D. Rose. 1974. "Nonattitudes and American Public Opinion: Examination of a Thesis," *American Political Science Review* 68:626-66.

Prothro, James W., and Charles M. Grigg. 1960. "Fundamental Principles of Democracy: Bases of Agreement and Disagreement," *Journal of Politics* 22:276-94.

Rockwell, George Lincoln. 1963. *This Time the World.* (no location) J.V. Kenneth Morgan.

Sarat, Austin. 1975. "Reasoning in Politics: The Social, Political, and Psychological Bases of Principled Thought," *American Journal of Political Science* 19:247-61.

Schlegel, Ronald P., and Don DiTecco. 1982. "Attitudinal structures and the attitude-behavior relation." In *Consistency in social behavior: The Ontario symposium.* Volume 2. Edited by Mark P. Zanna, E. Tory Higgins, and C. Peter Herman. Hillsdale, N.J.: Lawrence Erlbaum Associates, Publishers.

Schlozman, Kay Lehman, and Sidney Verba. 1979. *Injury to Insult: Unemployment, Class, and Political Response.* Cambridge, Mass.: Harvard University Press.

Schubert, Glendon 1965. *The judicial mind.* New York: Oxford University Press.

Schubert, Glendon. 1974. *The Judicial Mind Revisited* (New York: Oxford University Press).

Skokie Chamber of Commerce. 1977. *Skokie, Illinois.* Skokie, Ill.: Chamber of Commerce.

Skolnick, Jerome H. 1967. "Social Control in the Adversary System." *Journal of Conflict Resolution* 11:52–70.

Sniderman, Paul M. 1975. *Personality and Democratic Politics.* Berkeley: University of California Press.

Stouffer, Samuel C. 1955. *Communism, Conformity, and Civil Liberties.* New York: Doubleday.

Sullivan, John L., James E. Piereson, and George E. Marcus. 1978. "Ideological Constraint in the Mass Public: A Methodological Critique and Some New Findings." *American Journal of Political Science* 22:233–249.

—— 1979. "A Reconceptualization of Political Tolerance: Illusory Increases, 1950's–1970's," *American Political Science Review* 73:781–94.

—— 1982. *Political tolerance and American democracy.* Chicago: The University of Chicago Press.

Sullivan, John L., George E. Marcus, James E. Piereson, and Stanley Feldman. 1978–79. "The Development of Political Tolerance: The Impact of Social Class, Personality, and Cognition," *International Journal of Political Education* 2:115–39.

Sullivan, John L., James E. Piereson, George E. Marcus, and Stanley Feldman. 1979. "The More Things Change, the More They Remain the Same: Rejoinder of Nie and Rabjohn," *American Journal of Political Science* 23:176–86.

Sullivan, John L., George E. Marcus, Stanley Feldman, and James E. Piereson. 1981. "The Sources of Political Tolerance: A Multivariate Analysis," *American Political Science Review* 75:92–106.

Walker, Thomas G. 1978. *American Politics and the Constitution.* North Scituate, Mass.: Duxbury Press.

Wicker, Allen W. 1969. "Attitude Versus Action: The Relationship of Verbal and Overt Behavioral Responses to Attitude Objects," *Journal of Social Issues* 25:297–334.

Wray, J. Harry. 1979. "Comment on Interpretations of Early Research into Belief Systems." *Journal of Politics* 41:1173–84.

Zellman, Gail L. 1975. "Antidemocratic Beliefs: A Survey and Some Explanations." *Journal of Social Issues* 31:31–53.

Zanna, Mark P., E. Tory Higgins, and C. Peter Herman, eds. 1982. *Consistency in social behavior: the Ontario symposium.* Hillsdale, N.J.: Lawrence Erlbaum Associates, Publishers.

Appendix A   The Skokie Ordinances

ORDINANCE 994
AN ORDINANCE RELATING TO
PARADES AND PUBLIC ASSEMBLIES

WHEREAS, it is in the best interest of the Village of Skokie to provide for the safe and orderly movement of traffic and people so as to protect the residents of the Village of Skokie from disruption of essential services, such as fire protection, program participation, and the orderly pursuit of their activities.

WHEREAS, the President and Board of Trustees are of the opinion that the following regulations are necessary to provide for such purposes in order to promote the health, safety and welfare of the residents of the Village of Skokie.

NOW, THEREFORE, BE IT ORDAINED by the President and Board of Trustees of the Village of Skokie, Cook County, Illinois:

Sec. 1.   That Chapter 27 of the Code of Ordinances of the Village of Skokie be amended by the addition thereto of Article XIII Parades and Public Assemblies, as follows:

Article XIII   PARADES AND PUBLIC ASSEMBLIES

Sec. 27-51.   Permit Required.   No parade, public assembly or similar activity, where the number of participants expected may reasonably be assumed to exceed fifty (50) or more persons, and/or vehicles is permitted on any street or area of the Village unless a permit allowing such activity has been obtained from the Village Manager, or upon referral, to the President and Board of Trustees provided, however, that this Ordinance shall not apply to students going to and from school classes, or participating in educational activities under the immediate direction and supervision of school authorities or a governmental agency acting within the scope of its function, nor shall a permit be required for normal or scheduled activities of the Village.

Sec. 27-52. Application. Any person, partnership, voluntary association, corporation, or other organization seeking to obtain a parade or public assembly permit shall file an application with the Village Manager not more than ninety (90) days and not less than thirty days (30) before the date for which the parade, public assembly or similar activity is proposed.

Sec. 27-53. Contents. The application for a parade or public assembly permit shall contain the following information:

a) The name, address and phone number of the person signing the application.
b) If the parade, public assembly, or similar activity is proposed to be conducted for, on behalf of, or by an organization, the name, address, and phone number of the authorized and responsible leaders of the organization conducting the parade or public assembly, and name, address, and telephone number of the headquarters of the organization.
c) The date of the proposed parade or public assembly and the hours that it will commence and terminate.
d) The location of the assembly area and the time when the activity will begin to assemble.
e) The route to be travelled, starting point, and the termination point.
f) The approximate number of persons, animals and vehicles to participate in the parade, public assembly, or similar activity.
g) A statement as to whether the parade or public assembly will occupy all or only a portion of the width of the streets proposed to be traversed.
h) The interval of space to be maintained between units of such parade, public assembly or similar activity.
i) If the parade, public assembly or similar activity is designed to be held by and on behalf of, or for any person, partnership, voluntary association, corporation or other organization other than the applicant, the applicant for such permit shall file with the Village of Skokie a communication in writing from such person or from an authorized and responsible leader of such

organization authorizing the applicant to apply for the permit on behalf of such person or organization.

j) Any additional information which the Village Manager or President and Board of Trustees shall find reasonably necessary to a fair determination as to whether a permit should be issued.

Sec. 27-54. Insurance Required. No permit shall be issued to any applicant until such applicant procures Public Liability Insurance in an amount of not less than Three Hundred Thousand Dollars (300,000.00) and Property Damage Insurance of not less than Fifty Thousand Dollars (50,000.00). Prior to the issuance of the permit, certificates of such insurance must be submitted to the Village Manager for verification that the company issuing such insurance is authorized to do business and write policies of insurance in the State of Illinois.

Sec. 27-55. Late Applicants. The Village Manager or President and Board of Trustees, when good and compelling cause is shown therefor, may consider an application hereunder which is filed less than thirty (30) days before the date such parade, public assembly or similar activity is proposed to be conducted.

Sec. 27-56. Standards for Issuance. The Village Manager or President and Board of Trustees shall issue a permit as provided for hereunder when, from a consideration of the application and from such other information as may otherwise be obtained, it is found that:

a) The conduct of the parade will not substantially interfere with the safe and orderly movement of traffic in the area contiguous to the route.

b) The activity will not create an imminent danger of a substantial breach of the peace, riot, or similar disorder.

c) The conduct of the parade, public assembly, or similar activity will not portray criminality, depravity or lack of virtue in, or incite violence, hatred, abuse or hostility toward a person or group of persons by reason of reference to religious, racial, ethnic, national or regional affiliation.

d) There are available at the time of the parade, public assembly, or similar activity a sufficient number of peace officers to police and protect lawful participants in the activity and maintain adequate police protection in the rest of the Village of Skokie.

e) The concentration of persons, animals and vehicles at the assembly points of the parade, public assembly, or similar activity will not unduly interfere with the proper fire and police protection of, or ambulance service to areas contiguous to such assembly areas.

f) The activity will not interfere with scheduled Village functions or the normal pursuit of activities of the residents of the Village of Skokie.

g) The conduct of such parade, public assembly, or similar activity will not interfere with the movement of fire fighting equipment enroute to a fire.

h) The parade is scheduled to move from its point of origin to its point of termination expeditiously and without unreasonable delays enroute.

i) The parade, public assembly, or similar activity is not being conducted for an unlawful purpose or for the sole purpose of advertising any product, goods or event and is not designed to be held purely for private profit.

j) The applicant has complied fully with the insurance requirements set out in Section 5 of this Ordinance.

Sec. 27-57.   Time for Approval or Denial.   Following the receipt of an application or re-application, the Village Manager shall either within ten (10) working days, either issue such permit or deny same. In the event the Village Manager denies the application or re-application, the matter shall be referred to the President and Board of Trustees at a meeting scheduled not more than twenty-one (21) days after the denial of the permit application or at any special meeting of the President and Board of Trustees called for such purpose not more than twenty-one (21) days after the filing of the permit application. In the event the President and Board of Trustees concurs in the Village Manager's denial, the reasons therefor shall be stated and published in the minutes, and the Village Manager shall mail to the applicant within twenty-three (23) days after the date upon which the denial was made a notice of the action of the President and Board of Trustees stating the reasons for the denial of the permit. The action of the President and Board of Trustees shall be subject to judicial review in accordance with the provisions of the Administrative Review Act, Section 264 and subsequent sections of Chapter 110 of the Illinois Revised Statutes of 1975.

Sec. 27-58. Alternative Permit. The Village Manager or President and Board of Trustees in denying a permit application shall be empowered to authorize the conduct of a parade, public assembly, or similar activity on a date, at a time, at a location or over a route different from that named by the applicant. An applicant desiring to accept an alternate permit shall within two (2) days after notice of the action by the Village Manager and Board of Trustees file a written notice of acceptance with the Village Manager. An alternative permit shall conform to the requirements of and shall have the effect of a parade assembly permit.

Sec. 27-59. Notice to Officials. Immediately upon the issuance of a parade or public assembly permit, the Village Manager shall send a copy thereof to the following:

a) The Police Chief of the Village of Skokie.
b) The Fire Chief of the Village of Skokie.
c) The Corporation Counsel of the Village of Skokie.

Sec. 27-60. Contents of Permit. Each parade or public assembly permit shall state the following information:

a) Starting time.
b) Minimum speed.
c) Maximum speed.
d) Maximum interval of space to be maintained between the units of the parade or public assembly.
e) The portions of the streets to be traversed that may be occupied by the parade or public assembly.
f) The maximum length of the parade or public assembly in miles or fractions thereof.
g) Such other information as the Village Manager and Board of Trustees shall find necessary to insure the enforcement of this Ordinance.

Sec. 27-61. Duties of Permittee. A permittee hereunder shall comply with all permit directions and conditions and with all applicable laws and ordinances. One of the authorized and responsible leaders of the organization conducting the parade, public assembly or similar activity, shall carry the parade or public assembly permit upon his person during the conduct of the parade.

Sec. 27-62. Public Conduct During Parades, Public Assemblies or Similar Activities:

a) Interference.   No person shall unreasonably hamper, obstruct, impede or interfere with any parade, public assembly or similar activity, or with any person, vehicle or animal participating or used in such activity.

b) Driving Through Parades, Public Assemblies, or Similar Activities.   No driver of any vehicle shall drive between the vehicles or persons comprising a parade, public assembly, or similar activity when such vehicles or persons are in motion and are conspicuously designated as a parade, public assembly or similar activity; provided, however, that Fire and Police vehicles and ambulances may interrupt a parade in an emergency situation.

c) Parking on Parade or Public Assembly Route.   The Village Manager or President and Board of Trustees shall have the authority to prohibit or restrict the parking of vehicles along a highway or part thereof constituting a part of the route of a parade, public assembly, or similar activity. The Village Manager or President and Board of Trustees shall order the posting of signs to such effect and it shall be unlawful for any person to park or leave unattended any vehicle in violation thereof. No person shall be liable for parking on a street unposted in violation of the Ordinance.

Sec. 27-63.   Revocation of Permit.   The Village Manager or President and Board of Trustees shall have the authority to revoke a parade or public assembly permit issued hereunder if, at any time, facts are brought to the attention of the Village Manager or President and Board of Trustees which show that the parade, public assembly, or similar activity does not, or will not, comply with the standards for issuance as herein set forth.

Sec. 27-64.   Waiver of Provisions.   The President and Board of Trustees may, with the consent of all members of the Board present at any meeting thereof, waive any provision of this ordinance.

Sec. 27-65.   Penalties.   Any person who knowingly interferes with any person or organization lawfully conducting a parade or public assembly, or any person violating any of the provisions of this Ordinance shall be fined not less than Five Dollars ($5.00) nor more than Five Hundred Dollars ($500.00) for each offense.

Sec. 27-66. Separability. If any provision contained in this Ordinance is found to be invalid, such provision shall be deemed to be separable and shall not affect the validity of any of the remaining provisions of this Ordinance.

Sec. 27-67. Ordinance Repealed. All ordinances or provisions of ordinances in conflict with this Ordinance or any of the provisions of this Ordinance, are hereby repealed to the extent that they conflict with this Ordinance or any provision of this Ordinance.

Section 2. This Ordinance shall be in full force and effect from and after its passage, approval and publication, as required by law.

Adopted this 2nd day of May, 1977.

ORDINANCE 995
AN ORDINANCE PROHIBITING THE
DISSEMINATION OF MATERIALS WHICH
PROMOTE AND INCITE GROUP HATRED

Whereas, the dissemination of any material within the Village of Skokie which promotes and incites hatred against members of any group by reason of their race or national ancestry is repugnant to the local standards of morality of the people of the Village of Skokie.

Now, Therefore, It is Hereby Ordained:

Section: That Chapter 28 of the Code of Ordinances of the Village of Skokie be amended by the addition thereto of Section 28-43, as follows:

Sec. 28-43   Prohibition of materials promoting or inciting group hatred.

Sec. 28-43.1   The dissemination of any materials within the Village of Skokie which promotes and incites hatred against persons by reason of their race, national origin, or religion, and is intended to do so, is hereby prohibited.

Sec. 28-43.2   The phrase "dissemination of materials" includes but is not limited to publication or display or distribution of posters, signs, handbills, or writing and public display of markings and clothing of symbolic significance.

Sec. 28-43.3   The Corporation Counsel of Skokie is hereby empowered to seek an injunction in the Circuit Court of Cook County to restrain any person, group or organization from violating this ordinance.

Sec. 28-43.4   Any violation of this ordinance shall be deemed to be a misdemeanor and upon conviction thereof, any person found guilty shall be punished by a fine of not more than $500.00, or by imprisonment in the County Jail for not more than six (6) months, or by any combination of the foregoing for each offense.

Section 2:   This ordinance shall be in full force and effect from and after its passage, approval and publication as provided by law.

Adopted this 2nd day of May, 1977.

ORDINANCE 996
AN ORDINANCE PROHIBITING
DEMONSTRATIONS BY MEMBERS OF POLITICAL
PARTIES WEARING MILITARY-STYLE UNIFORMS

Whereas, public demonstration by members of political parties wearing military-style uniforms is repugnant to the tradition of civilian control of government and is repugnant to the standards of morality and decency of the people of the Village of Skokie;

Now, Therefore, It Is Hereby Ordained that Chapter 28 of the Code of Ordinances of the Village of Skokie be amended by the addition thereto of Section 28-42, as follows:

Sec. 28-42   Prohibition of demonstrations by members of political parties wearing military-style uniforms.

Sec. 28-42.1   No person shall engage in any march, walk or public demonstration as a member or on behalf of any political party while wearing a military-style uniform.

Sec. 28-42.2   "Political party" is hereby defined as an organization existing primarily to influence and deal with the structure or affairs of government, politics or the state.

Sec. 28-42.3   The Corporation Counsel of Skokie is hereby empowered to seek an injunction in the Circuit Court of Cook County to restrain any person, group or organization from violating this ordinance.

Sec. 28-42.4   Any violation of this ordinance shall be deemed to be a misdemeanor and upon conviction thereof, any person found guilty shall be punished by a fine of not more than $500.00, or by imprisonment in the County Jail for not more than six (6) months, or by any combination of the foregoing for each offense.

Sec. 28-42.5   The invalidity of any section or part of this ordinance shall not affect the validity of the remaining sections or parts.

This Ordinance shall be in full force and effect from and after its passage, approval and publication, as required by law.

Adopted this 2nd day of May, 1977.

Appendix B   The Questionnaire

THE UNIVERSITY OF WISCONSIN—MILWAUKEE
College of Letters and Science
Department of Political Science

N⁰ 2183

Civil Libertarian Project

INSTRUCTIONS: For each of the following questions please mark the answer that comes closest to the way you feel about the issue. There are no "right" or "wrong" answers — please answer the questions as honestly as possible. Answer each of the questions in the order in which it appears. If you wish to make additional comments on any of the specific questions or on the issues in general, use the space at the end of the questionnaire. Your opinions are extremely important for understanding these complex civil liberty issues — we greatly appreciate your cooperation!

We would like to begin with a few questions about your relationship with the American Civil Liberties Union (ACLU).   6 _1_

1a. About how many years have you been a member of ACLU? _____ years.   7 _ 8 _

1b. Why did you join the ACLU? That is, was there any **particular** cause that the ACLU was supporting or defending that prompted you to join the organization?
   ☐ Specific cause(s) – – → Which cause(s) _____
   ☐ No specific cause   9 _
   ☐ Don't remember

1c. Have you been very active in the affairs of the ACLU? For instance, have you done any of the following in the last five years?

	Yes	No	Don't Remember	
a. made financial contributions (beyond membership dues)	☐	☐	☐	10 _
b. written letters to ACLU leaders	☐	☐	☐	11 _
c. served in a leadership role	☐	☐	☐	12 _
d. attended local meetings of ACLU	☐	☐	☐	13 _
e. read ACLU newsletters and literature	☐	☐	☐	14 _
f. written letters to public officials at the urging of ACLU	☐	☐	☐	15 _
g. attended an ACLU party or benefit	☐	☐	☐	16 _
h. done volunteer work for ACLU (e.g., office assistance, phone calling, etc.) .	☐	☐	☐	17 _
i. participated in a court case or public hearing at the urging of ACLU . . .	☐	☐	☐	18 _

1d. The ACLU publishes a number of specialized newsletters and magazines that not all of the members receive. We would like to know if you have received any of these publications and, if so, how frequently you found the time to read them. For **each of the following** please check the most appropriate box.

	I have not received this publication	I received the publication and usually read it	I received the publication but rarely had time to read it	Don't Know	
a. Civil Liberties Review	☐	☐	☐	☐	19 _
b. Children's Rights Report	☐	☐	☐	☐	20 _
c. First Principles	☐	☐	☐	☐	21 _
d. Notes from the Women's Rights Project	☐	☐	☐	☐	22 _
e. Civil Liberties Alert	☐	☐	☐	☐	23 _
f. The Privacy Report	☐	☐	☐	☐	24 _
g. Civil Liberties	☐	☐	☐	☐	25 _

1e. Over the course of your membership, how satisfied have you been, in general, with the positions ACLU has taken on major issues?
   ☐ always in agreement   ☐ usually in disagreement   ☐ don't know   26 _
   ☐ usually in agreement   ☐ always in disagreement

2a. There are always some people whose ideas are considered bad or dangerous by other people. For instance, somebody who is against all churches and religion.

	Yes	No	No Opinion	
a. If such a person wanted to make a speech in your community against churches and religion, should he/she be allowed to speak or not?	☐	☐	☐	27 _
b. Should such a person be allowed to organize a march against churches and religion in your community?	☐	☐	☐	28 _
c. Should such a person be allowed to teach in a college or university, or not?	☐	☐	☐	29 _
d. If some people in your community suggested that a book he/she wrote against churches and religion should be taken out of your public library, would you favor removing the book, or not?	☐	☐	☐	30 _

209

2b. Or consider a person who is an admitted member of the Ku Klux Klan (KKK).

	Yes	No	No Opinion
a. If such a person wanted to make a speech in your community claiming that Blacks are inferior, should he/she be allowed to speak or not?	☐	☐	☐
b. If such a person wanted to organize a march against Blacks, should this march be permitted?	☐	☐	☐
c. Should such a person be allowed to teach in a college or university, or not?	☐	☐	☐
d. If some people in your community suggested that a book he/she wrote which said Blacks are inferior should be taken out of your public library, would you favor removing this book, or not?	☐	☐	☐

31 ___ (a) *32 ___* (b) *33 ___* (c) *34 ___* (d)

2c. What about a person who is an admitted Communist?

	Yes	No	No Opinion
a. Suppose this admitted Communist wanted to make a speech in your community. Should he/she be allowed to speak, or not?	☐	☐	☐
b. Suppose he/she wanted to organize a pro-Communist march in your community. Should this march be allowed to take place?	☐	☐	☐
c. Suppose he/she is teaching in a college. Should he/she be fired, or not?	☐	☐	☐
d. Suppose he/she wrote a book which is in your public library. Somebody in your community suggests that the book should be removed from the library. Would you favor removing it, or not?	☐	☐	☐

35 (a) *36 ___* (b) *37 ___* (c) *38 ___* (d)

2d. Consider a person who is an admitted member of a para-military organization (i.e., those who advocate doing away with elections and letting the military run the country).

	Yes	No	No Opinion
a. If such a person wanted to make a speech in your community, should he/she be allowed to speak, or not?	☐	☐	☐
b. Suppose he/she wanted to organize a march supporting this cause in your community. Should this march be allowed to take place?	☐	☐	☐
c. Should such a person be allowed to teach in a college or university, or not?	☐	☐	☐
d. Suppose he/she wrote a book advocating doing away with elections and letting the military run the country. Somebody in your community suggests that the book be removed from the public library. Would you favor removing it, or not?	☐	☐	☐

39 ___ (a) *40 ___* (b) *41 ___* (c) *42 ___* (d)

2e. And finally, what about a person who admits that he/she is a member of the Nazi party?

	Yes	No	No Opinion
a. Suppose this admitted Nazi wanted to make a speech in your community. Should he/she be allowed to speak, or not?	☐	☐	☐
b. Suppose this person wanted to organize a march in your community in support of Nazi beliefs. Should this march be permitted, or not?	☐	☐	☐
c. Should such a person be allowed to teach in a college or university, or not?	☐	☐	☐
d. If some people in your community suggested that a book he/she wrote should be taken out of your public library, would you favor removing the book, or not?	☐	☐	☐

42 ___ (a) *44 ___* (b) *45 ___* (c) *46 ___* (d)

3a. As you know, there are many groups in America that try to get the government or the American people to see things more their way. We would like to get your opinions toward what you perceive to be the **aims, objectives,** or **ideas** advocated by these groups. In particular, we would like your opinion on how significant the change in the American system of government would be if the ideas of the group were put into practice. Please rate each of the following groups in terms of the nature of the change in our system of government that would follow the implementation of their ideas.

Check only one answer in each column

	Communists	Nazis	Members of the Ku Klux Klan
The ideas, if implemented, would create a totally different and much worse system of government.	☐	☐	☐
The ideas, if implemented, would significantly change our system of government for the worse.	☐	☐	☐
I oppose the ideas but they would not change our system of government if they were implemented.	☐	☐	☐
I support the ideas but they would not change our system of government if they were implemented.	☐	☐	☐
The ideas, if implemented, would significantly change our system of government for the better.	☐	☐	☐
The ideas, if implemented, would create a totally different and much better system of government.	☐	☐	☐
No Opinion.	☐	☐	☐

47 ___ *48 ___* *49 ___*

3b How likely is it that the aims, objectives and ideas of these groups will have any impact on our political system in the foreseeable future?

Check only one answer in each column

	Communists	Nazis	Members of the Ku Klux Klan	
extremely unlikely	☐	☐	☐	50 ___
very unlikely	☐	☐	☐	
possible, but unlikely	☐	☐	☐	51 ___
very likely	☐	☐	☐	
extremely likely	☐	☐	☐	52 ___
No opinion	☐	☐	☐	

4. What do you think the Government should do about these organizations? For instance, should the Government engage in any of the following activities?

a. I would favor the Government taking the following actions against Communists (check **all** of the actions you favor).

☐ outlawing any organized Communist party — 53 ___
☐ prohibiting any Communist from running for public office — 54 ___
☐ engaging in covert surveillance of Communists (e.g., wiretapping) — 55 ___
☐ requiring that Communists register with the government — 56 ___
☐ ban all activities in public places by Communists — 57 ___
☐ ban public display of Communist symbols (e.g., hammer and sickle) — 58 ___

b. I would favor the Government taking the following actions against Nazis (check **all** of the actions you favor).

☐ outlawing any organized Nazi party — 59 ___
☐ prohibiting any Nazi from running for public office — 60 ___
☐ engaging in covert surveillance of Nazis (e.g., wiretapping) — 61 ___
☐ requiring that Nazis register with the Government — 62 ___
☐ ban all activities in public places by Nazis — 63 ___
☐ ban public display of Nazi symbols (e.g., swastika) — 64 ___

c. I would favor the Government taking the following actions against the Ku Klux Klan (check **all** of the actions you favor).

☐ outlawing any organized Ku Klux Klan party — 65 ___
☐ prohibiting any member of the Ku Klux Klan from running for public office — 66 ___
☐ engaging in covert surveillance of the Ku Klux Klan (e.g., wiretapping) — 67 ___
☐ requiring that members of the Ku Klux Klan register with the Government — 68 ___
☐ ban all activities in public places by the Ku Klux Klan — 69 ___
☐ ban public display of Ku Klux Klan symbols (e.g., burning cross) — 70 ___

5. Different people have different ideas about what kinds of speech should be protected under the First Amendment to the U. S. Constitution. We are interested in getting your opinion about whether particular types of speech **should** be protected under the First Amendment. For each of the following types of speech, please indicate whether you believe it should definitely be protected, probably be protected, probably not be protected, or definitely not be protected by the First Amendment. That is, please mark the blank which comes closest to your opinion for each of the following types of speech.

Should this type of speech be protected by the First Amendment?

	Definitely should be	Probably should be	Probably should not be	Definitely should not be	No opinion	
a. "symbolic speech," such as burning one's draft card in protest of the war in Vietnam	☐	☐	☐	☐	☐	71 ___
b. Obscene or profane speech	☐	☐	☐	☐	☐	72 ___
c. speech supportive of an enemy of the U. S.	☐	☐	☐	☐	☐	73 ___
d. speech extremely critical of the American system of government	☐	☐	☐	☐	☐	74 ___
e. speech extremely critical of the First Amendment to the U. S. Constitution	☐	☐	☐	☐	☐	75 ___
f. speech extremely critical of particular minority groups	☐	☐	☐	☐	☐	76 ___
g. speech advocating the overthrow of the U. S. Government	☐	☐	☐	☐	☐	77 ___
h. speech **designed** to incite an audience to violence	☐	☐	☐	☐	☐	78 ___
i. speech which **might** incite an audience to violence	☐	☐	☐	☐	☐	79 ___

6. Many public demonstrations pose a threat of violent reactions from crowds. Consider a demonstration that is itself peaceful, but which attracts a hostile crowd. Should the police be allowed to stop the demonstration in order to avoid violent crowd reactions? If so, at what point should the demonstration be stopped?
(Please check one of the following boxes.)

6 _2_

☐ the police should not be allowed to stop the demonstration
the police should be allowed to stop the demonstration when . . .

7 ___

    ☐ a crowd begins to form
    ☐ members of the crowd begin to taunt the group
    ☐ the crowd appears to be on the verge of violent reaction
    ☐ a member of the crowd picks up a rock
    ☐ a rock is thrown in the direction of the demonstrators
    ☐ the demonstrators begin to fight with the crowd
☐ no opinion

7. We would like to get your reactions to a number of possible circumstances that might involve applications for permits to hold a march or demonstration.

    a. For instance, what if a Black civil rights group asked to be allowed to hold a march in a White Southern community — would you oppose or support granting a permit?

8 ___

    ☐ Strongly Support   ☐ Support   ☐ Oppose   ☐ Strongly Oppose   ☐ No Opinion
    b. Suppose the Palestine Liberation Organization (PLO) sought to march in a Jewish community. Should a permit be granted?

9 ___

    ☐ Strongly Support   ☐ Support   ☐ Oppose   ☐ Strongly Oppose   ☐ No Opinion
    c. Should the Ku Klux Klan be granted a permit to march in a Black community?

10 ___

    ☐ Strongly Support   ☐ Support   ☐ Oppose   ☐ Strongly Oppose   ☐ No Opinion
    d. What if the Nazis asked to be allowed to hold a march in a White Protestant community? Would you support or oppose granting a permit in such a circumstance?

11 ___

    ☐ Strongly Support   ☐ Support   ☐ Oppose   ☐ Strongly Oppose   ☐ No Opinion

8a. A professor from Northwestern University has written a book, "The Hoax of the Twentieth Century," in which he claims that the number of Jews murdered in World War II is far fewer than the commonly accepted 6-7 million figure. Have you heard about this book?

12 ___

    ☐ Yes   ☐ No   ☐ Can't Remember

8b. In your opinion, should this book be available in your local public library or should it be prohibited?

13 ___

    ☐ Should be available   ☐ Should be prohibited   ☐ No opinion

8c. Have you taken any action with regard to the controversies surrounding this book? If so, what action?

_____
_____
_____
_____

9a. One issue that is of particular concern to us is that of the Nazi controversy in Skokie, Illinois (a suburb of Chicago). How familiar are you with this issue?

    ☐ Not familiar

14 ___

    ☐ Somewhat familiar   What is your opinion on this controversy?
    ☐ Very familiar   _____

_____
_____
_____

9b. In Skokie, the Nazis sought a permit to hold a public rally. If it were up to you to decide, would you grant the permit application or deny it?

15 ___

    ☐ Grant   ☐ Deny   ☐ No opinion
    Why?_____

_____
_____

9c. What do you think would happen if the Nazis are allowed to march in Skokie?

_____
_____
_____
_____

9d. The officials in Skokie passed a law in response to the Nazi application that required anyone wanting to speak, parade, or demonstrate to apply for a permit. The permit would be denied if, in the opinion of the village officials, the proposed speech portrays "lack of virtue" in others or "incites hostility." Were you aware that such a provision existed in the Skokie law?

    □ Yes   □ No   □ Can't Remember   16 ____

9e. Do you favor or oppose such a law being passed?

    □ Strongly Favor   □ Favor   □ Oppose   □ Strongly Oppose   □ No Opinion   17 ____

9f. In the same city, anyone who wants to hold a public march must also post a $350,000 insurance bond (although this requirement can be waived by the City). This requirement applies to everyone, not only the Nazis, and since insurance companies rarely will write such insurance, few bonds have been posted. Were you aware that such a provision existed in the Skokie law?

    □ Yes   □ No   □ Can't Remember   18 ____

9g. Do you favor or oppose such a law being passed?

    □ Strongly Favor   □ Favor   □ Oppose   □ Strongly Oppose   □ No Opinion   19 ____

9h. Is a law that requires a permit and an insurance bond compatible or incompatible with the First Amendment to the U. S. Constitution, in your opinion?

    □ Yes, compatible   □ No, incompatible   □ Don't Know   20 ____

9i. Would you favor changing the First Amendment to the Constitution to include a specific prohibition on speech that portrays a lack of virtue or incites hostility toward particular political or ethnic groups?

    □ Yes   □ No   □ No Opinion   21 ____

Why? _____

_____

_____

_____

10a. The ACLU has entered the dispute over the Nazis in Skokie. Are you familiar with the ACLU's activities on this issue?

    □ Not familiar   □ Somewhat familiar   □ Very familiar   22 ____

10b. The ACLU is currently representing the right of the Nazis to march in Skokie. Do you agree or disagree with this action?

    □ Strongly Agree   □ Agree   □ Disagree   □ Strongly Disagree   □ No Opinion   23 ____

Why? _____

_____

_____

_____

10c. Many people have resigned their membership in ACLU over the Nazi controversy, while others have recently joined the organization because of ACLU's position on this issue. Have you recently resigned from, joined, or taken other action with regard to the ACLU because of the Nazi issue? (Please answer only with regard to the Nazi issue.)

    □ Neither joined nor resigned because of the Nazi issue   24 ____

    □ Recently joined because of the Nazi issue

    □ Recently resigned because of the Nazi issue

    □ Recently let my membership expire because of the Nazi issue

    □ Intend to let my membership expire because of the Nazi issue

10d. Have you recently resigned from, joined, or taken other action with regard to the ACLU because of an issue other than the Nazi issue?

    □ Neither joined nor resigned because of other issues   25 ____

    □ Recently joined

    □ Recently resigned

    □ Recently let my membership expire

    □ Intend to let my membership expire because of the Nazi issue

What was (is) the issue? _____

_____

_____

_____

_____

_____

FOR PROJECT
USE ONLY

11. What are the most important sources of your information on the Skokie controversy? Please indicate whether you have gotten a great deal, only some, or no information about Skokie from each of the following sources.

	A great deal of information	only some information	no information
26 ___ a. television news	☐	☐	☐
27 ___ b. community organizations	☐	☐	☐
28 ___ c. ACLU literature and newsletters	☐	☐	☐
29 ___ d. churches/synagogues	☐	☐	☐
30 ___ e. newspapers	☐	☐	☐
31 ___ f. magazines	☐	☐	☐

32 ___ 33 ___   (Any newspaper in particular? Which one? _____)

34 ___ 35 ___   (Any magazine in particular? Which one? _____)

36 ___ 37 ___
38 ___ 39 ___
40 ___ 41 ___
42 ___ 43 ___

Below are a number of statements about civil liberties and politics in America that we have heard frequently. We are interested in your reaction to these statements. Although we realize that the statements may not correspond perfectly to your opinions, we would appreciate it if you could indicate whether you agree strongly, agree, disagree, or disagree strongly with the statement **taken as a whole**. After each statement please check the box that comes closest to the way you feel.

	Agree Strongly	Agree	Disagree	Disagree Strongly	No Opinion
44 ___ 12a. Police should be allowed to conduct a full search of any motorist arrested for an offense such as speeding.	☐	☐	☐	☐	☐
45 ___ 12b. In their fight against crime the police should be entitled to use wiretaps and other devices for listing in on private conversations.	☐	☐	☐	☐	☐
46 ___ 12c. The C.I.A. should be able to prevent any former employees from writing about the agency without the C.I.A.'s prior approval.	☐	☐	☐	☐	☐
47 ___ 12d. The use of tax funds to support parochial schools involves compulsory taxation for religious purposes and thus violates the First Amendment.	☐	☐	☐	☐	☐
48 ___ 12e. Students who shout down speakers to achieve their aims subvert the principles of academic freedom.	☐	☐	☐	☐	☐
49 ___ 12f. Membership in the John Birch Society by itself is enough to bar an applicant from appointment to the police force.	☐	☐	☐	☐	☐
50 ___ 12g. Court calendars are so crowded that the right to trial by jury should be restricted to persons accused of major crimes only.	☐	☐	☐	☐	☐
51 ___ 12h. In light of present standards of justice and humanity, the death penalty has become "cruel and unusual punishment" in violation of the Eighth Amendment.	☐	☐	☐	☐	☐
52 ___ 12i. A man should be denied unemployment compensation if fired from his job for growing a beard.	☐	☐	☐	☐	☐
53 ___ 12j. High school students are within their rights when they express political opinions, circulate petitions and handbills, or wear political insignia in school.	☐	☐	☐	☐	☐
54 ___ 12k. Government consolidation of dossiers on individual citizens violates the right to privacy.	☐	☐	☐	☐	☐
55 ___ 12l. A radio station which permits the reading of an anti-Semitic poem over the air should have its F.C.C. license revoked.	☐	☐	☐	☐	☐
56 ___ 12m. A woman has a private right to decide whether to have a child or undergo an abortion.	☐	☐	☐	☐	☐
57 ___ 12n. The "separation of church and state" clause of the First Amendment should be used to eliminate the tax-exempt status of religious institutions.	☐	☐	☐	☐	☐
58 ___ 12o. Countries that discriminate among their citizens on the basis of religion should be denied U. S. foreign aid.	☐	☐	☐	☐	☐

13. The U. S. Supreme Court has recently heard an appeal from an unsuccessful applicant to the University of California—Davis Medical School. In this case — the Baake case — affirmative action programs are challenged because they are alleged to be discriminatory. How familiar are you with this issue?

59 ___   ☐ Very familiar   ☐ Somewhat familiar   ☐ Unfamiliar

What is your opinion on this issue? _____

_____

_____

_____

14. We are faced with many problems in this country, none of which can be solved easily. Some of these problems are listed below. For each problem, please tell us how important the issue is to you. That is, mark the box for each issue that most closely represents your position.

	not important	slightly important	moderately important	very important	extremely important	no opinion	FOR PROJECT USE ONLY
a. solving economic problems (unemployment, inflation, etc.).	☐	☐	☐	☐	☐	☐	60 ___
b. improving and protecting the Nation's environment	☐	☐	☐	☐	☐	☐	61 ___
c. halting the rising crime rate	☐	☐	☐	☐	☐	☐	62 ___
d. solving the energy problem	☐	☐	☐	☐	☐	☐	63 ___
e. protecting individual civil liberties . .	☐	☐	☐	☐	☐	☐	64 ___
f. improving the conditions of Blacks . .	☐	☐	☐	☐	☐	☐	65 ___
g. military preparedness	☐	☐	☐	☐	☐	☐	66 ___
h. honesty in government	☐	☐	☐	☐	☐	☐	67 ___

15. Returning to the Nazis, have you taken any of the following actions in the last year with regard to whether the First Amendment guarantees the Nazis the right to hold public marches? (Please answer not in terms of your actions concerning Nazi **ideas** but rather in terms of your actions concerning the **First Amendment issue**).

	I have done this	I have not done this	Can't remember	
a. participated in demonstrations opposing the right of Nazis to hold public marches.	☐	☐	☐	68 ___
b. joined a group to actively oppose the right of Nazis to hold public marches. .	☐	☐	☐	69 ___
c. intentionally increased my donations to groups opposing the right of Nazis to hold public marches	☐	☐	☐	70 ___
d. contacted government officials to oppose the right of Nazis to hold public meetings	☐	☐	☐	71 ___
e. organized people to oppose the right of Nazis to hold public marches . . .	☐	☐	☐	72 ___
f. participated in demonstrations supporting the right of Nazis to hold public marches.	☐	☐	☐	73 ___
g. joined a group to actively support the right of Nazis to hold public marches .	☐	☐	☐	74 ___
h. intentionally increased my donations to groups supporting the right of Nazis to hold public marches	☐	☐	☐	75 ___
i. contacted government officials to support the right of Nazis to hold public marches	☐	☐	☐	76 ___
j. organized people to support the right of Nazis to hold public marches . . .	☐	☐	☐	77 ___
k. other (please specify) _____				78 ___

16. Have you ever actively demonstrated because of a political issue?

☐ Yes – – –→ What was the issue and what was your position? _____   79 ___

☐ No

☐ Can't remember

17. In the past ACLU has defended political groups representing a wide variety of political viewpoints, including members of the Ku Klux Klan, White Citizens' Council, Communists, etc. In your opinion, when should ACLU decline to defend political groups? That is, what do you think ACLU's policy should be regarding the kinds of groups and ideas it will defend?   6 __3__

_____

_____

_____

_____

_____

18. What in your view is the proper function of the American Civil Liberties Union?

_____

_____

_____

_____

_____

19. Many people living in the United States had personal experiences with the Nazis in the 1930's and 1940's. We would like to know what kind of experience you have had with the Nazis, if any. Have you, a member of your family, or a close personal friend had any of the following experiences with Nazis? (Please mark all that apply for you, for members of your family, and for close personal friends.)

	I experienced	A member of my family experienced	A close friend experienced	No such experience
a. a victim of Nazi discrimination	☐	☐	☐	☐
b. loss of job, livelihood	☐	☐	☐	☐
c. physical abuse	☐	☐	☐	☐
d. confinement in a concentration camp	☐	☐	☐	☐
e. death caused by Nazis	☐	☐	☐	☐
f. fled home because of Nazis	☐	☐	☐	☐

20. NBC recently televized a story entitled "Holocaust" about the experiences of Jews under the Nazi government in Germany. Did you happen to see the series?
☐ Yes
☐ No
☐ Don't remember
(IF YES) Did the series affect your opinion on the issue of marches by members of the Nazi party? If so, how?

_____

_____

_____

We would like to conclude with a few questions about your background.

21. What is your current age? _____ years old.

22. What is your sex? ☐ Female ☐ Male

23. What is your race? _____

24a. What is your religious preference?
☐ Protestant – – → Please specify denomination _____
☐ Catholic
☐ Jewish – – – → Please specify whether Orthodox, Conservative, Reform _____
☐ None
☐ Other – – – → Please specify _____

24b. How often do you usually attend church or synagogue?
☐ more than once a week
☐ once a week
☐ two or three times a month
☐ once a month
☐ at least once a year
☐ less than once a year
☐ never

25. Please indicate your birthplace and the birthplace of your parents below. If you or either of your parents were born outside the U.S. please indicate the year in which you or they immigrated to the United States.

	Country of birth	Country where mostly raised	Year of Immigration
Me	_____	_____	_____
My Father	_____	_____	_____
My Mother	_____	_____	_____

26. Do you consider yourself to be a member of any particular ethnic group? If so, which one? _____

                                                          _____

27. What kind of work do you normally do? That is, what is your job called? (Please be as specific as possible. If retired, please refer to the last major job you held.)

     _____

28a. Please indicate the highest grade in elementary school or high school that you finished and got credit for (use 0 to indicate no formal school). _____

28b. Did you ever complete one or more years of college for credit — not including schooling such as business college, technical or vocational school?

       ☐ Yes – – –→ How many years did you complete? _____
                     Do you have any college degrees?   ☐ Yes   ☐ No
                     What degree or degrees? _____
                     From what college or university is your undergraduate degree?

       ☐ No

29. Below is a scale on which the political views people might hold are listed. Where would you place yourself on this scale? Please mark the point on the scale that best describes you.
       ☐ radical left
       ☐ extremely liberal
       ☐ liberal
       ☐ slightly liberal
       ☐ moderate, middle of the road
       ☐ slightly conservative
       ☐ conservative
       ☐ extremely conservative
       ☐ radical right
       ☐ don't know

30. What is your current place of residence?
    City:_____ State _____

31a. About how many states have you lived in during your life? (Count only those states that you live in for at least one year.) _____ states

31b. About how many countries have you lived in? (Count only those countries that you lived in for at least one year.) _____ countries

32. Generally speaking do you consider yourself a Republican, a Democrat, an Independent, or what?
       ☐ Republican
       ☐ Independent
       ☐ Democrat
       ☐ Other (Please specify) _____

33. Are you a member of any of the following organizations?

	Yes	No
a. Common Cause	☐	☐
b. Jewish Defense League	☐	☐
c. Sierra Club	☐	☐
d. Concerned Jewish Citizens	☐	☐
e. NAACP	☐	☐
f. Anti-Defamation League of B'nai B'rith	☐	☐
g. Friends of the Earth	☐	☐

FOR PROJECT USE ONLY

50 ____

51 ____

52 ____ 53 ____

54 ____
55 ____ 56 ____
57 ____
58 ____ 59 ____

60 ____ 61 ____

62 ____ 63 ____
64 ____ 65 ____
66 ____ 67 ____

68 ____ 69 ____

70 ____ 71 ____

72 ____

73 ____
74 ____
75 ____
76 ____
77 ____
78 ____
79 ____

80 ___

THANK YOU VERY MUCH FOR YOUR TIME AND COOPERATION.
IF YOU WOULD LIKE A COPY OF THE SUMMARY VERSION OF
OUR REPORT, PLEASE PUT YOUR NAME AND ADDRESS BELOW.

_____

_____

_____

_____

ADDITIONAL COMMENTS

ADDITIONAL COMMENTS CONTINUED

_____
_____
_____
_____
_____
_____
_____
_____
_____
_____
_____
_____
_____
_____
_____
_____
_____
_____
_____
_____
_____
_____
_____
_____
_____
_____
_____
_____
_____
_____
_____
_____

Index

Abelson, Robert P.: 171
abstract attitudes and concrete opinions: 137, 184
  contextual influences on, 145-146, 156-157
  slippage between, 142-146
    among those with intolerant attitudes, 156-157
    within the Skokie-Nazi context, 145-159
acquired behavioral predispositions: 97, 161, 171
Ajzen, I.: 171
Albrecht, Stan L.: 171
Alien and Sedition Acts of 1798: 1, 16
American Civil Liberties Union:
  membership survey, 47-49
  leadership survey, 49
Andersen, Christi: 131
Anderson, Ronald E.: 131
antidemocratic ideas: 9, 10
atheism, tolerance of: 11
attitude-behavior relationship: 97-98
  bivariate relationships, 166-168
  conceptual models of, 161-164
  conditional models of, 162-164, 171-178
  empirical relationship, 166-171, 184
  multivariate relationships, 167-171
  path model of, 167-171

Bagehot, Walter: 4
Bagozzi, Richard P.: 171
Barnum, David G.: 35, 41, 164, 186, 187, 188
Beauharnais v. Illinois: 34, 44-45, 108

behavioral responses to the Skokie-Nazi conflict: 81-82, 164-165
belief systems: 129-139, 184
  and the abstract-concrete beliefs problem, 143
  constraint in, 129-139
Bell, Leland V.: 25, 42
Bem, Daryl J.: 171
Bennett, Stephen Earl: 131
Bennett, W. Lance: 140n
Bentler, P. M.: 171, 180
Berman, John J.: 171
Bishop, George F.: 131, 159
Borgida, Eugene: 171
Brandenberg v. Ohio: 31, 33, 43-44n
Brill, Alida: 59, 60, 68, 106, 132, 192
Brown, Steven R.: 139n
Burnkrant, Robert E.: 171

Campbell, Angus: 131, 139n
Campbell, Bruce: 171
Campbell, Donald T.: 97, 161, 171
Caute, David: 17, 190
Chaplinsky v. New Hampshire: 31, 34, 44-45n
Chicagoland's Community Guide: 23
Chicago Park District: 28, 34
Chong, Dennis: 21n, 106
civil liberties:
  and Skokie ordinances, 41-42
  attitudes toward, 121-126
clear and present danger: 44-45n, 46n
Cohen vs. California: 32, 42-43n, 108
Collin, Frank: 23, 26, 27, 28, 29, 30, 31, 34, 72,
Collin v. Smith: 32, 34, 44n

221

Common Cause:
  differences from ACLU members:
    in tolerance, 56, 64–65, 137
    in structure of attitudes, 133
  differences from mass public, 64–65
  membership survey, 49
communists: 10
  support for repression of, 117–121
Communist Party U.S.A.: 10
consensus, democratic: 114, 123–126,
  137–139, 184–185, 186–192
contingent consistency, between attitudes and behavior: 171
Converse, Philip E.: 131, 139, 129, 132,
  134, 180
Crockett, Harry J.: 14, 15, 16, 59, 68,
  126, 132, 139n
cultural homogeneity, and democracy:
  3–4
Cutler, Stephen J.: 139
  conceptualization of, 59–60
  consensus on tolerance, 65, 67–68,
    186–192
  differences from masses,
    in belief system constraint, 131
    in political activism, 61
    in resources, 60
    in tolerance, 14–17, 61–64, 67
  influence on public policy, 14, 16–17
  intolerance of, 16–17, 67, 68
  tolerance of, 15–16, 67, 137–139
  subculture of, 16
elitist theory of democracy: 14–17, 68,
  71, 186–192
extremist groups: 10–13

Dahl, Robert A.: 3, 5, 16, 106, 109
Davis, James A.: 14, 139
Defectors, from ACLU:
  attributes of, 86–95
Defection from ACLU:
  rates of defection, 72–74, 81–82,
    83–86
Defections rates, according to:
  attitudes toward ACLU involvement
    in Skokie, 90

attitudes toward Skokie ordinances,
  90
attitudes toward the heckler's veto, 90
attitudes toward the Nazis, 95
education, 89
experience with Nazism, 89
free assembly attitudes, 90, 91
free speech attitudes, 90, 91
gender, 88
general libertarian beliefs, 90, 91–92,
  95–98
ideological self identification, 92
leadership position, 95
occupation, 89
organizational loyalty and involvement, 93, 95, 96–97
race, 89
reasons for joining ACLU, 92, 93
region of residence, 89
religious affiliation, 89, 95–96
state of residence, 89
DeFleur, Melvin L.: 162
democracy, key elements of: 5–9
demonstrator-community conflict: 172
discriminant functions: 151, 152
disliking groups and intolerance: 65,
  67–68
DiTecco, Don: 171

Easton, David: 4, 139
economic development, and democracy:
  2–3
Edwards vs. South Carolina: 116
elites:
  and the democratic creed, 15,
    137–139

factor analysis: 115, 121, 126, 129, 133,
  135
Fazio, R.: 171
fighting words doctrine: 31, 34, 42n,
  44n, 45–46n
Field, John O.: 131
First Amendment: 10, 31
Fishbein, M.: 171
free assembly: 7, 42, 90, 91

support for,
  as a function of other tolerance atti-
    tudes, 152
  impact on behavior, 166–171
  measurement of, 116–117
free speech: 7, 42, 90, 91, 108
  support for,
    applied, attitudes, 143
    impact on behavior, 166–171
    measurement of, 110–115
Frideres, James, 171
Funder, David C.: 171

General Social Survey: 60, 61
German-American Bund: 24
Gibson, James L.: 171
government oppression:
  support for, measurement of, 117,
    121–122
Grigg, Charles M.: 13, 59, 105, 129,
  143, 161
group libel: 30, 33, 41, 43–45n
  ACLU members' opinion of, 74
Guttman scaling, 114, 126

Hamlin, David: 26, 27, 73, 86
Hand, Learned: 4
Haque, Khondaker E.: 129
heckler's veto: 116
Herman, C. Peter: 161
Herzon, Frederick D.: 132
Higgins, E. Tory: 161
hurdles, to attitude-behavior consis-
  tency: 162, 163, 159–178

Illinois Civil Liberties Union: 72
  defection rates within, 85–86
intolerance, in public policy: 17
Inglehart, Ronald: 3, 133
insurance bonds:
  Chicago, 28
  Skokie, 28, 30, 31, 32, 41
  ACLU members' opinions of, 74
institutional structures, and democracy:
  4, 190–192
iron law of oligarchy: 191

Jackman, Mary R.: 129
Jackman, Robert W.: 68
Jennings, M. Kent: 69n
Jewishness:
  as a contextual variable in the
    attitude-behavior relationship,
    175–178
Jewish Defense League: 27, 31, 41
Jukam, Thomas O.: 160

Kahle, Lynn R.: 171
Kaufman, Robert L.: 139n
Key, V. O.: Jr.: 14, 190
Kish, Leslie: 54
Ku Klux Klan: 14, 17, 88, 117
  support for repression of, 117–121

Lane, Robert E.: 131
LaPiere, R. T.: 162
Lawrence, David G.: 107, 141, 162, 163
League of Women Voters: 23
legitimacy: 6–7
liberal-conservative, belief systems: 131
linkage models: 141, 160–161
Lipset, Seymour Martin: 3
Lucas, J. Anthony: 71
Luttbeg, Norman: 132, 143

Madsen, Douglas: 139
majority tyranny: 12
marketplace of ideas: 7–9
Mann, Jim: 71
Marcus, George: 9, 10, 20n, 67, 105,
  131, 139, 156, 159n, 218
Marcus, Gregory B.: 139
Margolis, Michael: 129
Maslow, A. H.: 3
mass intolerance: 14–16, 67
McCarthyism: 16, 17
McClosky, Herbert: 21n, 59, 60, 106,
  123, 132, 192
McGuire, William J.: 171
measurement error: 56–58, 65, 68
member reactions to the Skokie-Nazi-
  ACLU conflict:

opinions toward
    Skokie ordinances, 74–81
        the proper role of ACLU, 98–104
menticide: 34
Mill, John Stuart: 7, 8, 9
Miller, Warren E.: 160
Mississippi ACLU: 88
Muller, Edward N.: 10, 160

National Lawyers Guild: 87
National Socialist Party of America
    (NSPA): 18, 23, 26, 27, 28, 29,
    30, 31, 34, 41, 72
    support for repression of, 117–121
Navasky, Victor S.: 17
Nazi Party of America: 2
Nazi movement in the United States:
    24–27
Neier, Aryeh: 73, 87, 88
Nie, Norman: 129, 131, 133, 159n
Niemi, Richard G.: 69n
Nunn, Clyde Z.: 14, 15, 16, 59, 68, 126,
    132, 139n

obscene speech: 114, 136
Oldendick, Robert W.: 131
order versus liberty, attitudes toward:
    123–126
Oskamp, Stuart: 171

Page, Benjamin I.: 160
Pierce, John C.: 131
Piereson, James E.: 9, 10, 20, 67, 105,
    131, 133, 156, 159, 163
pluralism: 189
political competition: 1, 5–9
political conflict: 1–2, 7, 110–114
political culture and democracy: 4
political opposition, right to oppose: 5,
    106, 109, 135
political association, measurement of
    support for: 117, 121
prerequisites of democracy: 2–4
Prothro, James W.: 13, 59, 106, 129,
    143, 161
public contestation: 5–9

Rabjohn, James N.: 129, 133, 159n
rationales for opposing Nazi rights:
    74–81
rationales for supporting Nazi rights:
    81–82
religious freedom and separation of
    church and state, measurement of
    support for: 126, 135
rights: 6, 12
    of freedom from government inter-
        vention, 135
    of political opposition, 39–40, 135
    of the political right, measurement of
        support for, 126
Rockwell, George Lincoln: 24–25, 26,
    73
Rose, Douglas D.: 132

samples:
    ACLU membership, 47
    ACLU leadership, 49
    Common Cause, 49
    representativeness of, 54, 94
    weighting, 54
Sarat, Austin: 144
Schlegel, Ronald P.: 171
Schlozman, Kay Lehman: 6
Schubert, Glendon: 133, 159
Seligson, Mitchell A.: 10, 160
Shapiro, Robert Y.: 160
Sheth, D. L.: 139
Skokie Chamber of Commerce: 23
Skokie-Nazi conflict: 18, 19, 28–41
    local reaction to, 35–41
    impact on ACLU, 71–86, 98–104
Skokie ordinances: 30–34
    ACLU member's opinions of, 74–75
        as a function of abstract attitudes,
        146–151
        impact on political behavior,
        166–171
    ACLU members' knowledge of, 74
    and democracy, 41–42
Skolnick, Jerome H.: 6
Sniderman, Paul M.: 139
social desirability, in tolerance
    responses: 56, 58, 68

Socialist Workers Party: 117
Speckart, George: 171, 180
Stouffer, Samuel C.: 12, 17, 59, 61, 68, 106, 123, 132, 163
Stouffer measures of tolerance: 61–67
Sullivan, John L.: 9, 10, 20, 67, 105, 131, 133, 139n, 156
Sullivan, Piereson, and Marcus approach to measuring tolerance: 10–12, 65
Symbionese Liberation Army: 14
symbolic speech, right to: 32, 33, 43, 114

Tabb, David: 131
target group selection: 10–12
temporal stability of attitudes: 129, 139n
Terminiello v. Chicago: 45–46, 109
threat of Nazis:
  as a conditional variable in the attitude-behavior relationship, 174–178
  to Jews, 26–28
Tinker v. Des Moines Independent School District: 43n, 109, 123
tolerance, political:
  abstract-concrete inconsistency, 108–109
  activity-based approach to, 12, 107–109, 110–114, 126, 129
  and value conflict, 99–104, 108–109, 136–139, 173
  and democracy, 1–2, 9, 10
  change in, 14

conceptualization of, 105–110, 183–184
context of, 107–109
dimensionality of beliefs, 133–136
group-based approach to, 12, 107, 110, 126, 129, 163
levels of, 12–14
measurement of, 105–110, 183–184
of anti-democrats, 10
political limits of, 9–12
subdimensions of, 106–110
Stouffer measures of, 110, 126, 129, 134
Tuchfarber, Alfred J.: 131
tyranny of the majority: 2, 160

utilitarianism: 99–104, 171–172
United States v. O'Brien: 108, 114
values, conflict among: 143–146
Verba, Sidney: 6
Violence, fear of:
  as a contextual variable in the attitude-behavior relationship, 172–174, 176–178

Walker, Thomas G.: 116
Warner, Lyle G.: 171
Westie, Frank R.: 162
Wicker, Allen W.: 161, 171
Williams, J. Allen, Jr.: 14, 15, 16, 59, 68, 126, 132, 139n
Wray, J. Harry: 132

Zanna, Mark P.: 161, 171
Zellman, Gail L.: 22, 164

About the Authors

James L. Gibson received his Ph.D. from the University of Iowa in 1975. He is currently Associate Professor at the University of Houston. In addition to his work on political tolerance, he is engaged in a study of the transformation of the political party system in the United States, the initial results from which have recently been published by Praeger Special Studies. He also is conducting research on the processes of decision making employed by judges and those within other political institutions. He has contributed to the *American Political Science Review*, the *American Journal of Political Science*, and the *Journal of Politics*, among several other journals.

Richard D. Bingham is Professor of Political Science and Director of the Urban Research Center at the University of Wisconsin–Milwaukee. He has authored or coauthored several books on urban innovation, state and local government, and public administration. His articles have appeared in the *Urban Affairs Quarterly*, the *Journal of Politics*, the *Western Political Quarterly*, and the *American Political Science Review*, and elsewhere.